BRICKS & BROWNSTONE

THE NEW YORK ROW HOUSE

BRICKS & BROWNSTONE

THE NEW YORK ROW HOUSE

Charles Lockwood & Patrick W. Ciccone

with Jonathan D. Taylor

Foreword by the New York Landmarks Conservancy
Essay by Fran Leadon

Photography by Dylan Chandler

RIZZOLI
NEW YORK

New York · Paris · London · Milan

CONTENTS

FOREWORD

THE NEW YORK LANDMARKS CONSERVANCY

The first edition of *Bricks & Brownstone* was published in 1972, when New York City's preservation movement was still in its infancy. Just a year earlier, the New York Landmarks Conservancy was founded to advocate for New York's architectural treasures, complementing the designation work of the New York City Landmarks Preservation Commission, itself created only in 1965. By providing the financial and technical assistance needed to save and restore buildings, the Conservancy has worked to ensure that New York's extraordinary historic architecture continues to have a vibrant life in the city of the present.

Bricks & Brownstone has served as a guide to understanding the complex nature of New York's row houses and as a template for their restoration. The Conservancy's preservation projects have included some of the very subjects so lovingly illustrated in this book, such as the James Watson House; the Merchant's House and its neighbor, the Samuel Tredwell Skidmore House; Sylvan Terrace, a set of wood-framed row houses in the Jumel Terrace Historic District; and many more modest row houses throughout the city.

In the nearly fifty years since *Bricks & Brownstone*'s initial publication, the built environment of New York has continued to evolve. In response to threats of wanton demolition of our historic architecture, the Conservancy has advocated for the designations of hundreds of new landmarks and historic districts—many of which are filled with row houses—and its Historic Properties Fund has aided the restoration of row houses in historic districts across the city. Historic districts continue to be the vibrant urban neighborhoods they have always been and illustrate the importance of the row house to New York's cultural, social, and economic life.

As New York City will, no doubt, undergo more changes in the twenty-first century, the revised and expanded *Bricks & Brownstone* will continue to be an indispensable resource for the historian, preservationist, those fortunate enough to live in a New York row house, and those who admire them from near and far.

ESSAY

BRICKS & BROWNSTONE: A RESTORATION

Fran Leadon

On Friday around lunchtime, March 6, 1970, Charles Lockwood and the photographer Robert Mayer were standing on West Eleventh Street in Greenwich Village, preparing to shoot the doorway of a Greek Revival row house, when a similar house just eight doors to the east exploded. The terrorist organization the Weather Underground had been using the house as a bomb factory, and two of the Weathermen had made a crucial mistake. Their improvised device, an iron pipe packed with dynamite, went off prematurely, killing them and a third collaborator who had just walked through the front door. Lockwood and Mayer set up a tripod on the sidewalk across from the raging inferno and snapped away. Both received credit for the black-and-white photo that dominated the front page of the next morning's *New York Times*.

The explosion that rocked Eleventh Street proved only a momentary interruption in Lockwood's dogged exploration of New York City's neighborhoods, a project that began as a college thesis and was published, in 1972, as *Bricks & Brownstone*.

Most of the row houses Lockwood documented had been built in the years spanning the opening of the Erie Canal in 1825 and the completion of the Brooklyn Bridge in 1883, those heady decades when the city's population skyrocketed from barely 150,000 to over two million people. By the end of the nineteenth century those houses had coalesced into a utopia of uniformity: row after row, block after block, a brick-and-brownstone world of endlessly repeating stoops, doorways, parlors, bedrooms, and discreet back gardens.

After 1900, New Yorkers, having immersed themselves in an exciting new metropolis of subways, automobiles, electricity, refrigeration, and telephones, yearned for the "French flats" (apartment buildings) that were springing up everywhere and seemed more in step with a taller, faster, modern city than did the brownstones of the gaslight era. By 1920, when Edith Wharton, in *The Age of Innocence*, described the brownstone of the nineteenth century as a bland coating of "cold chocolate sauce" defacing the city, single-family row houses had begun to seem quaint and outmoded. In the decades that followed, once-elegant row houses were cut up into apartments and, poorly maintained, went to seed. "Today, they are mostly rooming houses, sometimes partly business establishments with dressmakers or low price dentists using them for offices," Melrose Gower wrote in the *Washington Post* in 1937. "Dingy and drab, they do not suggest rundown gentility, nor down-at-the-heels respectability: they suggest only cheap lodgings of the most somber sort."

Then came expressways, which provided the escape routes for a post–World War II mass exodus to the suburbs, where a landscape of gas stations, shopping centers, and horizontally planned, detached houses promised easy living. The vertical row houses—so many stairs!—left behind in the city faded even further into grimy obscurity as, one by one, stoops were shorn off, cornices disappeared, and brackets and newel posts went missing.

But already a counter-migration was underway, as writers, editors, artists, teachers, engineers, and architects, many of them with young children in tow, discovered, or rediscovered, the joys of city living. You had to park your car on the street instead of in a carport, but it was so easy to walk around Brooklyn Heights or Park Slope, and so pleasant to sit on the stoop in the evening. There were so many neighbors close by, not to mention the butcher right across the street, the bakery down the block, and the school right around the corner. And climbing all those stairs, day in and day out, kept you in shape.

Those early brownstoners weren't a racially diverse group—one survey in 1971 put their number at 99 percent white—and they were generally more prosperous than the average New Yorker. As they founded block associations, community gardens, and day care centers, they instigated a social transformation that both saved neighborhoods from the wrecking ball and also unleashed the forces of what eventually would be called gentrification.

The effect on the city was profound. What began as a quirky rejection of Robert Moses's bulldoze-first, ask-questions-later urban-renewal initiatives of the 1950s and 1960s had, by the 1970s, become a mainstream movement. Bankers, brokers, physicians, and movie stars (Dustin Hoffman lived next door to the house the Weathermen destroyed) commandeered Greenwich Village and Brooklyn Heights, with houses priced accordingly. And so it went, in Cobble Hill and Carroll Gardens, Chelsea, and the Upper West Side: old row houses were *in*. "Brownstoning," the *New York Times* proclaimed in 1973, "is no longer the novelty it once was."

But in less fashionable neighborhoods, affordable houses were still plentiful—if you had the resources to pay cash or were lucky enough to finagle a mortgage. ("Many bankers . . . are not inclined to lend money for housing in areas of the city where they 'feel' property values are going down," Joy and Paul Wilkes complained in their 1973 nut-and-bolts guidebook *You Don't Have to Be Rich to Own a Brownstone*. "It is still difficult to convince them that once renovation sets in, values go up.") In 1970, Lockwood himself bought a gorgeous Italianate brownstone on South Oxford Street in Brooklyn, just steps away from Fort Greene Park. The house had originally gone on the market a full century earlier, in 1869, for the then-extravagant price of $30,000. Lockwood got it for just $21,000.

Today, it's hard to imagine a time, really not so long ago, when row houses were considered obsolete. Single-family houses in Boerum Hill or Park Slope are so expensive, they're beyond the reach of all but the wealthiest buyers. In neighborhoods like Bedford-Stuyvesant, where generations of middle-class African American homeowners preserved single-family row houses long before brownstoning became fashionable, prices run in the millions. Today a New York City row house embodies not decay and malaise but prosperity, a development that would have been inconceivable when, in 1955, Truman Capote moved to Brooklyn Heights and then half-apologized with the famous line, "I live in Brooklyn. By choice."

How wonderfully ironic that *Bricks & Brownstone* has itself become a landmark. Patrick W. Ciccone began work on this edition as Lockwood's collaborator and took over after Lockwood died in 2012. Though sturdily constructed, Lockwood's treatise—written when he was only in his early twenties—is now almost a half-century old, and was in need of some loving restoration. Ciccone has spruced things up, correcting a few mistakes that dated to the first edition, expanding sections of the book devoted to the late nineteenth and early twentieth centuries, and commissioning new photographs from the keenly observant Dylan Chandler. Ciccone's painstaking work has brought *Bricks & Brownstone* back to life, and no doubt Lockwood would have been pleased that a new generation of readers will inspect the pediments, consoles, quoins, and swags that are described so winningly in its pages.

It's tempting to think of this new edition of *Bricks & Brownstone* as a kind of victory lap, but time, not to mention the quirks of politics, culture, and money, continue to nibble away at New York's domestic cityscape. Explosions like the one Lockwood witnessed in 1970 are, thankfully, rare, but buildings, especially buildings in such a lively real estate market, exist in a state of continuous, incremental change. Even after decades of preservation efforts, historic houses are still demolished or altered past recognition. If a house lies outside the boundaries of an historic district, it's as vulnerable as ever, and even houses within historic districts are susceptible to interior gutting as new homeowners replicate the succulent pages of *House & Garden* and *Dwell*. And while the city's Landmarks Preservation Commission continues to create new historic districts and expand the edges of existing ones, its efforts do not go far enough: recently designated historic districts have tended toward the tiny and tentative, with piecemeal boundaries, and one longs for the sweeping dragnet approach that, in 1965, created the comprehensive forty-seven-block Brooklyn Heights Historic District.

In the end, we value these houses not just for their bricks and brownstone but for the stories they tell. The carpenters, bricklayers, and stone carvers who built the houses, and the families that first lived in them, speak to us as we stroll through the city's neighborhoods. Those folks have been gone for a long time, but many of their houses are still there, and every time we refurbish a bannister, replace a cornice, or straighten a tilting iron railing, we bring them back to life.

INTRODUCTION

Patrick W. Ciccone

New York is a city of houses. This may not be obvious in a city now more famous for its skyscrapers and apartment buildings, not to mention its loft buildings and tenements. However, it is the row house that remains the essential building block for understanding New York's form.

Row houses were the vanguard of urban development in both Manhattan and Brooklyn for 150 years, during New York's boom from a small port city at the end of the eighteenth century into the world's greatest metropolis at the opening of the twentieth. Houses were the first wave of construction to be built by real estate speculators after outlying farmland was divided into building lots. Though the street grid created the armature of the city's future shape, it was row houses that fleshed out that form into buildings.

Houses in Manhattan were built from the Battery north along Broadway to Bond Street and Washington Square and Greenwich Village, then were constructed in great numbers up the spine of the island on Fifth and Madison Avenues and side streets, then to the East and West Sides and uptown across Harlem. In Brooklyn, row houses were built on the Heights down to South Brooklyn and east to Clinton Hill and south to Park Slope, then out to Bedford-Stuyvesant and Crown Heights and Eastern Parkway, and along the spokes of the trolley lines miles from the Brooklyn Bridge deep into the borough. Though many sections of the city, especially in Manhattan, have since been rebuilt, often many times over, these houses remain the markers of New York's scale and urbanity against which newer buildings must be measured.

The original *Bricks & Brownstone* is nearly a half-century old. It began life in 1969 when Charles Lockwood, then an undergraduate at Princeton University, walked into the Donnell Library Center in Midtown Manhattan and asked for a book about New York brownstones. There was none. The subject became his undergraduate thesis, which he researched in libraries, on the streets, and inside the houses of sympathetic owners. In 1972, the original edition of the book was published, with the subtitle *A Guide to Architectural Styles and Interior Decoration for Period Restoration*. The book was intended not just as history but as a restoration template for "brownstoners," the name for owners who since the 1950s had been renovating houses in Manhattan and Brooklyn.

I began working with Charles as a graduate student at Columbia University's Graduate School of Architecture, Planning and Preservation in 2006. Charles had lived in Southern California for nearly three decades at that point, but New York row houses remained his obsession. His long plan was to revise *Bricks & Brownstone*. Though subsequent editions had appeared over the years, they left the original text and images untouched, adding only color photograph plates and walking tours. Charles died from cancer at the age of sixty-three in 2012, and he generously let me take the reins of the new edition after his passing, an exciting but terrifying prospect for me, as the book had come to be known as the Brownstone Bible.

Those familiar with the earlier editions will recognize Charles's text for the Federal, Greek Revival, and Italianate eras presented effectively intact as the book's first three chapters, with some revisions and correction of factual errors. I have added sources and years for quotations where possible, which makes the great depth of the original scholarship clearer. The other major change is that I have also, for space reasons, excised much of the information about the Gothic Revival and its row house styles, once a separate chapter. Gothic Revival row houses were rare, and I have incorporated information about the Gothic Revival and its influence on house architecture into the third chapter on the brownstone era.

Though the original book covered 1783 to 1929, the post-1875 years were treated in a somewhat rushed manner, especially compared against the much more detailed earlier chapters. (Charles had run out of writing time as well as funds for further research.) The chronological balance has been restored by the two new chapters dealing with the span from 1873 to 1893, and from 1893 to the new terminus of 1917. My hope is that the post–Civil War history of row houses has been given its full due and that the new chapters mesh with the familiar fabric of the book. My collaborator on this work, Jonathan D. Taylor, has been invaluable in this process, and the new version would have been impossible without him.

The most noticeable change is the striking new color photography by Dylan Chandler. Though this is a history book, it is also a guide for unlocking the cityscape of present-day New York, and it is my hope that these photographs surprise even the most knowledgeable New York urbanists with the unexpected beauty of the city's houses. And I also hope that the photographs show that it is possible to preserve historic row house interiors—it is now all too common for house interiors to be wholly gutted, with only their facades left intact, something that landmarks law by its nature does regrettably allow for private interiors.

A word about what has still been left out: though mansions and architect-designed town houses do feature in the book, its true subject is the vernacular row house, built by speculators and architect-builders. While individual town houses are an extension of the New York row house tradition, they really stand alone and are described in detail in Robert A. M. Stern's histories of the city's architecture. *Bricks & Brownstone* also does not cover in detail the subsequent history of early twentieth-century row house alterations, a subject taken up in Andrew S. Dolkart's 2009 book, *The Row House Reborn: Architecture and Neighborhoods in New York City, 1908–1929*. To my knowledge, no published work yet comprehensively covers the division of the city's row houses into boardinghouses, apartments, and single-room occupancies—arguably an equally significant role in the history of the city's housing as their original, often brief lives as single-family homes.

It would be impossible to introduce this volume without remarking that the New York City of today is vastly different from the New York City of the early 1970s, the lens through which the original manuscript was drafted. At that time, the preservation of much of the city's historic architecture and neighborhoods was an open question. Many brownstone neighborhoods had been redlined as part of racist housing policies, making it impossible to finance work on houses through banks and, it was thought, condemning them to their demise as slums. The Landmarks Preservation Commission had been established only in the previous decade, and the designation of historic districts comprising some of the city's most important row house neighborhoods occurred as the book was being written. Though reinvestment in many of these neighborhoods had begun, their future was not assured.

Today, some fifty years later, the city is awash in wealth of vastly unequal distribution, and historic row houses are among its most expensive real estate. In many ways, this is a reversion to the economic stratification these houses represented when they were first constructed. "New York is fast becoming a city of only the very rich and very poor," the *American Architect and Building News* wrote in 1878, a lament that will sound familiar to New Yorkers of almost any era. According to the magazine, the row house itself was to blame, as the city's 25-by-100-foot building lots encouraged the construction either of houses for single families "in which only the rich can afford to live" or, on the same size parcel, a tenement that housed many families at once, often in substandard conditions. It was in the latter where the vast majority of the city's nineteenth-century population lived. The row house—at least in its original single-family form—was never home to more than a fraction of New York's population. Nevertheless, the row house epitomized the city's potential urbanity and grace even if it remained out of reach for almost all.

Indeed, though this book describes the real estate development forces and vicissitudes of architectural tradition and style that brought the city's houses into being, such history would ultimately be empty if the subject did not resonate so deeply with New York's sense of collective identity and place. That point was made eloquently by the greatest of New York City architecture writers, Ada Louise Huxtable, in her 1964 *Classic New York: Georgian Gentility to Greek Elegance*. Part history, part walking tour, part preservation polemic, this volume was (and remains) one of the direct inspirations for *Bricks & Brownstone*. "A city in its most real sense, is its buildings," Huxtable wrote in that book's introduction. "The structures that its inhabitants have erected for their use and pride—even the buildings that have come and gone—and the way in which those buildings are disposed upon the streets and squares are the source of its personality, its style, and its distinguishing stamp." I hope these pages show that New York's row houses form irreplaceable components of the city's character, past, present, and forever.

I

1783–1830

THE FEDERAL STYLE & EARLY NEW YORK

When the British Army evacuated New York in 1783, the city bore little resemblance to the thriving metropolis it had been before the Revolutionary War. Few American towns suffered as much destruction as New York did during the long British occupation, which had begun in 1776. Fire had destroyed over one-quarter of all buildings in the small city, then clustered near the Battery, and charred rubble and fallen timbers remained in vacant lots for several years after the end of the war. Wharves had fallen into disrepair because of the virtual halt of trade during the war.

A drastic drop in population during the British occupation dramatically reflected New York's decline. A prosperous city with 25,000 inhabitants in 1775, New York's population had dropped to 12,000 by 1783. Of the remaining residents, many were living in "Canvas Town," a miserable collection of shanties and huts, which started, according to the *New-York Mirror*'s description a half century later, when "the ruins on the southeast side of the town were converted into dwelling places by using the chimneys and parts of walls which were firm, and adding pieces of spars with old canvas from the ships."

Nonetheless, New York recovered rapidly. By 1790, its population rose to 33,000, and, between 1789 and 1790, the city served as the U.S. capital. Its wealth multiplied as merchants rebuilt the city's shipping facilities and looked to trade in the Caribbean, Europe, and East Asia. At the same time, the city experienced a modest building boom, which replaced dwellings destroyed by fire and began to house the rapidly growing population. The number of dwellings in the city increased from an estimated 3,000 in 1783 to nearly 5,000 in 1790 and, only four years later, had nearly doubled to 9,000. In 1794 alone, 850 wood and brick houses were completed in the city.

By 1800, New York was the secondmost populous city in the nation, surpassed only by Philadelphia. Boston, once the nation's largest city, had slipped to third place. Meanwhile, New York had grown northward a mile from the Battery to the vicinity of

Stuyvesant Fish House, 21 Stuyvesant Street, Manhattan (1803–4). This handsome house has the doorway, Flemish-bond brick front, and pitched roof with dormer windows characteristic of the Federal style. National Historic Landmark and New York City Landmark, also within St. Mark's Historic District.

the present-day City Hall, albeit with many vacant lots and gardens still sprinkled among the dwellings. A jumble of narrow, irregular streets served the growing city. Broadway, which by then extended as far north as the present-day Astor Place, was New York's best-known street, an unusual 70 feet wide and, in some places, bordered with poplars. In the words of James Fenimore Cooper's imaginary "English gentleman" in his 1828 *Notions of the Americans: Picked Up by a Travelling Bachelor*, Broadway was "the fashionable mall of the city, and certainly, for gaiety, the beauty and grace of the beings who throng it . . . may safely challenge competition with most if not any of the promenades of the old world."

Despite Cooper's praise for Broadway, early nineteenth-century New York was a small and backward community when compared to the magnificent city of only several decades later. Even the city's most elegant dwellings lacked such conveniences as running water, furnaces, toilets, and cooking ranges that were to be taken for granted in the 1850s. Pigs foraged for garbage in the muddy, rutted, unlit streets. The Bowery was a country road lined with old Dutch farmhouses linking the farms of the Bronx and Westchester County with the city. Canal Street was still a canal, an unfinished project of the Dutch, designed to shorten the distance for ships between the Hudson River and Long Island. New Yorkers picked blackberries on present-day Bleecker Street, and fishermen hauled their nets ashore from the Hudson River at a beach at the foot of Greenwich Street.

NEW YORK'S UNFORESEEN RISE

In the early years of the nineteenth century, few New Yorkers foresaw the phenomenal growth about to overtake their prosperous, but still markedly rural, city. In 1806 a Lutheran church, in financial difficulties, refused a gift of six acres of land at Broadway and Canal Street as not worth the expense of fencing. Only three decades later, that intersection would be the center of the city's most fashionable shopping district. The Commissioners' Plan of 1811 proposed a gridiron of streets from today's Houston Street—then the very northern edge of the city—to 155th Street, setting the shape of all future development in a regular fashion of "beauty, order, and convenience." Nevertheless, the commissioners explained that the "whole island" had "not been laid out as city" because it was improbable New York would ever need to expand farther:

> It may be a subject of merriment that the commissioners have provided space for a greater population than is collected at any spot this side of China . . . and it is improbable that for centuries to come the grounds north of Harlem Flat will be covered with homes.

This comfortable small-town attitude of the city's residents did not last long into the nineteenth century. By the 1820s, New Yorkers boasted about the splendid destiny of their city, especially after the 1820 census ranked New York as the nation's most populous. In 1829 one newspaper proudly contrasted New York with the United States' other leading cities, Boston and Philadelphia:

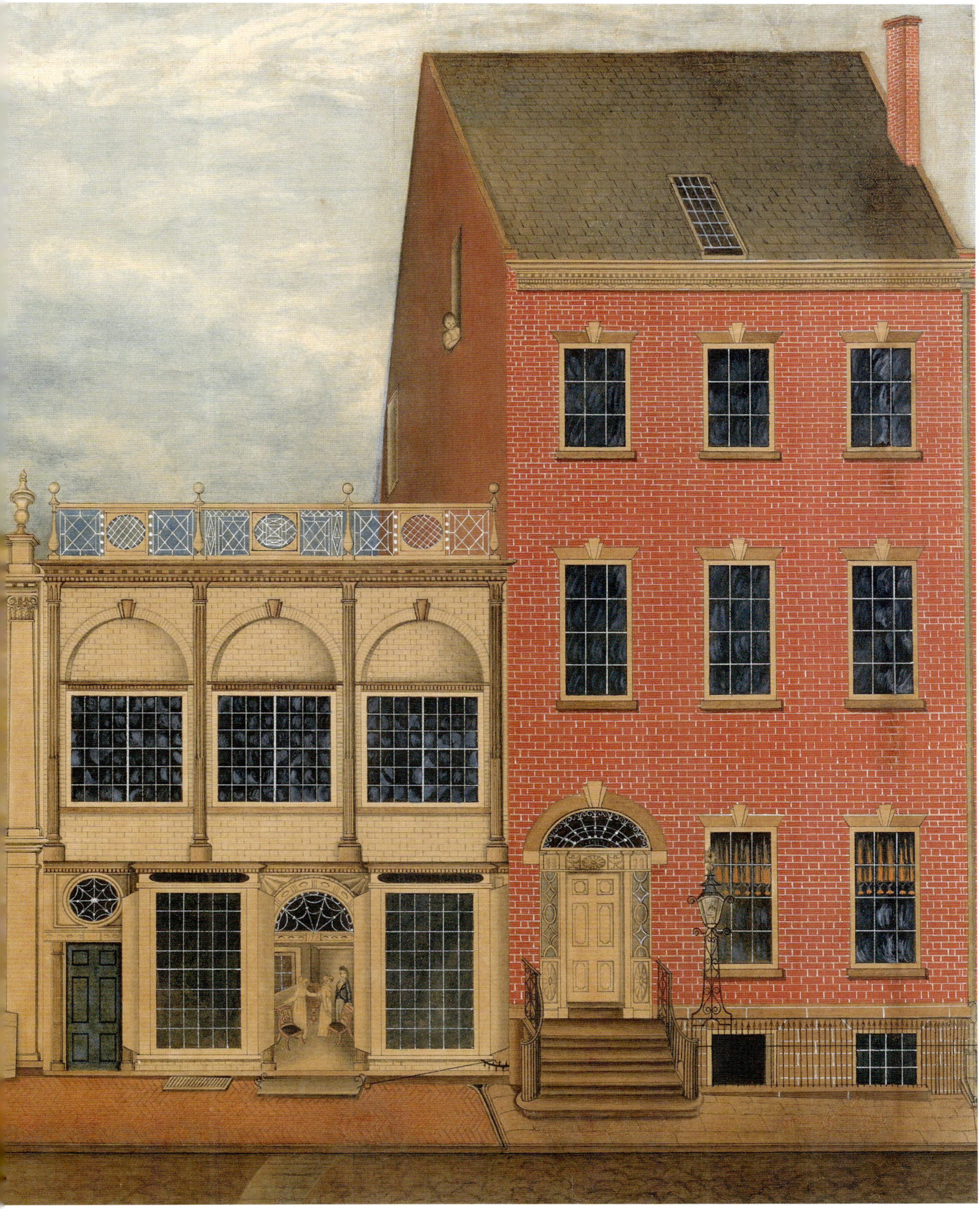

> We do not measure our steps as they do in Philadelphia. We do not study fluxions and eat cod for salmon as they do in Boston. . . . There is more life and spirit and variety in New-York in one day, than in all other cities put together in a fortnight. New-York is Athens revived. . . . Everybody wants to know what's the news? So did they of Ancient Athens. . . . How would the people of Baltimore, or the readers of Philadelphia, or the classiques of Boston get along in the world, if they had not a New-York—a great, active, bustling, ever curious New-York to furnish them with topics and news; to show them the way of living and moving, and to tell them what is fashionable in politics or pantaloons—in commerce or in coats and corsets?

Looking into the city's future, the *New-York Mirror* in 1835 foresaw:

> What enormous and magnificent edifices will . . . be erected! What splendid hotels! What charming private residences! What majestick city halls, courts, colleges, libraries, academies. . . . What fine rows of buildings! What streets and squares! What parks, theatres, opera houses, arcades, and promenades! . . . In short, situated as our city is—commanding, as it does, the trade of the western continent—with

Previous pages: House on Fulton Street, Manhattan (1816). The print shows the house and workshop of celebrated cabinetmaker Duncan Phyfe on the left, with the adjacent Federal-style house on the right delineated in remarkable detail, perhaps the earliest surviving depiction of a typical New York row house front. Note especially the brownstone splayed lintels above the windows, with contrasting marble or limestone keystones.

Above: Broadway, view north from Bowling Green (1828), as depicted in a print from several decades later. Lower Broadway and the area around the Battery were New York's most fashionable neighborhoods in the late eighteenth and early nineteenth centuries. Fortunate residents enjoyed splendid Battery Park and the view overlooking New York Bay, but the area was only a five- or ten-minute walk from the East River and Hudson River docks and countinghouses.

> all the wealth of the world rushing into its bosom by means of railroads, canals, steamers and packet ships—will not this become one of the most wealthy, populous and splendid cities of the globe?

THE REASONS FOR THIS GREAT GROWTH

The enormous growth of New York's share of American foreign and domestic trade fueled the city's prosperity and, in turn, a rapidly increasing population and building boom. Between 1800 and 1830, the value of foreign goods passing through New York increased more than 400 percent. The city's share of the nation's foreign trade rose from 9 percent in 1800 to 37 percent in 1830 and reached a staggering 62 percent by 1860. Oliver Wendell Holmes Sr. appraised the city's geographic and economic destiny: "Sagacious old Dutchmen! To fix on this tongue of land—a tongue that laps up the cream of the commerce of a continent!"

A splendid natural harbor, New York's geographic position, the hard work of the city's merchants, and, most critically, the construction of the Erie Canal accounted for New York's dominance of American domestic and foreign commerce. The city's commercial growth began after the War of 1812. During the war, when trade between Europe and the United States had come to a virtual standstill, American industry, still in its infancy, had been unable to meet the domestic demand for manufactured goods. By the end of the war, in 1815, there was a large and ready market for such goods from Europe. Meanwhile, the concurrent Napoleonic Wars prevented British manufacturers from selling to their usual European markets, and huge inventories had accumulated in their warehouses. At the end of these wars with Napoleon and the United States, British manufacturers dispatched veritable fleets of ships to America and, significantly, mostly to New York.

The federal customs revenue generated in New York jumped from $500,000 in 1814 to $14,000,000 in 1815. In one three-day period alone, in 1815, sixty-five British vessels docked at New York. Looking back at one boom year, 1816, one New Yorker recalled that "this year will be ever memorable with commercial men in this city, for the prodigious importation of merchandise, of every description, from Europe, which gave an impulse to business that was felt by all classes." New York was the first American city to offer shippers and passengers alike a regularly scheduled transatlantic packet to Europe. In 1817 the Black Ball Line operated four ships in transatlantic service and sailed to Liverpool, England, on the first of every month. By the next year, several additional ship lines sailed for Liverpool and, altogether, offered a departure every week. With this expertise in trade and the European connections, planters in the Southern slave states sent their valuable cotton crop to New York, where it was then shipped to British or New England textile mills.

However, the Appalachian Mountain range blocked trade between the rapidly growing Midwest and the East Coast. The several mountain passes offered only limited land routes for settlers moving West. In the United States of the early nineteenth century nearly all roads were narrow and rutted, muddy when it rained, and virtually impassable in winter. Twenty miles a day was good progress when shipping goods by wagon. Even though the turnpikes of the period did provide a few adequate roads and reasonably fast travel, the tolls were so high that commerce generally followed the slow inland waterways instead.

With the completion of the Erie Canal in 1825, the trouble-free water link between the Great Lakes and Hudson River made New York the terminus for the shipment of crops and goods from the Midwest and the entrepôt of manufactured goods moving in the opposite direction. Whereas it took $120 and three weeks to ship a ton of wheat, itself worth $40, from Buffalo to New York City by land, on the Erie Canal the shipping cost dropped to $6 a ton for grain and the time to eight days. At the Erie Canal's dedication ceremony, New York's Common Council addressed the city and New York State in the form of prophecy: "[T]here will be no limits to your lucrative extensions of trade and commerce. The Valley of the Mississippi will soon pour its treasures in this great emporium, through the channels now formed and forming."

THE BUILDING BOOM OF THE 1820s AND 1830s

This flourishing domestic and foreign trade brought prosperity and enormous population growth to New York. The city's population increased from 124,000 in 1820 to 203,000 in 1830, reached 313,000 in 1840, and 516,000 in 1850! To accommodate this growing population, the city raced northward on Manhattan in a continual building boom, interrupted only by occasional depressions or wartime economic uncertainty.

After a modest recession in 1817–18, the construction boom started in earnest about 1820. New Yorkers were fascinated by their city's awesome growth. One gentleman's journal noted that in 1824 "more than 1600 new houses were erected, nearly all of them of brick or stone." In 1830 Philip Hone, mayor of the city from 1825 to 1826 and a well-to-do merchant whose two-million-word journal gives a fascinating view of New York in the 1830s and 1840s, observed that "our country at large, and particularly this city, is at this time prosperous beyond all former example . . . real estate, up and down town, equally high; houses in great demand, at advanced rents."

New Yorkers soon realized that the only unchanging aspect of their bustling city was change itself. In 1839 Hone wrote in his journal that "the pulling down of houses and stores in the lower parts [of Broadway] is awful. Brickbats, rafters, and slates are showering down in every direction. There is no safety on the sidewalks." Hone concluded that "the spirit of pulling down and building up is abroad. The whole of New York is rebuilt about once in ten years."

New York's ceaseless northward growth and rebuilding of existing areas soon obliterated all traces of its Dutch past as New Amsterdam. As early as 1797, the *American Gazetteer* noted that "there are remaining a few houses built after the old Dutch manner." James Fenimore Cooper in *Notions of the Americans* in the 1820s observed that "a few old Dutch dwellings yet remain, and can easily be distinguished by their little bricks, their gables to the street, and those steps on their battlement walls . . . invented, in order to ascend to regulate the iron weathercocks at every variation of the fickle winds." In a startling sign of the city's growth, Cooper estimated that "there are not five hundred buildings in New-York, that can date further back than the peace of '83" less than a half century before.

THE FEDERAL ROW HOUSE FRONT

The architectural style of row houses built during the prosperous period between the Revolutionary War and the 1830s became known as the Federal style. Based primarily on the work of the Adam brothers in Great Britain, the Federal style was a direct architectural link to the pre-Revolutionary tradition, derived from the English Georgian style. In its simplicity, the Federal-style row house followed the classical tradition in architecture of the eighteenth century, an influence also pervasive in that period's literary classicism and in the scientific work of such men as René Descartes and Isaac Newton. The classical tradition in architecture sought principles worthwhile in all times and circumstances. British architects in this tradition looked to the ruins of Greece and Rome not to idealize or to copy the specific era but to find universal principles and forms that were appealing beyond shifts in architectural fashion.

The pervasive British influence in American architecture in the late eighteenth and early nineteenth centuries confirmed that the Revolutionary War had been a political, not cultural, revolution, and visitors from Great Britain to the United States noted the similarity of

155 and 157 Willow Street, Brooklyn Heights (ca. 1825). These Federal-style houses evoke the long-vanished dignity of early nineteenth-century New York's houses and streets. Brooklyn Heights Historic District.

24
Clinton

Opposite: 24 Middagh Street, Brooklyn Heights (1820s). This charming Federal-style house, with a richly detailed front doorway, is one of the finest remaining early nineteenth-century frame houses in New York. Building codes requiring masonry construction in Manhattan made it illegal to construct frame dwellings below the fire line, meaning few wood dwellings were built there after the 1820s. Though still relatively rare, more examples of wood row house construction survive across the East River. Brooklyn Heights Historic District.

Right: 29 East Fourth Street, Manhattan (1831–32), photographed in 1936, now the Merchant's House Museum. This photograph, taken for the Historic American Buildings Survey (HABS), shows the Seabury Tredwell House only three years after Tredwell's youngest daughter, Gertrude, died in the house at the age of ninety-three. She was born there in 1840 and lived in the house her entire life. The original furniture from before the Civil War and all the interiors were left intact at her death, a remarkable time capsule of an otherwise lost New York. The house was completed in 1832, and its exterior is in the late Federal style, a more ostentatious variation of the long-lasting Federal style, while the interior is mostly executed in the ascendant Greek Revival style. National Historic Landmark, New York City Landmark, and New York City Interior Landmark.

British and American architectural styles. James Fenimore Cooper's traveling bachelor observed that "the Americans have not yet adopted a style of architecture of their own. Their houses are essentially English," and English visitor John Lambert in 1814 remarked that "the houses in the Broadway are lofty and well built. They are constructed in the English style and differ little from those of London at the west end of town; except that they are universally built of *red* brick."

"Excepting in a few low quarters," wrote Englishman Andrew Bell, in 1838, New York was distinguished by its "cheerful" and "neat" row houses. In the early nineteenth century, New York houses were modest in scale and simple in architectural ornament—particularly compared to similar dwellings of later decades. This handsome simplicity of the Federal style showed that the classical ideals of architectural restraint were influential. Moreover, the high cost of hand labor made elaborate architectural forms and details too costly except for the finest houses, and social customs in New York did not yet demand an ostentatious dwelling. The narrow front of a row house also discouraged a pretentious architectural treatment. "The exterior necessarily presents a narrow, ill-arranged facade, that puts architectural beauty a good deal at defiance," observed Cooper. "The most that can be done with such a front is to abstain from inappropriate ornament, and to aim at such an effect as shall convey a proper idea of the more substantial comforts, and of the neatness that predominate within."

Brick. The front of Federal-style row houses usually was red brick, ordinarily laid in Flemish bond, which showed alternately the long side and the end of the brick. The doorway and window trim of brownstone, granite, or marble was modestly detailed and barely broke the planar smoothness of the facade. During the early nineteenth-century hegemony of the Federal style, the brick fronts of New York row houses were usually painted red or occasionally gray or cream with false mortar lines in white added between the bricks. "The inhabitants of New York inherit the taste of their Dutch ancestors for fresh paint; every house of any pretension is annually coated with scarlet or grey, the divisions of the bricks are picked out with white," observed English author Sarah Mytton Maury. Cooper praised the practice, which he deemed "scarcely alters their original appearance, except by imparting a neatness and freshness that are exceedingly pleasant." Later, in 1852, Charles Astor Bristed in *The Upper Ten Thousand: Sketches of American Society* sneered at the effect, stating that the "flaring vermilion" brick with "each individual brick picked out in white lead . . . disfigures a great deal of New York."

Basement and Stone Trim. The row house rose above a high basement of brick, blocks of brownstone with a plain surface and sharply beveled joints, or rusticated blocks of brownstone or marble. In the early nineteenth century, the same dark red sandstone, or brownstone, that would later epitomize luxury and architectural sophistication—and would of course become a name for row houses themselves—was then an inexpensive local substitute for the marble or limestone of pretentious buildings. The brownstone basement, door, and window trim presented a pleasing contrast of color and texture on the red-brick house front, and in her 1832 *Domestic Manners of the Americans*,

Opposite top: Hollow urn newel posts, 56 West Tenth Street, Greenwich Village (1831–32). Wrought-iron hollow urns graced the stoop railings of many fine New York row houses in the 1820s and 1830s, but unfortunately most have disappeared. Greenwich Village Historic District.

Opposite bottom: Boot scraper, 59 Morton Street, Greenwich Village (1828). Few streets in early nineteenth-century New York were paved, and in wet weather or winter they turned into a muddy morass. Greenwich Village Historic District.

English novelist and writer Frances Trollope wrote that the city's builders "are now using a great deal of a beautiful stone called Jersey freestone; it is of a warm rich brown, and extremely ornamental to the city wherever it has been employed."

Throughout the early nineteenth century and particularly after the opening of extensive marble and granite quarries near New York City in the 1820s, fine row houses employed costly and classically more appropriate marble for street-front trim rather than the local brownstone. "Since the discovery of the vast quarries of white marble in Westchester County, the effect is everywhere manifest," reported one newspaper in 1828. "The brown sand stone of New Jersey is quite neglected in domestic architecture, compared with its former exclusive use," observed one New Yorker the same year. The light-colored marble and granite "now introduced into buildings . . . have conduced much to improve the aspect of the city." Some marble- or granite-front row houses were built in the late 1820s and early 1830s and immediately excited comment. In 1833, the *New-York Mirror* praised marble-front dwellings as "another improvement" in the city and applauded "the employment of a nobler and more durable material in building" than brick. Observing that nearly all the city's row houses had brick fronts, the newspaper bemoaned the comparably scarce "numbers of private houses upon which no cost has been spared, except the cost of erecting them of a material which defies the tooth of time."

The emergence of marble-front row houses and elaborate large dwellings in the 1820s revealed the decline in fashion for the simplicity of the long-lived Federal style and the demand for architectural grandeur to match the city's unparalleled prosperity. Reflecting this rising taste, one newspaper wrote in 1827:

> Elegant pillars, pilasters, pediments, caps, steps, sills, etc., many of them presenting the most ingenious specimens of architecture and carved work, are among the striking embellishments which adorn numbers of newly erected houses. While these things impart an aspect of peculiar richness and beauty, they . . . are as creditable to the taste of our citizens, as they are to the skill and ingenuity of our artists.

These lavish marble fronts and elaborate ornament, however, appeared only on a handful of the city's most costly dwellings.

Stoop and Ironwork. On most Federal-style dwellings, the front doorway entrance provided one of the few enriching touches on the street facade. Because the first floor—also known as the parlor floor—was above the street over a high basement, a low flight of brownstone or marble steps known as a "stoop" led to the front door. The original Dutch settlers of New Amsterdam, as New York was then called, brought the concept of the stoop, as well as its name (from the Dutch *stoep*), from the Netherlands, where the continual threat of flooding made the elevation of the principal floor above ground a practical necessity. Because New York faced little threat of flooding, many simple early Dutch houses in New Amsterdam were in fact built without them. New Yorkers thus viewed the stoop as an ornamental feature that brought a simple architectural grandeur by elevating the first floor of houses several feet above the street. The stoop also served a critical practical as well as decorative function. Because Manhattan and Brooklyn blocks rarely had service alleys behind the houses, as in fine streets in Philadelphia or Baltimore, the doorway under the stoop provided a much-needed separate service entrance to the kitchen by way of the basement hallway.

In the early nineteenth century, well-to-do New Yorkers had already discovered the pleasures of stoop sitting on warm evenings. During evening parties in hot summer months, "it is customary to sit out of doors on the steps that ornament the entrances of the houses," wrote British naval officer Frederick Fitzgerald De Roos in 1827. "On these occasions, friends assemble in the most agreeable and unceremonious manner. All sorts of cooling beverages and excellent confectionary are handed round, and the greatest good humour and gaiety prevail."

Cooper, however, panned stoops as "hideous excrescences . . . found disfiguring the architecture, cumbering the side-walks, and endangering the human neck," though admitting that New Yorkers "cherish the clumsy inconvenient entrances." Nevertheless, besides providing the important service entrance, the stoops, wrote Cooper, "compensate, in a slight degree, for the pain of ascent . . . by their admirable neatness, and the perfect order of their iron rails and glittering brass ornaments." The safety considerations that required handrailings for the stoop and a fence separating the sidewalk from the dug-out areaway made for exceptionally handsome hand-wrought ironwork on the city's early nineteenth-century row houses.

In the 1820s and 1830s, the front fences for the areaway had pineapple, pine cone, or acorn finials on top of the vertical iron shafts or on the top and bottom railings between the shafts. The stoop railing's newel post usually was a four-sided hollow cage, which either rose directly from the sidewalk or sat on a modest stone pedestal, often a section of a column. The hollow-cage newel posts often employed picturesque "Gothick" arches on their sides, and in a further display of early nineteenth-century artisans' skills, were topped by a small pineapple or by a large, hollow urn, itself terminating in a pineapple, the symbol of hospitality. Built-in boot scrapers usually were a part of the stoop railing or newel post and indicated that most of the city's early nineteenth-century dwellings originally were built on unpaved streets. Although very few hollow-cage newel posts or hollow urns have survived to the present day, handsome wrought-iron stoop railings and areaway fences occasionally remain on Federal dwellings otherwise lacking in prominent architectural features.

Doorway. The elegant front doorway, usually the most elaborate feature of the restrained row house front, reflected the good taste and fine workmanship of the early nineteenth century. The usual Federal-style doorway had a delicately leaded rectangular toplight and, often, leaded sidelights. The single wood door had six or eight deeply set panels, often edged with a delicate egg-and-dart pattern or beading, and brass or silver doorknob and knocker. The fanlight doorway, commonly associated with the Federal style, was used in New York only in the 1820s and early 1830s, when late Federal houses adopted more elaborate design and ornament. Doorway size and ornamentation

Dormer windows, 52 West Tenth Street, Greenwich Village (1830–31). Greenwich Village Historic District.

Top left: Doorway, 39 Charlton Street, Manhattan (1827). This impressive entry shows the grander configuration of the Federal doorway, with a leaded toplight recessed beneath the lintel and surrounded by elegant moldings. Below, Ionic colonnettes and sidelights with delicate tracery flank either side of the paneled door. Charlton-King-Vandam Historic District.

Top right: Doorway, Merchant's House Museum, 29 East Fourth Street, Manhattan (1831–32). In the late 1820s and early 1830s, large New York row houses in the late Federal style had doorways with richly ornamented fanlight and sidelight windows, Ionic columns, and arched stone moldings.

Left: Doorway, 24 Charlton Street, Manhattan (ca. 1825). In the 1820s, the doorways of modest row houses had rectangular toplights for ornament rather than the elaborate fanlight and sidelight arrangement commonly associated with Federal-style houses. Charlton-King-Vandam Historic District.

Opposite: Doorway, 59 Morton Street, Greenwich Village (1828). This widely admired doorway epitomizes the elegance and good taste of the Federal style with its leaded fanlight and sidelight windows, colonnettes at each side of the door, and stone arched lintel above the elaborate fanlight window. Greenwich Village Historic District.

59

depended upon the size of the dwelling and its date of construction. The high cost of hand labor, even then, reserved the highly decorated doorway for the houses of the rich. Elaborate doorways also became stylistically more acceptable in the late 1820s and early 1830s, partly as a reaction to the simplicity of the long-lived Federal style and partly because of the wealth accumulating in the city, which encouraged more elaborate houses.

Windows. On most row houses, windows were modest in scale, small-paned, and double-hung, usually six-over-six. The first- and second-floor windows of the Federal house were nearly the same size, unlike the row houses of the mid-nineteenth century in which windows diminished in size on the upper, less important floors. Shutters or window blinds, usually painted green, added a cheerful note to the front and, when shut, offered some relief from winter winds or summer sun.

The occasional late Federal house of the late 1820s and early 1830s introduced parlor windows that dropped to the floor, later a typical feature on Greek Revival houses. Here, windows either were double-hung, i.e., six-over-six, or triple-hung, i.e., six-over-six-over-six. These long windows added a note of grandeur to the rich facade and brought more light and air into the large parlors of these houses. To shield the parlor from the view of passersby, iron guardrails were added to the lower two or three feet of the window, sometimes extending as a balcony across the entire parlor-floor front. Largely gone today, these iron guardrails or balconies exhibited late Federal or Greek Revival designs of great beauty.

Brownstone or marble lintels over the windows and door were a decorative touch and usually reflected the degree of facade embellishment established by the doorway. Often the flat lintel over a door followed the design of the window lintels. On the many houses where the basement and first floor have been converted into a storefront, the stone lintels of the second-floor windows often are the only obvious clue that the building is a much-altered early nineteenth-century row house.

Cornice and Dormers. The Federal row house usually was smaller in scale than the comparable houses of succeeding decades. Most houses built before 1830, as well as modest houses constructed well into the 1830s, followed the same general design: two full stories over a basement topped by a pitched roof with two dormers. On the pitched-roof house, the cornice at the roofline provided a casing for a gutter whose drainpipe ran down the street front. To minimize the visual intrusion of these drainpipes, a single pipe sometimes emptied the gutters of the two houses on either side. An important visual element, the cornice clearly marked the top of the house front and, thereby, defined the facade's proportions by its width and height. The cornice also added a note of richness to the restrained facade. The 12-to-18-inch-high fascia board, which stretched from one side of the facade to the other, usually was a plain and flat surface except for occasional fluting. In most houses, an egg-and-dart or dentil molding appeared just below the fascia board.

Above the cornice, the two dormer windows, aligned over the solid piers of the wall, pierced the pitched roof and made the attic a lighted and well-ventilated area. Characteristic of the Federal style, the dormers took a variety of handsomely simple forms and architectural ornament. On a single row house or several houses in a row, the pitched roof and two dormers lent a picturesque distinction to the streetscape quite lacking in the streets entirely lined with flat-roofed houses of succeeding styles.

Few pitched roofs now remain on the city's surviving Federal-style row houses. With the city's constantly rising land values, many house owners replaced the pitched-roof attic with a full third floor and new cornice. A later-style cornice or third-floor lintel on an otherwise Federal-style row house will indicate the addition of a third floor and, to the architecturally knowledgeable, the approximate date of this addition. Some alterations, however, were more careful than others, and the new cornice and window lintels copy the original forms.

FEDERAL-STYLE HOUSE PLANS AND INTERIOR DESIGN

In the early nineteenth century, the typical row house was 20 to 25 feet wide and, for the sake of adequate lighting and ventilation, only two rooms deep. With a usual 35 to 40 foot depth on a typical 100-foot-deep lot, row houses had a substantial backyard or garden.

Inside, a generic house plan for New York had stabilized by the 1820s. On the basement floor, there was a front room, accessible from under the stoop, and a rear kitchen, opening onto the garden. On the first (or parlor) floor, the stoop entrance led to a small vestibule then into the hallway, or directly into the hallway, which in turn opened on to the connected front and rear parlors. On the second floor were front and rear bedrooms. All floors were typically connected by a single stairway, save in the case of rarer grand houses with a separate service stairway at the rear.

Basement and Garden. The basement front room is the only room of the city's early nineteenth-century row houses whose original use cannot be definitely established. Travel accounts of several Englishmen in the United States place the dining room in the front room of the basement floor, convenient to the kitchen in the adjacent back room. One Englishman, Joseph J. Gurney, observed in 1841 that the dining room was in the basement front room and the first floor was totally given over to two parlors:

> The private houses . . . are generally of neat red brick-work, four stories high, besides the basement. This last [floor] in New York generally contains the dining-room; so that we descend to dinner. . . . The drawing room . . . usually occupies the whole of the first story, being divided in two by large folding doors. These apartments are often very spacious.

Only for formal dinner parties, a rare occasion in early nineteenth-century New York, did the servants set up a table in the handsome back parlor and bring the food up the stairs from the kitchen below. It was difficult to serve meals in this rear parlor from the basement below, and a formal dining room in the back parlor with heavy table and breakfronts would have prevented the family from opening the sliding doors between the parlors and using the full expanse of the front and back parlors for the usual receptions and dancing parties.

The back parlor of Philip Hone's elegant row house at 235 Broadway, opposite City Hall Park, likely was a reception room rather than a formal dining room. After a party at the Philip Hone residence, Mrs. Basil Hall (Margaret Hunter Hall), a British visitor to the United States, observed in 1827 that "there were two large rooms open, communicating by folding doors and handsomely furnished and lighted. Quadrilles were danced in both rooms."

On the other hand, other early nineteenth-century travelers in the United States stated that the rear parlor was a formal dining room and the front room of the basement a nursery or an office. Frances Trollope in 1832 remarked that "in nearly all the houses the dining and drawing-rooms are on the same floor, with ample folding doors between them," and, according to a British writer under the pen name of Mrs. Felton in 1842, "[T]he dining and drawing rooms are situated on the lower [first] floor, and so arranged, as by throwing open a large pair of folding doors, to form one splendid apartment." Furthermore, the French naturalist and artist Jacques-Gérard Milbert, who traveled to the United States in 1815 and lived and taught in New York until 1823, called the front room of the basement *"la nursery"* and *"le logement des enfants,"* and the well-informed Cooper wrote that "the basement contains a nursery and the usual offices."

Despite the contradictory evidence of these sources, the front basement room's convenience to the kitchen and the small pantry-like rooms between the front room and the kitchen indeed suggest that it was an

Following pages: Garden, Merchant's House Museum.

informal dining room in the 1820s and 1830s. Besides, the handsome mantels and wood paneling in the front basement room of an early nineteenth-century row house were architectural features too elaborate for rooms of such an ordinary function as a nursery or office.

In the 1820s and 1830s, the first-floor rear parlor probably functioned as a formal dining room only for occasional dinner parties, and, significantly, it was in these festive circumstances that such distinguished British visitors as Trollope and Felton visited the city's row houses. Only with the ready availability of servants from waves of European immigration after the 1840s and the widespread appearance of the dumbwaiter in large row houses in the 1850s and 1860s did the rear parlor actually become the usual formal dining room, freeing the front basement room for use as an informal dining room for breakfast and supper and occasionally as an office or nursery.

Unlike later houses, the modest Federal row house lacked a furnace and rarely had a cellar for storage. Often, the wide-plank floor of the basement family room and kitchen sat on a cheap subflooring that rested on the bare earth. The Federal row house nevertheless had considerable storage space. Many houses of the period have vaults, about 10 feet wide and 20 feet long, extending underneath the street in front of the house to store food and, in wet weather, dry firewood as well. Placed several feet below the level of the basement, these vaults had comfortable, 8-to-10-foot-high ceilings and were constructed of stone and brick rubble held together by mortar. One usually entered the vault through a door under the stoop and walked down a steep flight of wood or stone steps.

By the mid-nineteenth century, gardens or backyards would be dug out so as to be on the same level as the basement. In the early nineteenth century, this practice was unknown, and a sunken areaway with steps led from the garden to the back door of the basement. In many houses of the Federal period, the kitchen had a small, several-foot-high food-storage vault sunk into the garden between the kitchen's two windows and directly accessible, like a cupboard, from the kitchen. The relatively low and constant temperature of these vaults was, of course, a great help in food preservation.

Parlor Floor. On the first floor, the front door usually led directly into a long and narrow hallway along the side of the house or, in some large row houses of the period, a large vestibule and a second doorway. This "little vestibule, which may be some 12 feet long, by 8 in width," wrote Cooper, was "entirely unfurnished, and appears only constructed to shelter visiters [*sic*] while the servant is approaching to admit them through the inner door. The general excellence of the climate, and, perhaps, the customs of the country, have, as yet, prevented the Americans from providing a proper place for the reception of the servants of their guests: they rarely wait, unless during the short calls, and then it is always in the street."

This vestibule led into a side hallway, with the stairway to the second-floor bedrooms placed at the end, rather than the center as in later decades, to better receive daylight from a rear window placed between the first and second floors.

Above: Kitchen, Merchant's House Museum. The rear room of the basement floor facing the garden served as the kitchen in early nineteenth-century row houses, a location that would remain fixed in row house plans, modest or grand, for the rest of the century. Here, the Merchant's House kitchen is staged with a later cast-iron stove in the hearth, an advance over the more difficult to control—not to mention more dangerous—open-hearth cooking.

Following pages:
The identical pair of buildings at 37 and 39 Charlton Street (1827) are two of the most impressive Federal-style row houses surviving in Manhattan. Charlton-King-Vandam Historic District.

Plans: 37 Charlton Street, Manhattan (1827), in a floor plan drawn by the Historic American Buildings Survey (HABS) in 1936. This plan shows the typical configuration of a more substantial Federal row house. On the basement floor sit the dining room and kitchen, connected by a pantry. The service entry below the stoop is at the bottom right of the basement plan, which connects via a long hallway to the kitchen and garden at the rear. The grandest rooms, the front and rear parlors, sit on the first, or parlor, floor, connected by swinging double doors. The stoop entrance is shown at the bottom right of the parlor floor plan; visitors first entered a vestibule before passing through another doorway into the hall. The stair, as typical in many Federal houses, was at the rear of the hallway. The second and third floors feature bedrooms at the front and rear. The second- and third-floor bathrooms shown on this plan were added at a later date, replacing closets. Before the introduction of water carried by the Croton Aqueduct from Westchester County to Manhattan in 1842 and a sewage system begun in 1849, all houses, even the grandest, had privies in the rear yard.

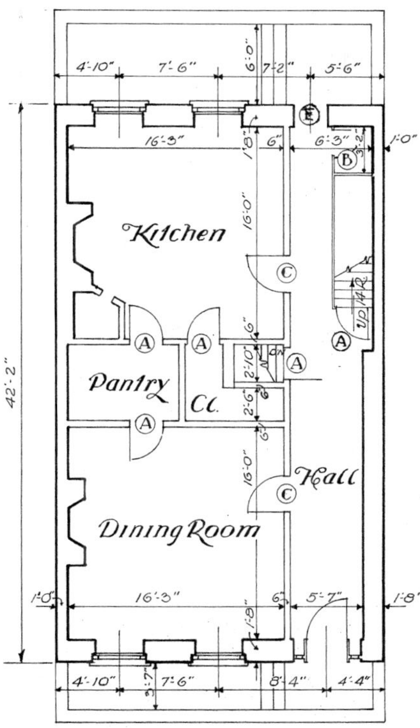

Basement

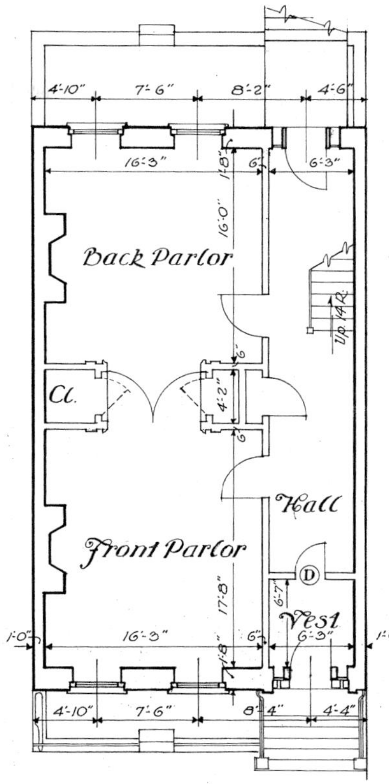

First Floor

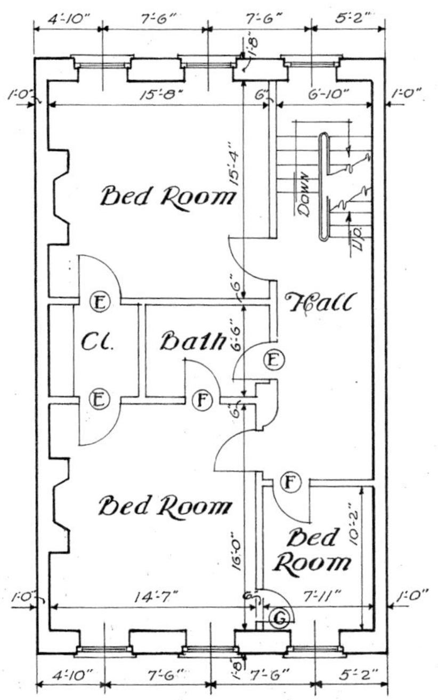

Second Floor

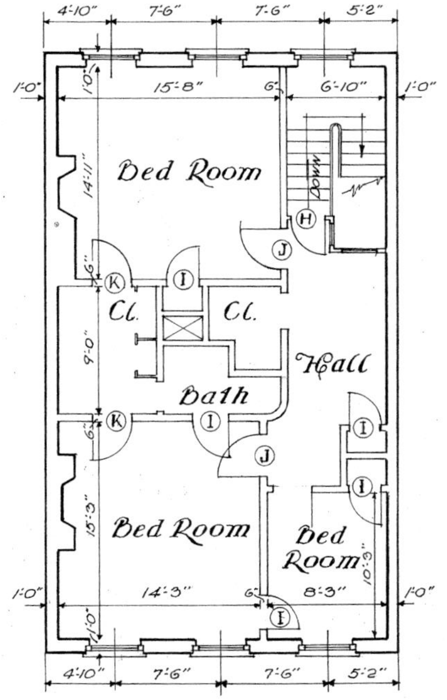

Third Floor

The front and back parlors, nearly square and usually nearly identical in shape, opened off this long side hallway. In the early nineteenth century, visitors to New York always admired the elegance of the parlors, which displayed the richest architectural ornament, finest materials, and best furniture of the family house. In the 1820s Cooper described the parlors in the elegant row house of a New Yorker "in the first society of the country, and of what is here called an easy fortune," on then-fashionable lower Broadway:

> Each room is lighted by two windows; is sufficiently high; has [a] stuccoed ceiling, and cornices in white, hangings of light, airy, French paper; curtains in silk and in muslin; mantel-pieces of carved figures in white marble (Italian in manufacture, I should think); Brussels carpets; large mirrors; chairs, sofas, and tables, in mahogany; chandeliers; beautiful, neat, and highly wrought grates in the fireplaces of home work; candelabras, lustres, &c. &c., much as one sees them all over Europe.

Even the often-critical Frances Trollope remarked that "the dwelling houses of the higher classes are extremely handsome, and very richly furnished."

In the early nineteenth century, New Yorkers and visitors also admired the row houses of the city's middle-class families, which shared many qualities with their more elegant peers. "On entering the house of a respectable mechanic, in any of the large cities of the United States," wrote the Bohemian-born American author and journalist Francis Joseph Grund in 1837, "one cannot but be astonished at the apparent neatness and comfort of the apartments, the large airy parlors, the nice carpets and mahogany furniture." Cooper's thorough description of the "second-rate, genteel" row houses in New York is particularly charming:

> There is a species of second-rate, genteel houses, that abound in New York, into which I have looked when passing, with the utmost pleasure. They have, as usual, a story that is half sunk in the earth, receiving light from an area, and two floors above. The tenants of these buildings are chiefly merchants, or professional men, in moderate circumstances, who pay rents of from 300 to 500 dollars a year. You know that no American, who is at all comfortable in life, will share his dwelling with another. Each has his own roof, and his own little yard. These buildings are finished, and exceedingly well finished too, to the attics; containing, on the average, six rooms, besides offices, and servants' apartments. The furniture of these houses is often elegant, and always neat. Mahogany abounds here, and is commonly used for all the principal articles, and very frequently for doors, railings of stairs, &c. &c.

In an early nineteenth-century row house, these rooms typically had pleasing proportions. The relatively low cost of building lots made possible a 25-foot-wide lot even for some middle-class row houses. Despite the space devoted to the stair hallway from the front to the rear of the house, the rooms were fairly square in shape. Nine- and 10-foot-tall ceilings on the parlor floors enhanced the feeling of hominess and restraint evoked by these square rooms and modest forms.

Parlor Decoration. Within the modestly scaled parlors, such elements of interior design as mantels, doorways, or ceilings were characterized by restrained forms and enriched with occasional ornamental detail. On the first floor, rectangular double doors separated the front parlor and the back parlor and, in many cases, the front and back bedrooms on the second floor as well. In most Federal row houses, the double parlor doors were hinged. Although double doors, which slid into the wall on metal tracks, did appear in large row houses of the mid-1820s and in the Greek Revival parlors of late Federal dwellings, they did not displace the hinged parlor doors in modest row houses until the mid-1830s. In the 1820s, the enframement of the mahogany- or rosewood-veneer parlor doors consisted of pilasters, at each side, supporting a horizontal lintel with carved square end blocks and, in the center, usually, a large rectangular carved block. In the first-floor parlor, carved acanthus or oak leaves enriched these end and center blocks. These double parlor doors and their enframement with richly carved pilasters and center blocks evidence the simplicity of form, relieved by occasional ornamental details, so valued in the Federal-style dwellings.

A small antechamber separated the front parlor and back parlor, and some houses boasted two sets of doors for the two rooms. Fully opened, the two sets of double doors—or even the single pair of doors—formed handsome paneled walls. The fully opened doors concealed china closets or a small butler's pantry in the hallway. These sets of hinged double doors and the connecting hallways clearly defined the separateness of the front and back rooms. With the introduction of sliding doors in the 1820s these hallways—or "pantries," as they

Top: Parlor doorway, 39 Charlton Street (1827). Ionic pilasters, a richly carved rectangular center block, and square end blocks frame the doorway between the front and rear parlors. Two doors once sat in the opening, allowing the front parlor to be separated from the rear. When swung open, they concealed the closets located between the two parlors, visible here.

Bottom: Front-parlor door enframement, 39 Charlton Street.

This page and opposite: Mantels, 39 Charlton Street. The three mantels, respectively, show the difference in detail—and cost—between the mantel on the parlor (first) floor, bedroom (second) floor, and top (third) floor in a large Federal-style house. The front-parlor mantel, which sits at the center of the grandest public room, features rich contrasting marble. In the second-floor front bedroom, a similar mantel continues the same forms but in far less expensive wood. On the top floor, a simple painted-wood mantel with modest decoration surrounds the fireplace.

Following pages:
Rear second-floor bedroom used as an artist studio, 39 Charlton Street.

LAVAZZA
PREMIUM
DRIP COFFEE

SORIN

Entrance hallway, 155 Willow Street, Brooklyn Heights.

This page and opposite:
Front and rear parlor, 155 Willow Street, Brooklyn Heights.

Following pages:
Rear top-floor bedroom, 155 Willow Street. The room would have originally been divided in between the two dormers into much smaller rooms used as bedrooms by the servants.

were then called—disappeared on the parlor floor, and the space of two parlors flowed directly into each other.

Mantels. In the early nineteenth century, a wood-burning fireplace was the usual source of heat. Handsome marble or wood mantels graced most rooms in the Federal row house. Reflecting the overall architectural modesty of the period, the parlor mantels usually had a plain rectangular shelf supported by plain or fluted columns, flat side jambs, and a horizontal jamb, above the fireplace opening, usually ornamented by a deeply set panel in the center. The favorite materials were wood, white marble, a mixture of white and black marble pieces, or, as would become common in the Greek Revival style, black marble veined with gold.

Mantels were "highly ornamental, when tastefully constructed," but often "the magnitude of a chimney-piece does not always correspond with that of the room in which it is situated," architect Asher Benjamin wrote in his 1833 pattern book *Practice of Architecture*. "Columns are often employed in their decoration" and "in large apartments may sometimes be employed to advantage," but this impressive mantel style was "in small plain rooms, to be avoided." In their large scale and rich ornament, such mantels, with columns supporting the shelf, were inappropriate to a small and otherwise simply detailed room.

Following this sensible advice and, at the same time, keeping an eye on construction costs, row house builders in New York installed in the second-floor bedrooms handsome mantels of a simpler design than in the first-floor parlors. These mantels usually omitted the ornamental and costly columns that supported the shelf and instead relied upon their pleasing proportions and the paneled horizontal jamb above the fireplace opening for decorative effect.

In the early nineteenth century, firewood was sold from wagons that stopped at the street corners, and the servant who sawed the firewood into suitable logs and kept the fires burning usually was given the privilege of selling the ashes. Even then, long-burning anthracite coal, in an iron grate, began to replace wood as a source of heat in the city's large dwellings, a development evidenced by the reduced size of the fireplace opening and the appearance of ornamental iron screens in an occasional dwelling of the late 1820s and early 1830s.

The parlor walls were painted plaster, with a single foot-high molding or baseboard at the floor, enhancing the overall feeling of simplicity. Occasionally a room recalled the earlier Georgian tradition and was wood-paneled from floor to ceiling in small, deeply set panels. Where the walls met the ceiling, the cornice usually was two moldings, separated by several inches to make a coved form.

By the 1820s, elaborate interior embellishments in large row houses signaled the waning of restrained Federal-style forms. In 1829 the noted New York architect Minard Lafever wrote in his *Young Builder's General Instructor* that "carved mouldings have of late, become very fashionable in this city, and are indeed very beautiful, and thereby have excited the carvers to prodigious extravagances, both in the quality of work and position of the ornaments." Another evidence of the increasing splendor of row house parlors was the widespread appearance of a ceiling "centerpiece" or "centerflower," a plaster or stucco medallion consisting of foliate forms thrusting outward to a circular molding and placed in the center of the ceiling. "Centre Flowers may be classed among the finest order or Ornaments in interior furnishing, and is indeed as beautiful and produces as lively an effect as any other Ornament in Architecture," wrote Lafever.

Stairway. The stairway to the upper floors, as noted, was at the back of the long side hallway and was lit by a rear window between the first and second floors. The stairway rose to the second floor in graceful elliptical turns, a form emphasized by the simple handrail. Very often the round post took a simple baluster form and railing spindles lacked any turning. A semicircular niche, later erroneously termed a "coffin niche," usually graced the curving wall at the top and bottom of each flight. These cylindrical niches reputedly allowed a coffin to be carried from the second-floor parents' bedroom to the parlor without marring the walls, but actually were an ornamental feature that enhanced the elliptical form of the stairway and usually held a statue or lamp. "The plans of niches with cylindrical backs should be semicircular . . . as deep as may be necessary for the statues they are to contain," wrote Asher Benjamin in 1830 in *The Architect, Or Practical House Carpenter*.

Second Floor and Above. The second-floor bedrooms were plainer than the rooms on the parlor floor, though not spartan. Ceilings usually lacked the ornate centerpiece of the parlor-floor ceiling, and mantels seldom displayed the delicate fluting or classical foliate detail. On the second floor, the side of the hallway between the front and back bedrooms often originally was a clothespress, while the other concealed washbasins and chamber pots. On the top attic floor, bedrooms for the children and live-in servants were located under the pitched roof, all effectively undecorated.

Privy. There were no interior bathrooms in the days before indoor plumbing, with privies typically located in the rear yard. Before the introduction of water delivered through the aqueduct from Westchester County in 1842 (referred to as "Croton water"), bathing and toilet facilities were almost unknown in New York row houses. "Another defect in the American establishments is the want of cabinets de toilette," observed Cooper in the 1820s. "They are certainly to be found in a few houses, but I have occupied a bed-room five and twenty square, in a house, otherwise convenient, that had not under its roof a single apartment of the sort." Toilet facilities consisted of chamber pots in the pantries between the front and back bedrooms and a "bathing house" or privy in the backyard.

ARCHITECTS AND ARCHITECT-BUILDERS

Throughout the nineteenth century, architects rarely designed New York row houses. At that time, the professional architect—hired by a client to design a house, handle all legal details, and supervise construction—scarcely existed in the United States. Most builders purchased standard row house front and interior plans from amateur architects or ordinary draftsmen, or used builder's guides and pattern books.

In his 1864 *Autobiography,* architect James Gallier described the usual position of the architect in row house design in early nineteenth-century New York: "I found that the majority of people could with difficulty be made to understand what was meant by a professional architect; the builders, that is, the carpenters and bricklayers, all called themselves architects, and were at that time the persons to whom owners of property applied when they required plans for building; the builder hired some poor draftsman, of whom there were some half a dozen in New York at that time, to make the plans, paying him a mere trifle for his services."

Often, drawings were "but of little value": "[S]ome proprietors built without having any regular plan. When they wanted a house built they looked about for one already finished, which they thought suitable for their purpose; and then bargained with a builder to erect for them such another, or one with such alterations upon the model as they might point out." In the public mind, there was little or no difference between a builder and an architect or between an architect and a draftsman. The employment of an architect was considered a needless luxury, useful only for the design of a large public or commercial building or an extravagant mansion.

While not typical, high-style houses designed by architects were nevertheless built in New York in the first decades of the nineteenth century. Among the earliest such houses were those along State Street, facing the Battery, attributed to John McComb Jr. Other leading architects who occasionally designed New York's early nineteenth-century row houses were Josiah R. Brady, Samuel Dunbar, Minard Lafever, Calvin Pollard, Martin E. Thompson, and the firm of Ithiel Town and Alexander Jackson Davis.

For the most part, however, ordinary carpenters and masons and large-scale professional row house builders—with a crew of workmen performing their own specialty, whether bricklaying, cellar digging, or plastering—designed and built nearly all the city's houses. Very few houses were individually built for a particular family and its specifications. Because of their dual roles in control of both design and construction, the builders of the city's early nineteenth-century row houses might more accurately be termed architect-builders.

Houses constructed by architect-builders usually were slow to reflect national architectural ideals. Some architect-builders clung to a style for years after it had gone out of fashion, because they were hesitant to give up designs in which they had become skilled and to which their middle-class clients were accustomed. Stylistic change and innovation also occurred more slowly in less expensive Manhattan houses and in Brooklyn row houses, and in general there was a lengthy and gradual transition between styles.

Indeed, the design of the New York row house reflected tension between hewing to architectural style and the reality of speculative construction. Beginning with the boom of the 1820s, New York was a rich, ambitious, cosmopolitan, and fashion-conscious city, all of which tended to stimulate an elaborate, consistent architecture for row houses, often with rich decorative details. "The consequences of its rapid growth, and the extraordinary medley

2·6
9·0
10·0
7·8
17·0
22·0 front

of which its population is composed, serve to give something of a peculiar character to New-York," wrote Cooper in the 1820s. "It is the only city in the Union that has not the air of a provincial town."

City houses were also expected to be more ornate, formal, and fashionable than suburban or country houses. In the 1840s Andrew Jackson Downing, a prominent landscape gardener and sometime-architect in the Romantic Gothic Revival style, recommended that the country house "should always be furnished with more chasteness and simplicity than a townhouse; because, it is in the country, if anywhere, that we should find essential ease and convenience always preferred to that love of effect and desire to dazzle, which is begotten, for the most part, by the rivalry of mere wealth in town life." Downing advised leaving "the complex intricacy and richness of ornamental details to the more elaborate and showy life of those who live in fine townhouses."

However, the economic limitations of speculative construction imposed a bar on fashion and ornateness in New York dwellings. The architect-builder, usually speculating with his own money, resisted any departure from a proved and profitable design. And, the cost of convenient land in Manhattan and Brooklyn limited architectural extravagance; the architectural effect possible on the front of a 20- or 25-foot-wide house was obviously much less than for the four-sided freestanding house.

BUILDER'S GUIDES

Architects were far more influential in publishing builder's guides, where contemporary architectural styles used by builders were developed and spread, than in the design of buildings themselves. These builder's guides, or pattern books, were the source for the handsome up-to-date architectural style in the city's Federal and Greek Revival row houses. Written by professional architects, builder's guides described sound construction methods and illustrated doors, mantels, and cornices in popular styles that a builder could reproduce with local materials and labor. The builder's guides also inspired many of the row house plans sold to builders by architectural draftsmen.

Builder's guides originated in the seventeenth and eighteenth centuries. In colonial America, builders relied on the British pattern books of Batty Langley, Abraham Swan, William Pain, Peter Nicholson, George Andrew Cook, and Isaac Ware, among others. These guides were popularizations of books by the architectural leaders of the Renaissance tradition: Vignola, Andrea Palladio, James Gibbs, and Sir William Chambers.

Asher Benjamin's *The Country Builder's Assistant* (1797) was the first builder's guide by an American author. These American builder's guides borrowed freely from British and other American pattern books. "I have not, from prejudice, omitted anything useful contained in the books already published on this subject," wrote Owen Biddle in his 1805 builder's guide *Young Carpenter's Assistant*. "The proportion of the four Orders I have taken from Pain's work, with but little variations; and, for some of the Geometrical Problems, I am indebted to Peter Nicholson, whose works are held in deserved estimation." By the late 1820s, builder's guides by American authors began to appear in great numbers.

For a builder in an always fashion-conscious New York, line drawings of stylish doorways or mantels were especially important. Here the architect showed his talent for design and spread the latest architectural styles to builders in the city and country. Although some builders exactly copied designs in the builder's guides, they usually adapted them to their own taste and their workmen's skills and local building materials. "How very soon these [builders] got tired of copying the lessons in architectural books," wrote the *Builder* magazine in 1865, looking backward, "and began to develop 'patterns'—for so only can they be called—of their own."

The authors of builder's guides knew about the on-site adaptation of their designs. Discussing his design for a parlor door, Minard Lafever remarked that "in some instances, a drawing may appear exceedingly well; but when executed, will appear very deficient in all its parts" and "therefore, I do not wish my patrons to understand that I have introduced this Elevation for a perfect model, but for a guide by which they may be enabled to execute according to any variation agreeable to their own fancy." In a footnote to this paragraph, Lafever does remind the reader that "I say not a perfect model, but if well executed, would appear exceedingly well."

ROW HOUSE CONSTRUCTION

In the early nineteenth century, masons and carpenters built dwelling houses singly or in

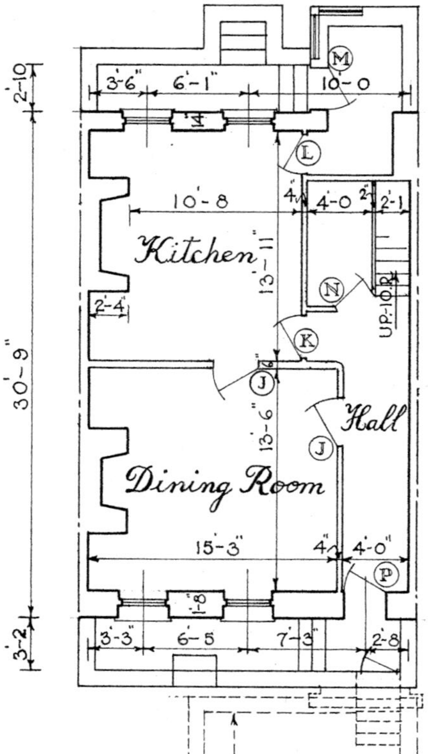

Basement

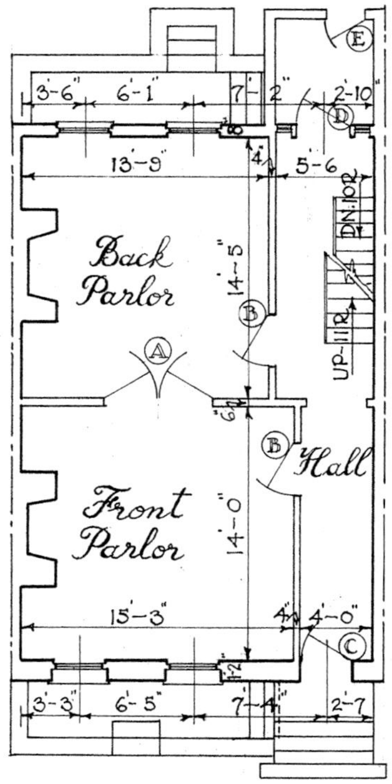

First Floor

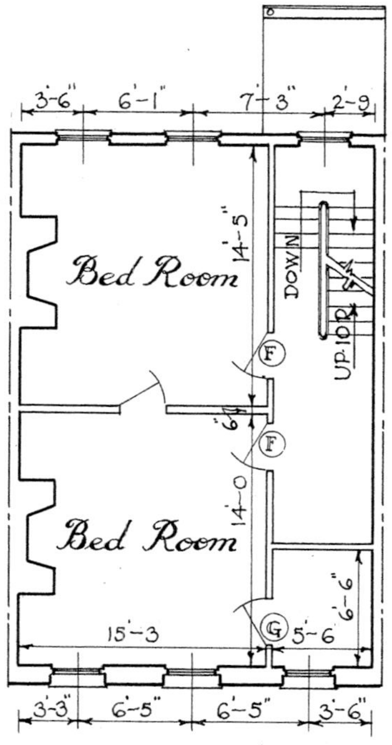

Second Floor

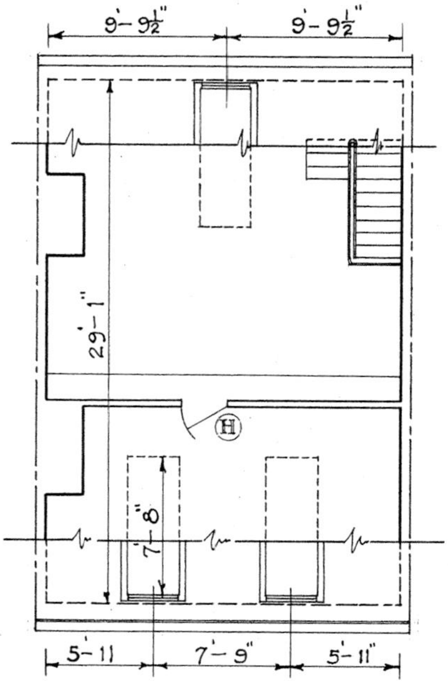

Attic

Previous pages: Elevation for a small house, possibly on Grand Street, Manhattan, likely 1820s. This drawing of a modest Federal-style house is extraordinarily rare, as most of the city's houses in the first decades of the nineteenth century were constructed without drawings, relying on building traditions and pattern books for ornamental details.

Right: 12 Commerce Street, Greenwich Village. Charming, modest row houses like this one must have inspired James Fenimore Cooper's often-quoted praise of New York's "second-rate genteel houses." Greenwich Village Historic District.

Opposite: Floor plan, 4 Grove Street (ca. 1833–34), Greenwich Village, as drawn by the Historic American Buildings Survey (HABS) in the 1930s. The modest but human-scale dimensions of the smaller Federal row house are evident, with nearly square front and rear rooms on every floor, including the front and back parlors, which are connected by swinging doors. The attic story sat between the steeply pitched gabled roof. After the 1820s, rising land prices made it impossible to build such houses in Manhattan ever again. Greenwich Village Historic District.

groups of two or three—as seen in the pleasant variety of doorways, stoop ironwork, and cornices on remarkably well-preserved Charlton Street in Greenwich Village. By the 1820s, professional builders erected rows of at least three or four houses on speculation, and in the subsequent decades builders turned to wealthy investors as the source of capital for speculative house construction, especially on the largest, fanciest dwellings.

Englishman Henry Bradshaw Fearon in 1818 noted the city's construction boom and described certain aspects of row house construction at the time:

> Building appears brisk in the city. It is generally performed by contract. A person intending to have a house erected contracts with a professed builder; the builder, with a bricklayer; and he, with all other necessary to the completion of the design. In some cases, a builder is a sort of head workman, for the purpose of overseeing the others; receiving for his agency seven-pence per day from the wages of each man; the men being employed and paid by him. There are occasional instances in which there is no contract, everything paid for according to measure and value.

This last sentence distinguished between "construction by contract," in which incentives existed to finish a house as quickly as possible and start another one, and "day's work," in which workmen were paid by the day and were expected, therefore, to do the highest-quality work.

The speculative builder started construction in the summer of one year and completed the house in the next March or early April so that it was rented or sold before May 1, the general moving day throughout the city at that time. Only the large, elaborately ornamented row houses or freestanding mansions took more than one year to build.

One reason for the important role of the mason and carpenter in row house construction in the early

WINGED VICTORY
GERMAN TANKS
FORTITUDE
GREEN BEACH

Previous pages: Front parlor,
131 Charles Street, Greenwich Village.

Left: Front second-floor bedroom,
131 Charles Street, Greenwich Village,
used as a sitting room.

This page: Interiors, 131 Charles Street, Greenwich Village.

nineteenth century was the simplicity of the house. Until the widespread introduction of plumbing and heating in the 1840s, almost the builder's entire effort was to erect well-built and handsome structures. With the appearance of complicated and expensive mechanical equipment to install in the 1840s and 1850s, the small builder lacked construction expertise and capital to build fine houses and slowly disappeared from the city's housing construction scene.

BUILDING CODES: FROM WOOD TO MASONRY

Fire was a constant threat to all eighteenth- and nineteenth-century cities. New York's frantic early nineteenth-century building boom partly was to replace business buildings and dwelling houses destroyed by the periodic large-scale conflagrations. "Scarcely a night passes without our citizens being awakened by the cry of 'Fire!' " remarked Philip Hone in 1829. To lessen the chance of disastrous fires, the city periodically passed ordinances that encouraged citizen participation in firefighting, required regular chimney cleaning and repairs, and forbade the storage of such combustible materials as hay, straw, or gunpowder within built-up areas.

In the late eighteenth century, the state and city also enacted building codes to aid in fire prevention. State laws of 1791 and 1796 declared that, thereafter, all buildings taller than two stories and a basement, south of Broome Street, be built of brick or stone with a tile or slate roof. Wood structures already standing within this "fire district" might remain unchanged; but if these wood structures became deteriorated, they had to be demolished or rebuilt under the new building regulations. In succeeding years, the city forbade the construction of wood structures of any height within the fire district and periodically extended the fire district to the north to include new areas of row house development.

These building codes soon affected the appearance of New York. The city's "houses were formerly built of wood, with shingle roofs," wrote one New Yorker about 1820, "but these are fast disappearing, and substantial brick houses, with slated roofs, rising in their places. . . . This interference on the part of the Legislature has introduced much neatness and regularity to the general aspect of the dwelling-houses." So effective were the building codes or fire-district regulations, combined with the continual rebuilding of the city's downtown areas, that in 1848 English author Sarah Mytton Maury remarked upon brick's near-total domination of Manhattan's building stock: "[W]ooden buildings are scarcely to be seen in the city of New York." However, some surviving brick houses in Greenwich Village from the early nineteenth century are in fact only brick-front dwellings, with a wood-frame structure still lying hidden behind the masonry facade.

131 Charles Street, Greenwich Village (1834). This house is a remarkably intact example of the Federal style, representing the long tradition of building in New York in the first decades of the nineteenth century. A later consoled lintel above the entry doorway replaced the plainer flat lintels that survive above all the window openings. The extra space at the left side of the elevation bridges the horse walk, whose entrance is visible to the left of the stoop. A carriage house sits behind the main house. New York City Landmark, also within Greenwich Village Historic District.

THE BATTERY

Federal-style row houses once covered most of Manhattan south of Washington Square. In the city's never-ending march northward, block after block of houses were built to accommodate the city's burgeoning population in the early nineteenth century. By 1830, city growth had passed Houston Street and extended into Greenwich Village and Astor Place. Nevertheless, New York's subsequent awesome growth and rebuilding have spared only a handful of these houses. In the past two centuries, commercial buildings and tenements of different eras have replaced most houses below Houston Street, excepting a handful of notable survivors, leaving Greenwich Village and the Charlton-King-Vandam area just south of Houston as one of the few neighborhoods with significant numbers of Federal-style houses.

The northward march of house construction began at the very southern point of Manhattan, the Battery. There, the James Watson House, at 7 State Street, is the city's finest remaining late eighteenth-century row house. Attributed to John McComb Jr., one of the architects of City Hall, the James Watson House was built in two sections: an eastern half, completed about 1794, and the western half, completed in 1806, with a curved three-story colonnade, which offers an elegant architectural solution to an oddly shaped, curving corner lot. The house's facade is typical of the period: redbrick laid in Flemish bond, with windows enhanced by splayed lintels with double keystones.

Once part of an elegant row of houses along State Street, the James Watson House is one of the few tangible reminders that the Battery and lower Broadway areas were once the city's finest residential districts in the late eighteenth and early nineteenth centuries. Indeed, the only other surviving relic of the era standing today is the Robert and Anne Dickey House at 67 Greenwich Street, a 40-foot-wide mansion constructed in 1809–10.

The Battery was one of the city's few parks, and on pleasant afternoons and evenings, the shaded winding paths were the favorite promenade of fashionable New Yorkers. It was only a short walk from New York's thriving waterfront and emerging Wall Street community. In 1827 a real estate advertisement for the "Substantial House" at 38 Broadway declared that " 'tis seldom a house is offered for sale in so central and desirable a situation," and in 1828 an advertisement in the *New-York Evening-Post* for a twenty-room mansion overlooking "the Battery, Castle Garden, the North river, the Bay" stated that "its situation is not excelled by any in this city."

As late as 1832, a writer described the "most finished house" in all New York as on "Greenwich near the Battery," apparently completed that year. The house was 37 feet wide with a central staircase. On the front, the "basement front and steps . . . caps, window sills and cornice" were white marble, and inside were "Italian marble mantels and mahogany doors" and "silver plated knobs on every door in the house"—a grandeur not "equaled by any house in the city."

7 State Street, James Watson House (1794–1806). This elegant Federal mansion at the far southern tip of Manhattan, attributed to architect John McComb Jr., is the only intact survivor of the fine houses that were once clustered around the Battery. New York City Landmark.

Just as this house was completed, shops, offices, and warehouses had already begun to invade the Battery area. Cooper reported in 1828 that "commerce is gradually taking possession of the whole of the lower extremity of the island, though the Bay, the battery, and the charming Broadway, still cause many of the affluent to depart with reluctance.' By the 1850s, a visitor to New York, one William Bobo, who described himself as "a South Carolinian, who Had Nothing Else to Do," observed, "Around this place was considered a few years back the most desirable to live at in the city, and all the wealth and aristocracy had their residences here if possible. Now, I believe, there is but one family who pretends to move in the upper story of society remaining."

Even as commerce invaded the Battery, many areas to the northeast, on today's Lower East Side, had fine houses, most of which were later demolished for tenements. The Edward Mooney House at 18 Bowery, at the corner of Pell Street in Chinatown, constructed between 1785 and 1789, still stands, reasonably intact, and is the oldest surviving row house in the city. *A Gazetteer of the State of New York* in 1842 described the handsome streets in the district: "East Broadway is a spacious and elegant street on the east side of town, and parallel with it are Henry, Madison, and Monroe-streets, all handsomely built up with private residences, in the neighborhood of the East River." A scattering of these houses, often heavily altered, remain on these same streets today.

ST. JOHN'S PARK

The city's most fashionable residential district in the 1820s was located near the present-day entrance to the Holland Tunnel, just south of Canal Street. Today, not a trace of St. John's Park, St. John's Chapel, or the fine row houses that once lined it remains.

In 1807, the Trinity Church parish built the handsome St. John's Chapel on Varick Street at the outskirts of the city. Many people saw the chapel as a folly—it was too fine and costly a structure for its unlikely surroundings at that time, overgrown fields and cow pastures. Several years later Trinity Church laid out St. John's Park, or Hudson Square, bounded by Varick, Beach, Hudson, and Laight Streets, and the surrounding streets attracted prominent and wealthy families, many of them fleeing the increasingly commercial lower Broadway and Battery areas. In the tradition of London's West End, the owners of the elegant row houses around the park actually owned the park, and only they had keys to open the park gates. Gramercy Park, laid out in 1831, was the only other private park in the city.

St. John's Park was "the fairest interior portion of this city," wrote one New Yorker in the 1820s: "The regularity of the elegant mansions surrounding it, together with the choice trees and shrubbery, and the costly and much admired metropolitan church of St. John's, with its lofty and beautiful spire, places this square at once as the most desirable residence, and most judiciously embellished spot contained in the city." The elegant park was planted with catalpa trees, cottonwood, horse chestnuts, and silver birches; gravel paths wound among the trees, shrubs, and many flower beds. Frances Trollope remarked that "the square is very beautiful, excellently well planted with a great variety of trees . . . and it will give some idea of the care bestowed on its decoration, to know that the gravel for the walks was conveyed by barges from Boston, not as ballast, but as freight." From the open doors of St. John's Chapel, one could look through the tree-shaded park and down Hubert Street to the sail-flecked, sparkling Hudson River.

This *rus in urbe* setting was to survive for only a few decades. Wealthy and socially prominent families began to leave St. John's Park in the 1850s, and nearby streets began to deteriorate. The fine houses facing the park continued to be occupied, for the most part, by families into the 1860s. However, the commercial encroachments that drove away the socially prominent families so as to be "above Bleecker"—the line between the commercial and the residential sections of the city on the eve of the Civil War—soon brought the area's complete destruction.

In October 1866, Commodore Cornelius Vanderbilt announced the purchase of St. John's Park for $1,000,000 and began to erect his massive St. John's Park Freight Depot. In this transaction, Trinity Church parish, which owned St. John's Chapel, received $400,000 for its share of the park, and each of the forty house owners on the park received about $13,000. Once the huge railroad freight terminal rose on the site of the park, the houses in the area became cheap boardinghouses. In the following years, factories and warehouses were built in the area, and one by one the once-fine Federal row houses were torn down. St. John's Chapel and several adjacent

Top: St. John's Chapel and Park, Manhattan, depicted in 1829. New Yorkers rightly hailed St. John's Park as a "spot of Eden loveliness and exclusiveness."

Bottom: Beach Street, opposite St. John's Park, Manhattan, photographed about 1866. In the 1820s, 1830s, and 1840s, palatial row houses of the wealthy and fashionable lined private St. John's Park. After the Civil War, Trinity Church and the house owners around the park effected the area's destruction as an exclusive residential area by selling the park to Commodore Cornelius Vanderbilt, who built the massive St. John's Park Freight Depot on the site. Even before the park's destruction, heavy rolling stock passed directly in front of the elegant mansions—the railroad tracks are visible as the lines in the otherwise muddy street.

houses survived until the era of World War I, when they were demolished by the city for the widening of Varick Street.

LE ROY PLACE AND DEPAU ROW

The block of Bleecker Street between Mercer Street and Greene Street was the first planned monumental blockfront in the city. In 1826 Isaac G. Pearson purchased the building lots on both sides of Bleecker between Mercer and Greene for $400 to $600 a lot. Renaming the block Le Roy Place, in honor of the prominent New Yorker Jacob Le Roy, Pearson constructed two fine rows of elegant houses on each side of the street. Built in a simple Federal style, the Le Roy Place houses had showy granite fronts and sold for the then-staggering $11,000 to $12,000 each. An 1827 real estate advertisement for the just-completed houses gives a rare description of their plan and appointments:

> FOR SALE OR TO LET, The elegant block of 3 story granite Houses, in Bleecker st. near Broadway. The lots are 25 by 100, and 25 by 125, and the Houses are 25 x 50 feet each; they are built in the most substantial and best manner, and are to be finished with plate glass, iron balconies, and piazzas to parlour windows, with marble chimney pieces in each story, mahogany sliding doors in the 1st, and folding doors in the 2d stories; 1st and 2d floors deafened and laid with narrow plank, pantries, wardrobes, drawers and shelves in each story; the garrets will be divided into bed rooms, entirely finished with hard walls, and the house will be completed with blinds, grates, bells, and every possible convenience by the first of May next. There are spacious vaults front and rear, with large cisterns and wells of excellent water in the yards; court yards in front to be enclosed with iron railings.

Pearson purposefully built the houses with a unified, impressive blockfront. The same advertisement continued:

> The block extends from Mercer to Greene sts., and it is intended to erect a block of Houses on the opposite side of Bleecker st. in a corresponding style, so placed as to make a distance of 80 feet between the two fronts, and one of the handsomest places for an elegant and genteel residence in the city.

The houses were set back a uniform 10 feet from the front lot line, leaving each house with a small front yard and giving the street a feeling of greater width and a more dignified scale than available in the usual crosstown street. In an 1831 print of one side of Le Roy Place, drawn by the architect Alexander Jackson Davis, the row houses are identical, except for two houses in the center, which are taller than the others and step out a few feet from the blockfront. On all the houses, a continuous areaway fence, balconies for the tall second-story windows, and a classically inspired balustrade at the roofline enforce the composition's visual unity and monumentality.

Several blocks away, on the south side of Bleecker Street, between Sullivan and Thompson Streets, Depau Row (1829–30) was another early monumental streetscape in New York. Built by Francis Depau, a merchant, and attributed to architect Samuel Dunbar, the restrained Depau Row houses together formed a blockfront united at the second floor with a continuous veranda. An 1833 real estate advertisement for "that valuable house and lot, known as No. 146 Bleecker street," in Depau Row stated: "The building is 25 feet, front and rear, and 54 feet deep. The lot is 125 feet deep. The house was erected in 1830, in the most elegant, and substantial manner, and is three stories high, of brick and a slated roof. There is a building in the rear containing a tearoom and a library, and a well and cistern in the yard. The house is every way calculated for a large and fashionable private family."

The planned regularity of these blockfronts was greeted warmly by contemporary observers. The fine houses of Le Roy Place, observed the 1831 guidebook *Views in New-York and Its Environs*, "afford a new evidence of the surprising improvements visible in the city" and "have a uniform color, and present an imposing appearance." By then, New Yorkers had begun to tire of the usual street built up haphazardly, "wherein each [house] is of different height and composed of different materials."

CHARLTON, KING, AND VANDAM STREETS

The finest concentration of Federal row houses survives on Charlton, King, and Vandam Streets, just south of Houston Street. The north side of Charlton Street offers the longest unbroken streetscape of row houses from the 1820s and 1830s in New York. Here, better than any block in the city, one sees the heterogeneous visual unity of the early nineteenth-century streetscape. Such modest houses typically were built in ones and twos by different architect-builders, without any formal design to align neighboring houses and form a monumental streetscape. The doorways

Top: Depau Row, Greenwich Village, proposal by Samuel Dunbar, late 1820s. The spectacular monumental blockfront, designed by Dunbar for Francis Depau and completed 1829–30, heralded a treatment of row houses as a uniform streetscape in the English terrace tradition. Note the five-bay-wide mansion at the center of the block, flanked by more typical yet still grand three-bay-wide row houses on either side.

Middle: Le Roy Place, Greenwich Village, north and south sides of Bleecker Street, between Mercer and Greene Streets (late 1820s), depicted in a print from 1831. Le Roy Place was the first planned monumental blockfront or terrace in New York.

Right: 153 Bleecker Street, Greenwich Village, at northeast corner of Thompson Street (ca. 1830), photographed about 1870. With its columned doorway porch, tall windows with shutters, and parlor window balcony and stoop railings, this house and others on the blockfront projected an air of wealth and leisure. These houses were replaced by tenements in the early twentieth century.

and stoop ironwork of the houses differ in design, the windows and doors are on differing levels, and the varying cornice lines emphasize the different heights of the houses. Nevertheless, despite the differences in the individual houses, the streetscape has a cohesive dignity because of common materials and proportions.

These three blocks are the remnants of a larger, but nevertheless distinct, area, originally bounded by Greenwich Street (which then faced the Hudson), King Street, MacDougal Street, and Vandam Street. In the late eighteenth and early nineteenth centuries, the Richmond Hill mansion sat on a high hill, with gardens, meadows, and woods, overlooking the Hudson River. Undoubtedly, it was one of the finest country estates in eighteenth-century New York, and served as George Washington's temporary headquarters in the summer of 1776 and later as the official residence of Vice President John Adams during Washington's presidency, when New York was the U.S. capital.

In 1794, Aaron Burr purchased the house, and his entertainments there were among the most lavish in the city at the time. By then, the northward growth of the city already approached the Houston Street area, and a road parallel to present-day Greenwich Street led directly to the still-small New York City to the south. In 1797 Burr platted today's Charlton, King, and Vandam Streets, dividing the 6-acre estate into the 25-by-100-foot building lots. After his notorious duel with Alexander Hamilton in 1804, Aaron Burr left New York in disgrace, and John Jacob Astor held the estate for him. In 1817 Astor purchased the estate from Burr and proceeded to develop the property. The Richmond Hill mansion was moved to the southeast corner of Varick and Charlton Streets, and its lofty hill was leveled. Building lots were laid out and sold to local architect-builders. Nearly all the surviving row houses in the area were erected in the early and mid-1820s by these builders on speculation rather than for their family residences. The original residents of the area were prosperous builders, lawyers, and merchants—the latter group usually dealing in foodstuffs at the wharves on the Hudson River, then just west of Greenwich Street. The Richmond Hill mansion became a theater in 1831, later a circus, a menagerie, and then a tavern and was finally demolished in 1849.

In the late nineteenth and early twentieth centuries, large industrial buildings invaded nearby streets of row houses, but these three blocks always retained a well-kept residential character. "Vandam Street . . . is an old-fashioned residence street," wrote one New Yorker in the 1890s, "and the well-kept three-story houses, with their polished door plates and brass knockers, are occupied by their owners, most of whom were born in them. It is a typical street of old Greenwich Village. There is scarcely any traffic, and the street is quiet and orderly."

THE FEDERAL TRADITION FADES

"The old New York streets were neither dark nor unlovely," wrote architectural critic Montgomery Schuyler in 1899. "They were gay and positively attractive, by reason of the architectural tradition that had grown up among the mechanics. The houses were more than decent; they were 'elegant.'" This essay, "The Small City House in New York" was one of the first historical appreciations of the charms of the city's unpretentious early nineteenth-century houses. The small New York house, wrote Schuyler, "owed its elegance to the ornament which was applied to it, very modestly and very sparingly, but none the less effectively."

By the 1830s, this tradition of sparing ornament was superseded in grander late Federal-style houses, whose greater ostentation signaled a shift in the city's long residential building tradition. In addition, the city's real estate economics—namely the high price of building lots—meant that the modest "second-rate genteel" houses so common in the first decades of the nineteenth century could be built no more. The handful of Federal survivors that stand today in Lower Manhattan are gracious reminders of a more orderly, self-confident era of architectural simplicity and good taste, which possess, as Schuyler deemed, a "decorum and refinement for which one would search any more modern quarter entirely in vain."

Top: 21–29 Vandam Street, Manhattan. The houses and streetscapes of early nineteenth-century New York have largely been obliterated by the subsequent two centuries of growth and change in Manhattan. This historic district just south of Houston Street is one of the few areas where substantial numbers of such houses survive together, giving a picture of the scale and pleasant variation of the city of that era. Charlton-King-Vandam Historic District.

Bottom: Doorway, 113 East Broadway, Manhattan, photographed in 1937 by Margaret Bourke-White. East Broadway, Henry Street, Madison Street, and Monroe Street on the Lower East Side had numerous grand Federal-style houses, many of which survived into the twentieth century relatively intact. Here, though the fanlight and entry door had already been lost, the doorway itself, including the Ionic colonettes and stoop ironwork, remained largely as it was a century before. Demolished.

10

II

1830–1850
THE GREEK REVIVAL

In 1832 a now-unknown architect-builder completed a row of several houses on East Fourth Street, just west of the Bowery, of which the Seabury Tredwell House, 29 East Fourth Street, now the Merchant's House Museum, is the only survivor. Despite its grand scale and elaborate ornament typical of the late Federal style, the balance of the house's exterior was part of the declining stylistic tradition. By the early 1830s, a new era in the architectural history of the city's row houses had already dawned.

Around the corner on Lafayette Place, builder Seth Geer had begun the spectacular Colonnade Row, nine houses in the Greek Revival style, faced with white marble and united by a monumental two-story colonnade running the length of the row. Nearby, on Washington Square North, three architect-builders worked on thirteen palatial row houses along the north side of the newly opened park. These thirteen redbrick houses clearly expressed the newly fashionable style in the fluted Doric columns of the doorway porches and in the Greek motifs on the iron front fences. Both sets of houses were among the very earliest examples of the Greek Revival style in New York City and set a high standard of taste and opulence in city row houses perhaps unequaled anywhere else in nineteenth-century United States.

With these splendid inspirations, New York architects and architect-builders abandoned the Federal and late Federal styles for the fashionable Greek Revival. The triumph of the Greek Revival style was so complete in New York that Englishman William Ross observed in an 1834 report on "The Street House of New York" that the "Greek mania here is at its height, as you infer from the fact that everything is a Greek temple from the privies in the back court, through the various grades of prison, theatre, church, customhouse, and state-house." This sudden and nationwide mania completely dominated American architecture from the late 1820s to the late 1840s. It swept from the East Coast into the Midwest as far away as Iowa and Wisconsin and was especially well received in the Deep South. So strong was the sway of ancient Greece and classical antiquity that by the end of the rage for the Greek, the United States had gained not only countless Greek Revival structures but also fifteen Romes, twelve Carthages, and twenty-seven Troys!

10 Washington Square North, Greenwich Village (1831–33). The Greek Revival–style mansions on the north side of Washington Square are some of the finest nineteenth-century row houses remaining in New York. These buildings epitomize the elegance of the Greek Revival style, in their freestanding columned doorway porches, smooth red brick fronts, and fine ironwork exhibiting the anthemion and Greek key. Greenwich Village Historic District.

NO STANDING
FIRE ZONE
PARKING
PERMITTED
TUES
ONLY

AN AGE OF REVIVALS

The Greek Revival style introduced an age of revivals to American architecture. Although the Greek Revival row house was quite similar in appearance to the Federal, its design expressed a far different aesthetic intent. The Greek Revival, and indeed all revival styles, self-consciously recalled a distant time or place and its architecture. A revival style tried to evoke an "association" that stimulated the emotions. For Andrew Jackson Downing in his famous manual *The Architecture of Country Houses*, revival styles provided "another source of pleasure to most minds, which springs not from beauty of form or expression in these styles but from personal or historical associations connected with them; and which, by a process half-addressed to the feelings and half to the intellect, makes them in the highest degree interesting." A revival style rejected the classical tradition's idea that forms were beautiful only in themselves and, instead, accepted the Romantic concept that forms were beautiful for the emotions they evoked. Buildings ideally evoked a tantalizingly distant time or place and often took on asymmetrically massed facades, rich ornament, and dark building materials, which recalled the much-admired Picturesque countryside.

Previous pages: 20–26 Willow Street, Brooklyn Heights (ca. 1846). Brooklyn Heights Historic District.

Above: Ernest and Helen Fiedler and their children, 38 Bond Street, a family portrait painted by Francis H. Heinrich ca. 1850. In the 1830s and 1840s, the Bond Street area probably was the city's most desirable neighborhood. Elegant row houses and mansions, sometimes with showy marble or granite fronts, graced the serene tree-lined streets and cost a staggering $20,000 to $30,000. Despite the splendor of this family scene, wealthy households were already abandoning Bond Street for newly developed districts further uptown by the date of this painting.

The evocation of an ancient Greece made the Greek Revival style as much a part of the Romantic tradition as the Gothic Revival country house or church. Indeed, the Greek Revival was a watershed style: as Romantic classicism, it combined severity and light-colored materials of the classical tradition with the distant historical evocation of ancient Greece. In 1835 Philip Hone described the moonlit appearance of a Greek Revival–style hotel he owned in Rockaway, Long Island, in Romantic terms: "The view was unspeakably grand. The broad red moon, setting over the tops of the mountains of Neversink, threw a solemn light over the unruffled face of the ocean, and the lofty columns of the noble piazza, breaking the silver streams of light into dark and gloomy shadows, gave the edifice the appearance of some relic of classical antiquity."

ORIGINS OF THE GREEK REVIVAL

The Greek Revival style was the culmination of an interest in classical antiquities that emerged in the middle of the eighteenth century with archaeological discoveries in Italy. Excavations at Pompeii and Herculaneum gave Europe its first view of life in classical antiquity and focused attention on ancient Rome and, through Rome, ancient Greece.

Archaeologists, many of them also architects, published the results of their discoveries. In Great Britain, for instance, the Society of Dilettanti sponsored the publication of Robert Wood's *Ruins of Palmyra* (1753) and *Ruins of Balbec* (1757), Robert Adam's *Ruins of the Palace of the Emperor Diocletian at Spalatro in Dalmatia* (1764), and Richard Chandler's *Ionian Antiquities* (1769). Most important of their publications was James "Athenian" Stuart and Nicholas Revett's four-volume *Antiquities of Athens*, issued between 1762 and 1816, a detailed study of ancient ruins in Greece with numerous illustrations and restorations. From this and similar books, British and American architects frequently borrowed details for their designs and builder's guides. Minard Lafever wrote of the *Antiquities of Athens* that "perhaps there are none superior to it," and Alexander Jackson Davis found that "this is a work of great value indeed, and quite indispensable to the architect."

International interest in ancient Greece increased in the early nineteenth century after Thomas Bruce, the 7th Earl of Elgin, British ambassador to Ottoman-held Greece, received permission to take "a few blocks of marble with inscriptions and figures" from the Acropolis of Athens. With several hundred men and part of the British fleet in the Mediterranean, Lord Elgin removed almost all of the sculptured metopes, the frieze, and the tympanum from the Parthenon and also part of the front porch and a caryatid from the Erechtheum. His loot, dubbed the Elgin Marbles, excited a widespread interest in ancient Greece among the educated throughout Europe and the United States. In addition, the Greek War for Independence in the 1820s evoked international sympathy for the Greek patriots and kindled even greater interest in the civilization of ancient Greece, especially in the United States, itself only recently freed from foreign domination.

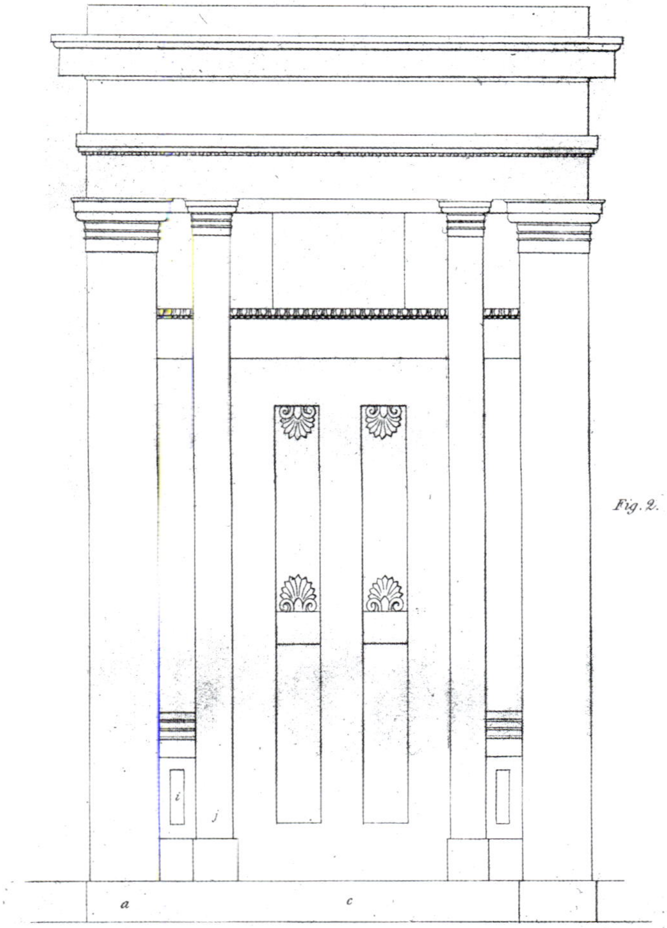

Fig. 2.

EMERGENCE OF THE GREEK REVIVAL IN THE UNITED STATES

Since the early eighteenth century, American architects had worked with classical designs of Renaissance and later of direct Roman inspiration. In 1785 Thomas Jefferson, with the aid of the French architect-archaeologist Charles-Louis Clérisseau, had designed the Virginia State Capitol, closely modeled on the Maison Carrée, a first-century A.D. Roman temple at Nîmes. Jefferson, at the time the U.S. ambassador to France, wrote that the Maison Carrée "is allowed without contradiction to be the most perfect and precious remain of antiquity in existence." His Virginia State Capitol was the first monumental building in the United States to be modeled on an entire temple. William Thornton's 1791 design for the U.S. Capitol in Washington, D.C., also revealed an ancient Roman inspiration in the shallow dome of the Rotunda modeled after the dome of the Pantheon in Rome and in the Roman hemicycle form of the Senate and House of Representatives chambers.

Even in the late eighteenth century many Americans were familiar with the architecture of ancient Greece, for as early as 1770 the Carpenters' Company of Philadelphia owned a copy of Stuart and Revett's *Antiquities of Athens*, a book also in Thomas Jefferson's library. At that time scholars throughout the world considered ancient Greek architecture and culture an offshoot of the Roman. Accordingly, architects neglected Greek motifs until the German art historian and archaeologist Johann Joachim Winckelmann proved beyond doubt that, in fact, Greek culture and architecture had profoundly influenced that of ancient Rome.

Architects and government leaders had also begun to look for a style with more American and more democratic connotations than the Federal style, too specifically British in its origins. American nationalism was on the rise, stimulated by the successful defense of American independence in the War of 1812 against Britain and by the general surge in nationalism in the Western world following the French Revolution and Napoleon's final defeat at Waterloo.

By the 1820s, the once-fashionable Roman influence in architecture had lost favor with many Americans. Napoleon had used the Roman triumphal arches, fasces, and eagles in his Empire style. A style associated with the despot Napoleon and imperial Rome was unsuitable for the new American republic and its democratic ideals. The Greek Revival style, on the other hand, recalled the democratic city-states of ancient Greece and, in its simple forms and spare ornament, was a style that could be appreciated by all Americans.

The Second Bank of the United States (1819–24) in Philadelphia was the first building where the entire front of a Greek temple was copied completely and, therefore, is regarded as the first fully developed American example of the Greek Revival style. Designed by William Strickland, this large, marble-faced bank had Doric porticoes, inspired by the Parthenon at Athens, and marked the first great triumph of the Greek Revival style over the Federal style and Roman influence of the early nineteenth century. Visitors to Philadelphia described the bank

Opposite:

Top left: Doorway, 4 Washington Square North, Greenwich Village (1832–33). The freestanding doorway porch, with fluted columns supporting a heavy horizontal entablature, appeared only on the finest houses. Greenwich Village Historic District.

Top right: Doorway, 15 Washington Square North. Demolished.

Bottom left: Doorway, Minard Lafever's *The Beauties of Modern Architecture* (1835).

Bottom right: Doorway, 24 Willow Street. Brooklyn Heights Historic District.

as "chaste," "noble," and "majestic" and often considered it the most beautiful building in the United States at that time. "The two great truths of the world," declared Nicholas Biddle, the president of the bank, "are the Bible and Grecian architecture."

THE GREEK REVIVAL IN NEW YORK

During the 1820s, Greek Revival motifs occasionally appeared on churches or commercial buildings in New York—notably Martin E. Thompson's Phoenix Bank (1825) on Wall Street, his Church of the Ascension (1827–29) on Canal Street, Josiah R. Brady's Second Unitarian Church (1826) at Mercer and Prince Streets, and Ithiel Town's Bowery Theatre (1825).

Greek Revival touches also appeared on occasional New York row houses in the late 1820s. An 1829 elevation drawing by Martin E. Thompson shows a Greek Revival doorway porch of Doric columns and an entablature on an otherwise Federal-style row house. An 1827 real estate advertisement for a "3 story House, being one of the range of 12 houses now erecting . . . on Fourth-street, opposite to Washington square" stated that "the fronts and rears of the whole range are to be finished in the same style as the front of the Bowery Theatre." These fine houses on the south side of Washington Square had Greek Revival doorways with flat pilasters and entablatures with laurel wreaths.

Several years before Greek Revival–style row houses began to be constructed in New York, designs in that style, mainly ornamental and detail work, also appeared in American builder's guides. The sixth edition of Asher Benjamin's *American Builder's Companion* (1827) pictured several Greek ornamental details. Figure 5 of Minard Lafever's *The Young Builder's General Instructor* (1829) is a "Grecian" front doorway, which, on each side of the door, consists of fluted Greek Doric

Above: Ironwork detail, Cushman Row, 416 West Twentieth Street (1839–40). Chelsea Historic District.

Top right: Ironwork, detail from parlor window balcony, 21 Washington Square North, Greenwich Village (1835–36). A handsome combination of the anthemion and the Greek key on a wheel, the classical symbol of eternity. Greenwich Village Historic District.

Opposite: Cast-iron veranda, 3 and 4 Gramercy Park West (ca. 1850). This veranda, or porch, attributed to architect Alexander Jackson Davis, employs the entire repertoire of Greek Revival ornament with dazzling richness. Gramercy Park Historic District.

Following pages: 12 and 11 Washington Square North, Greenwich Village (1831–33). Greenwich Village Historic District.

columns that, together with pilasters at each side, support a flat entablature. This handsome "Grecian doorway" would become a popular form on the city's costly row houses.

Nevertheless, New York was slower than other cities to adopt the Greek Revival style on a large scale, mainly because of the conservative influence of architects like John McComb Jr. working in the long-lived classical tradition. The city's architect-builders also were hesitant to abandon the Federal style to which their workmen and their cautious house-buying customers had become accustomed over decades.

Alexander Jackson Davis's work in the 1820s and 1830s played a large part in the style's acceptance. Davis claimed in his daybook that he introduced the Greek Revival style to New York dwellings in a row of houses on Bleecker Street, since lost. The monumental Colonnade Row on Lafayette Place, begun in 1832 and often attributed to Davis, dramatically showed the elegance of the Greek Revival style for row houses, as did the row on Washington Square North, whose architect is not definitively known.

THE GREEK REVIVAL ROW HOUSE FRONT

At first glance, the Greek Revival row house front appeared to be nearly identical to that of the Federal style. Like the Federal dwelling, the Greek Revival row house had the warm redbrick facade, set off by brownstone or white-marble trim, and relied on the contrasts of these materials and on the pleasing proportions of the street front and its parts for architectural effect. Unlike the vernacular Federal style, however, the Greek Revival was a thoroughly self-conscious style. Once architects and architect-builders deliberately evoked associations of ancient Greece in New York row houses, they adopted urban forms suitable to the increasingly powerful city and its well-to-do residents.

The Greek Revival row house sought a greater dignity and monumentality than did the Federal row house. Higher ceilings made for a taller, hence more impressive, house, and a full third floor replaced the pitched roof and dormer window arrangement of earlier years. "A style less tawdry and more in consonance with the rules of good taste has been introduced," reported the *New-York Evening Post* in 1833. "These ugly projections from the roofs, called dormant [*sic*] windows, which in many streets disfigure almost every private building, have been generally banished from the new edifices." The flat roofline also was thought to make for a more coherent streetscape with a continuous roofline. "To judge of our principal street, Broadway, you would think that the first object with every person about to build, had been to measure with his eye the houses adjacent and take care to order his to be several inches higher or lower than his neighbor's," observed the *Evening Post* in 1828. "But in those [houses] now erecting, or lately erected, this old, ugly, and absurd custom is avoided."

To enhance the large, smooth expanses of the row house front, lampblack was mixed with the mortar to minimize the joints between bricks. The rectangular window lintels and sills were simple in form and spare in ornament and were almost flush with the facade. Only the projection of the door enframement and stoop broke the planar unity of the row house front, and its severity served to underline the smoothness of the facade in contrast.

The Greek Revival row house evidenced a simplicity of forms and ornament that, architectural theory then held, alone could be grasped easily by the mind. The difference between the elaborate late Federal doorway, marked by a many-paneled door and leaded fanlight and side windows, and the plain, rectangular transom and single-panel door of the Greek Revival doorway epitomized the emergence of the pervasive ideal of architectural simplicity through monumentality.

Under these ideals, New York's once-admired City Hall, with its rich classical ornament, was now scorned. The building, according to the *New-York Mirror* in 1834, was "deformed with a mass of gingerbread," echoing the earlier sentiments of a visitor to the city in the 1820s who found that the "prevailing defect" of New York's architecture was the "absence of simplicity and grandeur."

On the other hand, *Philadelphia Monthly* in 1827 admired that city's Second Bank of the United States because the viewer "is forcibly struck with the grand appearance of the front" and "the unity and entireness of view under which it is presented to him. The platform with its gradation of steps, the massive yet well-proportioned columns, the long line of entablature, and surmounting pediment, are embraced by the eye at the first glance."

Doorways and Enframements. In New York row houses, the Greek Revival style first appeared in the late 1820s in the front doorways of otherwise Federal-style dwellings as delicate Ionic colonnettes separating the door from the sidelights and supporting the architrave and a lacy toplight. By the 1830s, large houses featured a handsome doorway porch consisting of freestanding and generally fluted Doric or Ionic columns supporting a heavy horizontal entablature. The Doric order was preferred to the Ionic because of its massive scale and simple forms, and from a Picturesque standpoint, Minard Lafever admired the Doric order for "the bewitching variety of light and shade."

The high cost of cutting fluted columns and building a freestanding porch limited this doorway treatment to only the finest row houses. In most row houses, the doorway treatment consisted of rectangular pilasters set flat against the facade and supporting a horizontal entablature scaled to the pilasters. Sometimes, a triangular pediment replaced the conventional horizontal entablature and an anthemion (a honeysuckle motif) or a palmette (a stylized palm frond) projected from the peak of the pediment as an acroterion. On some houses of the 1840s, the outside edge of the doorway pilaster sloped outward as it neared the base, and protruding Greek ears usually marked the top corners of the enframement. The rectangular pilaster was a far simpler form for the builders' workmen to execute than the ideal freestanding and fluted column, and thus saw far greater use than the freestanding doorway porch.

On some dwellings, the doorway enframement simply was four wood boards nailed together, but typically it was of the local brownstone or a light-colored limestone, granite, or marble. In the 1820s, a costly pale gray stone was preferred to brownstone for doorway porches and window trim. Architectural fashion changed by the early 1840s. Under the ascendant Romantic movement, so-called Picturesque dark colors were fashionable, and brownstone replaced light-colored marble for doorway and window enframements on most new dwellings. "The flights of steps at the front doors, of a reddish brown sandstone . . . have a remarkably handsome appearance. Sometimes they are to be seen, at every successive door, along an extensive street," wrote one admiring English traveler in the 1840s.

A recessed doorway enhanced the monumentality of the street front by introducing a dramatic recessed dark volume to the otherwise flat and modestly ornamented front. The recessed doorway also offered a sheltered space for visitors between the outdoors and the interior of the house. The richly detailed leaded fanlight and sidelights, characteristic of the Federal doorway, disappeared with the advent of the Greek Revival row house. The transom, which replaced the fanlight doorway, and the sidelights were plain panes of glass separated by wood muntin bars. In another simplification of form, the door was typically a single vertical panel, two vertical panels, or three horizontal panels, usually edged with an egg-and-dart molding, rather than the six- and eight-panel doors of Federal-style row houses.

Ornament and Ironwork. The Greek Revival row house relied on handsome ornament for much of its aesthetic impact. The most popular motifs were the fret, or Greek key; the acanthus leaf; and the anthemion, the stylized honeysuckle. The decorative repertoire also

Elevation drawing, Samuel Tredwell Skidmore House, 37 East Fourth Street, Manhattan (1844–45).

. Principal . Elevation .

included the meander, an endless fret design; the guilloche, a border of two or more bands interlaced in a repeating pattern; floral forms in double relief, usually a rosette with a slender, several-inch-long foliate form extending above and below; the lyre; an upright obelisk; and sharp-pointed geometric cones.

Because it was easier to shape iron into elaborate forms than to carve them in stone, most ornament appeared in ironwork, usually in the stoop railings and areaway fences. Some ironwork was hand wrought, but machine-made casting became available in the 1830s and soon replaced the costly hand-wrought iron on all but the finest houses. In the *Practice of Architecture* (1833), Asher Benjamin devoted a page to "a series of designs for Fences, Window Guards, &c." in handsome Federal and Greek Revival styles and, at this early date, said that "in this construction a view was had to their being made of cast iron." By the 1840s, advertisements for factory-made stoop railings and front fences appeared in the New York and Brooklyn directories. The ironwork illustrated in these advertisements survives on many houses throughout the city today.

Some of the most beautiful Greek Revival–style ironwork was on the parlor-window balcony, a feature introduced on New York row houses about 1830. Because grand houses were now built 5 or 10 feet deeper to create large parlors suitable for entertaining, parlor windows in turn dropped to the floor to provide more light and air to the large rooms, with an iron balcony placed in front as a privacy screen. This two-window-wide balcony offered splendid opportunities for ironwork decoration. Though most are gone because of decay and wartime scrap-iron drives, the few remaining parlor-window guards and balconies in Manhattan and Brooklyn show the ironwork and Greek Revival decorative motifs in perhaps their most elaborate and imaginative forms.

Cornice. The cornice enriched the plain street front and also defined the top of the row house, just as the rusticated basement indicated the lower limit. The simplest cornice treatment was a flat horizontal board, known as a fascia, across the full width of the house just below the roofline. Above the fascia board the builder usually added dentiled molding, an ornamental row of small toothlike blocks. The dentiled cornice often had another decorative molding such as the egg and dart, an egg-shaped ornament alternating with a dart-like form, or the leaf-and-tongue, often combined with the bead and reel.

The Greek Revival row house typically had an attic story lit by small windows that unobtrusively pierced the fascia board of the cornice. Carved-wood or cast-iron laurel wreaths sometimes encircled these windows, a motif also found on windowless cornices or on the horizontal entablature of doorway porches. These windows usually have not survived intact. To make the attic another fully usable and rentable floor, the openings have been enlarged over the years into small double-hung or casement windows, thus cutting into the ornamental cornice molding above and below the fascia board, or completely replaced by a full story added to the house.

Verandas. Ornamental ironwork in New York row houses attained its fullest development in the 10-to-12-foot-tall porches or verandas

Opposite: Back porches or tearooms, 20–26 Willow Street (1846), Brooklyn Heights. A view of the tearooms that often appeared as rear extensions on New York row houses in the 1840s and 1850s. Brooklyn Heights Historic District.

Following pages: Merchant's House Museum, 29 East Fourth Street, Manhattan (1831–32). With its unaltered rooms and original Tredwell family furniture, the Merchant's House Museum offers a rare glimpse of the well-to-do New York family's house and lifestyle in the early nineteenth century. National Historic Landmark, New York City Landmark, and New York City Interior Landmark.

across the width of the row house front. Slim vertical roof supports and several-foot-high railings employed Greek Revival style ornament with a freedom and richness rarely seen in the city's row houses at that time. Apparently at variance with the era's ideal of architectural severity, the lacy cast iron of the veranda offered a pleasing contrast with the plain brick row house front. These verandas also pointed out the degree to which machine technology served, and indeed shaped, row house architecture of the period.

Such verandas appeared throughout New York State, Pennsylvania, and Ohio in the 1840s and 1850s but saw the most imaginative and widespread use in such Southern cities as Charleston, Savannah, Mobile, and particularly New Orleans. In New York, cast-iron verandas also appeared on the Italianate-style row houses of the 1850s. The veranda often was employed in New York on row houses in a *rus in urbe* setting. In an era that idealized the rugged countryside and nature, the verandas denoted the countryside, even in the city, and were deemed particularly appropriate to row houses facing a park or with handsomely planted 10-to-20-foot-deep front yards. Probably the finest remaining row house verandas survive on 3–4 Gramercy Park West. Attributed to Alexander Jackson Davis, these verandas employ a full repertoire of Greek Revival motifs with a dazzling richness.

GREEK REVIVAL HOUSE PLANS AND INTERIOR DESIGN

The New York row house of the 1830s and 1840s, except for several small changes for added comfort and grandeur, featured the same basic floor plan as houses of the previous era: on the basement floor, a dining room in the front, kitchen in the back; on the first (or parlor) floor, front and rear parlors, with the rear parlor occasionally used as a formal dining room; and on the upper floors, bedrooms and servants' rooms.

Within the same plan, however, floor heights increased, often dramatically. The basement ceiling increased from 7 or 7½ feet to 8 or 9 feet, making the front dining room more spacious and, in turn, raising the parlor floor farther from the street for a more impressive house. In the first-floor parlors, ceilings rose to 11 or 12 feet, and in large houses reached a spectacular 14 feet. In the late 1820s, sliding parlor pocket doors, which rolled out of sight into the walls on metal tracks, appeared in the lavish Greek Revival–style parlors of otherwise late Federal row houses and, within a few years, had replaced folding doors in the parlors of all but the simplest dwellings. Minard Lafever's *The Modern Builder's Guide* (1833) carried a design for sliding parlor doors, enframed by handsome flat pilasters and entablature, which appeared in many Greek Revival row houses in New York. The sliding parlor doors and high ceilings introduced a feeling of unusual spaciousness and a free flow of space between the front and back parlors.

The interior design of the Greek Revival row house carried the same simple forms relieved by occasional rich ornament seen on the street fronts. Walls were of plaster painted a light color and relieved by simple baseboards, a plaster cornice at the ceiling, and perhaps a simple, unmolded chair rail around the room at waist height. The floors were of light-colored wood planks, often 1 foot wide and 1 inch thick.

In some fine row houses, as at the Merchant's House on East Fourth Street, a pair of Ionic or Corinthian columns, supporting a horizontal entablature, replaced the flat pilaster and entablature enframement for parlor doors. In other Greek Revival row houses, a double pair of columns replaced the sliding door and wall between the front and back parlors.

In the early nineteenth century, the stairway to the second floor had occupied the rear of the side hallway, at the back of the house, and was lit by a window at the landing between the first and second floors. In the 1830s, the stairway instead was often located at the center of the hallway and lit by a skylight in the roof several floors above. When only identical front and back parlors occupied the first floor, the space at the back of the hallway might have been a butler's pantry to the back parlor; when used as a formal dining room, a small servant's stairway behind the centrally located main stairway.

Tearooms. In the 1840s and 1850s, New York row houses sometimes had several-story-tall open galleries across the back of the house. On the first floor, French doors led from the splendid back parlor to the open porch, or a windowed porch known as the tearoom. Because of the several windows overlooking the backyard, the tearoom did not appreciably diminish the light or ventilation in the back parlor. When these porches reached the second floor, they were open porches separated from

Left: Front parlor, Merchant's House Museum. View from the formal dining room.

Above: Rear parlor, Merchant's House Museum, with original furniture.

Doorways, front parlor, Merchant's House Museum. The right door is false to provide symmetry. Behind it lies the rear side of the plaster lathe boards of the entry hall. The gas chandelier was installed later in the nineteenth century.

SACRED HARMONIST
Piano Forte or Organ

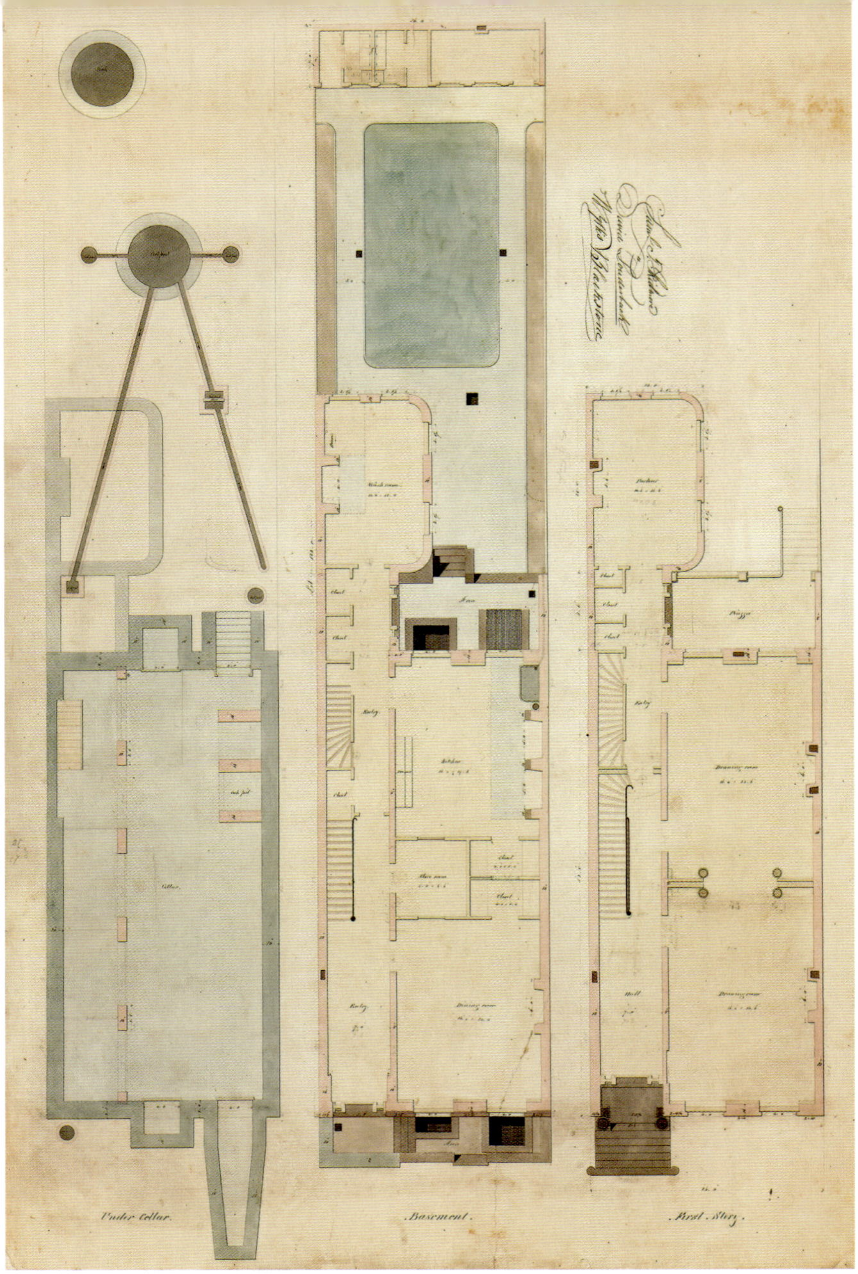

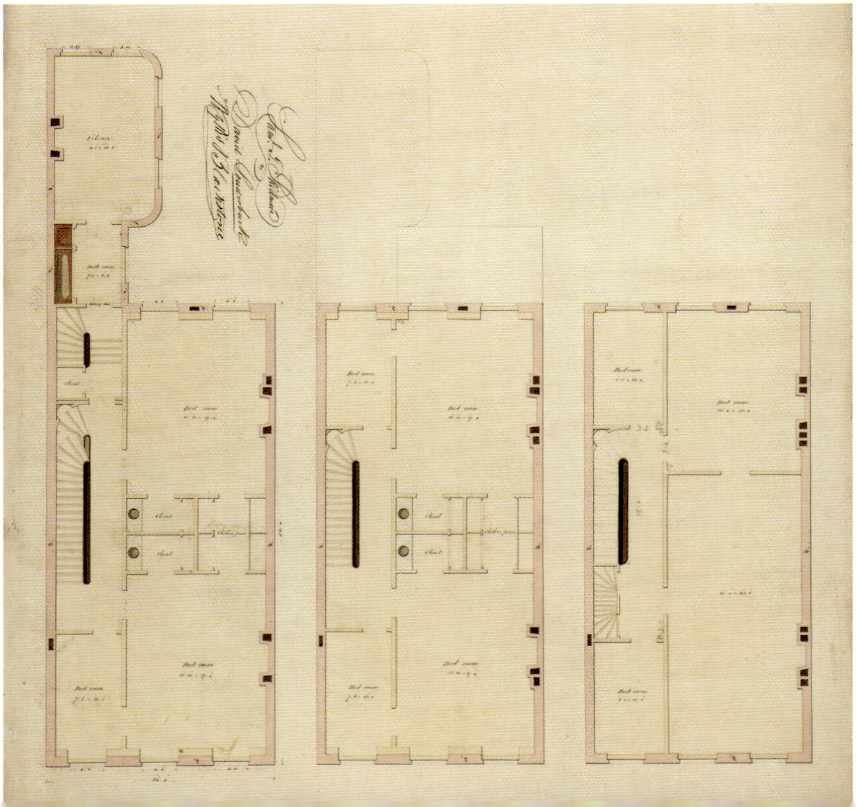

Top and bottom: Plans, Samuel Tredwell Skidmore House, 37 East Fourth Street, Manhattan (1844–45). This drawing is one of the most detailed surviving original plans for a New York row house, and detailed receipts also survive for the entire construction process. The plan is similar to the nearby 29 East Fourth Street, now the Merchant's House Museum. However, note the bathroom in the second-floor extension and washbasins in the closets of the second- and third-floor bedrooms—a new convenience following the introduction of Croton water in 1842.

Opposite, top and bottom: Bedrooms, second floor, Merchant's House Museum, with original family furniture.

Following pages: Ceiling centerpiece or rosette, Merchant's House Museum.

adjacent porches by a brick wall. Many galleries or tearooms did not survive or, at best, sagged and leaned, because builders did not always build them upon as firm a foundation as the house proper.

Doors. The doors usually were the most elaborate feature of the parlors. Each parlor door, usually mahogany or rosewood, had one large, deeply set panel or two long and narrow panels, impressive for the simple form and rich wood finish. The pilasters that supported the horizontal entablature had acanthus leaf capitals and, in many cases, an inset panel running the full length with applied Greek detail, such as the anthemion. The horizontal entablature also displayed Greek Revival motifs, such as the anthemion and Greek key, or several rows of egg-and-dart or dentiled molding. When the parlors employed a screen of Ionic or Corinthian columns, with or without the sliding parlor doors, the double parlors took on a richness and flamboyance hardly expected behind the severe street front.

Mantels. Mantels were massive, severe, and in design resembled the front doorway enframement, with pilasters and a horizontal entablature. Only in the finest dwellings did columns or caryatids, rather than pilasters, support the mantelshelf. Applied or carved Greek Revival details occasionally ornamented the mantel's smooth surfaces, and the preferred material was marble, especially black marble veined with yellow or gold. In rooms other than the parlors, and in the parlors of small houses, the mantel was a white-gray marble, a slate oiled to appear as black marble, or ordinary painted wood. In the early Greek Revival row houses of the early and mid-1830s, the mantels in rooms other than the parlors were typically still in the Federal style.

Plasterwork. In the parlor, the ceiling decoration usually was a cornice of simple molding or two moldings enclosing a rounded cove and an ornate and heavy sculptured centerpiece in the center. The centerpieces varied from a simple circular molding to stylized foliate forms reaching out from a central rosette to an outer edge, which varied from a plain molding to an elaborate arrangement of circular and polygonal forms within each other.

By the 1830s, ceiling cornices and centerpieces generally were larger and more boldly detailed than in earlier decades—partly to satisfy an emerging fashion for impressive dwellings and to complement the new scale of the high ceilings and larger rooms. "In adjusting the proportions of these cornices, the size and height of the rooms should be taken into consideration," wrote Asher Benjamin in the 1833 *Practice of Architecture*. With the higher ceilings and the greater distance between the viewer and the ceiling, ceiling plasterwork might be less precise in workmanship, as well as larger, than in earlier years. "When ornaments are liable to close inspection, every part should be well expressed and neatly furnished," warned Benjamin, "but when their situation is such that they can be seen only at a distance, the nice finish may be omitted, but their details must be strongly expressed."

The handsome ceiling plasterwork of a Greek Revival row house often was machine-made, rather than handmade, and of papier-mâché or stucco, rather than plaster. Just as factory-made cast iron replaced hand-wrought iron for stoop railings and areaway fences in the 1830s, steam-powered machinery mass-produced interior architectural ornament and doors and wood moldings. Quite often, factory designers copied their patterns directly from popular builder's guides, so some street-front and interior details exactly duplicate a plate in an Asher Benjamin or Minard Lafever pattern book.

Even the era's finest architects and ordinary builders took the shortcut of utilizing mass-produced interior ornament in New York dwellings. Alexander Jackson Davis noted in his price book for May 20, 1842, a purchase of machine-made ornament from John Gallier, at 592 Broadway, as "ornaments of Gallier in composition—honeysuckle, scroll, rosettes, wreath," and Martin E. Thompson's account book similarly records the purchase of "carved work" and "ornament" for several houses he designed.

BUILDER'S GUIDES AND THE GREEK REVIVAL

An outpouring of builder's guides in the late 1820s and 1830s featuring Greek Revival designs suitable for city houses helped assure the style's acceptance by New York's conservative architect-builders. The most influential and prolific author of the era remained the long-lived Asher Benjamin, while the other leading author was Minard Lafever of Brooklyn.

Lafever's first book, *The Young Builder's General Instructor* (1829), carried Federal-style designs that were clumsy in proportion and details and evidently modifications of contemporary New York row houses. In 1833 Lafever halted sales of

Left: Front parlor, 37 West Eleventh Street, Greenwich Village.

Above: Front parlor mantel, 37 West Eleventh Street, Greenwich Village.

Following pages:
Front parlor details, 37 West Eleventh Street, Greenwich Village.

Doorway into hall from front parlor, 37 West Eleventh Street, Greenwich Village.

GALERIE MAEGHT
GIACOMETTI

ARTFULLY MODERN RICHARD MISHAAN
GOODNOUGH

Mantel details, 37 West Eleventh Street,
Greenwich Village.

the book, because "though others seemed perfectly satisfied with the book, I myself was not." Lafever subsequently published *The Modern Builder's Guide* (1833) and *The Beauties of Modern Architecture* (1835), whose Greek Revival–style designs are nearly all original and are extraordinarily handsome in proportion and ornament.

In Greenwich Village and Brooklyn Heights, row house street fronts and interiors have details identical or nearly identical to designs in Lafever's guides. Whether handmade by craftsmen at the site or machine-made in a factory, these Lafever-inspired details reflect the importance of the builder's guides in row house ornament. The Merchant's House owes much of its handsome details to Lafever designs—indeed, so strongly do details of the front and the parlor echo designs in his guides that it once was thought that Lafever himself designed the house as part of a long row stretching to Lafayette Place. The arched late Federal doorway, set off with keystones and rustication blocks, is similar to Plate 42 in *The Young Builder's General Instructor*, the Ionic columns and entablature for the sliding double parlor doors resemble Plate 60 of *The Modern Builder's Guide*, and the plaster cornices of the parlor ceilings copy Plate 64 of *The Young Builder's General Instructor.* An occasional confusion of forms in the lavish parlors indicates that an architect-builder probably designed the house from Lafever prototypes.

Builder's guides largely were responsible for the successful adaptation of ancient masonry forms in such books as Stuart and Revett's *Antiquities of Athens* to nineteenth-century American materials and construction technology and to the scale of domestic architecture. "The style of building in this country differs very considerably from that of Great Britain, and other countries," wrote Asher Benjamin in 1806 in his preface to the first edition of *The American Builder's Companion*. "We do not conceive it essentially necessary to adhere exactly to any particular order, provided the proportion and harmony of the parts be carefully preserved. . . . We have ventured to make some alteration in the proportions of the different orders."

For easier construction, the builder often simplified the already modified designs. In New York row houses, it will be recalled, architect-builders usually substituted simple rectangular pilasters and entablature flush with the facade for the difficult doorway porch with freestanding columns. The American architects' modifications of Stuart and Revett's drawings for their own builder's guides, together with the builder's own changes at the construction site, resulted in a style that, if not totally classically correct, was structurally and economically practical for the period.

NEW YORK'S PROSPERITY IN THE 1830s AND 1840s

The 1830s and 1840s were largely a period of unparalleled prosperity and growth in New York, interrupted, however, by the Panic of 1837 and the protracted economic depression that followed it. During these decades of boom and bust, the city commanded unrivaled supremacy in foreign and domestic trade in the United States. As railroads began to replace rivers and canals in the 1840s for shipment of crops and

Top: Doors, from Minard Lafever's *Beauties of Modern Architecture* (1835). Notice the "battered" or outward-sloping sides that would become popular on New York row houses in the 1840s.

Bottom: Pocket parlor doors, Minard Lafever, *Beauties of Modern Architecture* (1835).

Pl. 14.
Engd by J.F. Morin, N-Y.

b
a
a
b

goods within the United States, New York became linked to a rail network connecting the city to the rest of the nation. In the decades before the Civil War, New York also attracted banking and insurance companies that were to make it the financial center of the nation and, in time, the world.

The bustling crowds and traffic-clogged streets awed residents and visitors to the city alike. Already in the mid-1820s, the city's "thrice told multitude" filled a western stranger with "amazement" that "240,000 [*sic*] people" could be living "in one place!" By 1850, that figure had doubled again, with more than half a million people residing on the island of Manhattan. The growth of Brooklyn, then a separate city, was equally staggering: from 21,000 in 1830, to 48,000 in 1840, to 139,000 in 1850.

The spectacular increase in population and wealth led to an unprecedented building boom. Row house construction swept relentlessly up narrow Manhattan Island to accommodate the city's ballooning population and those families fleeing the once-secluded downtown residential districts recently invaded by commercial activity. "The old downtown burgomasters, who have fixed to one spot all their lives," wrote Philip Hone in 1836, "will be seen during the next summer in flocks, marching reluctantly north to pitch their tents in places which, in their time, were orchards, cornfields, or morasses a pretty smart distance from town."

By the mid-1830s feverish speculation in land and building lots had seized New York, a mania also matched in cities and villages throughout the United States. Much of Manhattan had already been laid out in row house building lots, and according to one Frenchman, enough lots had been sold by 1835 to accommodate houses for two million people. A dizzy rise in all prices accompanied the nationwide speculative fever. "Everything in New York is at an exorbitant price," Hone wrote in 1836. "Rents have risen 50 per cent for the next year."

This bubble of false prosperity burst with the Panic of 1837, which initiated a several-year-long nationwide depression. In New York, hundreds of businesses failed, and thousands of workingmen lost their jobs. And in the Bond Street area, Hone saw "the sales of rich furniture, the property of men who a year ago thought themselves rich, and such expenditures justifiable, but are now bankrupt." Land values and construction activity suffered for several years. "Real estate is unsalable at any price; rents have fallen and are not punctually paid, and taxes have increased most ruinously," lamented Hone in 1837. The same year, he noted that building lots on the then-rural West Side, which had brought $480 a year earlier, had just sold for $50 each.

Prosperity returned to the nation and New York by the early 1840s, and the city's building boom and growth resumed its former hectic pace. "The city is spreading north . . . out of all reason and measure," wrote New York lawyer and diarist George Templeton Strong. The activity of architect-builders, who built row houses on speculation for sale to well-to-do businessmen, always suffered badly in a depression. Row house construction figures in New York from the 1830s and 1840s clearly reflect these periods of boom and bust. In 1834, 877 houses were completed in Manhattan, rising to 1,259 the next year, and 1,826 in 1836, the peak year before the Panic of 1837, when construction fell to 840 houses, before bottoming out at 674 houses completed in 1839. Production steadily increased to nearly 1,000 houses a year by 1841, with the annual number completed rising all the way to 1,980 in 1845. The annual tally never fell beneath 1,100 houses finished per year for the remainder of the 1840s.

BOND STREET

In the 1830s and 1840s, the city's most fashionable and best-known residential district was the Bond Street area. "In Houston, Bond, Bleecker, Fourth, and many other streets, large blocks of spacious and elegant houses are erecting or just completed," one newspaper observed in 1831, "and preparations for as many more are actively going forward." An 1829 real estate advertisement for an "elegant house and lot" on Bond Street asserted that "in point of eligibility of situation, convenience of arrangement and costliness of finish, this splendid establishment is not surpassed by any in the city." Elegant brick and marble-front row houses and mansions, the homes of some of New York's leading families, graced the area's serene tree-lined streets by the mid-1830s. "The elegance and beauty of this section cannot be surpassed in the country," wrote the *New York Morning Herald* in 1835.

Bond Street, a single 1,000-foot-long block, was the best-known street in the area. In 1820 Jonas Minturn built the first fine row house on Bond Street, No. 22, in a plain Federal style but with a startling white-marble front. By 1835 about sixty lavish row houses lined the block, ranging in style

Lafayette Place, view north from Great Jones Street (ca. 1866). A verdant and tranquil Lafayette Place was the setting for the spectacular white-marble Colonnade Row.

from Federal and late Federal to Greek Revival. In the 1820s, two trees had been planted in front of each house lot on Bond Street, and, by the 1850s, their foliage was so dense in summer that only the stoops of the houses and gaslights could be seen easily from carriages in the street.

The width and rectangular layout of streets in the Bond Street area were admired as an improvement over the jumble of streets in much of Manhattan south of Houston Street. "The streets in the lower and older portion of the city are very narrow and crooked, and what is more immediately inexcusable, are kept in very bad order," wrote British traveler John Morrison Duncan in the early 1820s. "The more modern streets are greatly superior in every respect; they are in general wide and straight, and the footwalks comparatively free of projections and encumbrances." Indeed, the irregular streets of the West Village, which today form a pleasant contrast with the ubiquitous grid, were considered old-fashioned by early nineteenth-century New Yorkers.

The Bond Street area's years of fashion were fleeting. By the late 1840s, elegant shops and hotels began to replace the fine dwellings along Broadway and marked the beginning of the area's decline as a residential neighborhood. "The mania for converting Broadway into a street of shops is greater than ever," wrote Philip Hone in 1850. "There is scarcely a block in the whole extent of this fine street of which some part is not in a state of transmutation." Fleeing this unwanted commercial intrusion, the rich and socially elect families abandoned their by then old-fashioned dwellings for showy brownstone-fronts of Fifth Avenue and Madison Square. By 1853, the *Builder* magazine observed that "Bond and Bleeker [*sic*] streets, that were then the *ultima thule* of aristocracy, are now but plebian streets."

After the Civil War, the Bond Street area lost all semblance of its patrician past. The elegant dwellings became "restaurants or private boarding-houses, barrooms or groceries, peculiar physicians' offices or midwives' headquarters." Other houses became sweatshops, lofts, or warehouses. "No street in the Metropolis has changed more than Bleecker," wrote Junius Henri Browne in the 1869 *The Great Metropolis: A Mirror of New York*. "The grand mansions stand conspicuously in the thoroughfare, with a semblance of departed greatness, and an acknowledgement of surrendered splendor."

THE COLONNADE ROW AND LAFAYETTE PLACE

Some of the first, and certainly the most spectacular, Greek Revival dwellings in New York were the nine marble-front houses known as Colonnade Row (1832–33). Built by Seth Geer and attributed to Alexander Jackson Davis, Colonnade Row was originally named La Grange Terrace in honor of the country house of the Marquis de Lafayette, and stood on then-secluded Lafayette Place. The street, 100 feet wide, had been cut in 1826 southward from Astor Place to a dead end at Great Jones Street.

Colonnade Row was a testament to the striking potential of the monumental blockfront and streetscape. In the tradition of the terraces and crescents in London and Bath, the nine houses of Colonnade Row were subordinated to the monumental two-story-tall colonnade running the full length of the row. A heavy bronze cornice reinforced the visual unity of the row (and, at the same time, concealed a pitched roof when viewed from below.) A rusticated basement and first floor visually balanced the two-story colonnade and the cornice. Here, the single row house gave up its individuality for the dignity of the row and streetscape.

Within the uniform blockfront of Colonnade Row, the detailing of the individual houses was remarkably sophisticated in concept and extravagant in execution. Doric columns framed front doorways, which were modestly recessed into the rusticated first floor and similar in appearance to the first-floor windows. Elegant cast-iron torches stood at each side of the modest several-step-high stoops. Laurel wreaths decorated the lintels, rectangular doorway, and second-floor parlor windows, and the capitals of the elaborate fluted Corinthian columns were deeply and freely cut. A drawing titled *Approaching what Lafayette Terrace ought to be*, by Davis, showed the houses with roof gardens and vine-covered overhead trellises, which never were built.

Before the row's construction, few houses had been built beyond Bleecker Street, and New Yorkers traveled uptown to marvel at the houses rising in near solitary splendor in the still rural area. In 1911 Montgomery Schuyler evoked Colonnade Row at the time of its construction:

> Even from the mellow gray of the relics of the mansions one can understand how electrifying must have been their effect upon New York when

Above: Colonnade Row, Lafayette Place. The nine white-marble mansions of Colonnade Row were some of the most extravagant—and beautiful—row houses erected in nineteenth-century New York and, indeed, anywhere in the United States. At their completion in 1833, the houses sold for a then-unheard-of $25,000 to $30,000.

Left: Colonnade Row (1832), photographed in the 1860s.

Following pages:
27 East Eleventh Street, Greenwich Village (1844–45). This handsome row house is an excellent example of the Greek Revival style. Greenwich Village Historic District.

> their "new-cut ashlar took the light" . . . in its glittering freshness of white marble. . . . There were not wanting critics to call the Terrace "Geer's Folly," and to predict that there were not millionaires enough in New York to live up to these splendors especially since "the splendors" were "so far away," almost two miles to the Battery. It is satisfactory to know that the enterprising builder confounded his critics and was rewarded for bestowing one of its chief ornaments upon the city by disposing of all the houses at a handsome profit.

The completion of Colonnade Row pointed to the city's rapid uptown growth and the decline of traditional residential districts closer to the Battery. In 1836, Philip Hone regretfully sold his home, 235 Broadway, opposite City Hall Park, and moved to 1 Great Jones Street, several blocks from the Colonnade Row, because "all" the downtown "dwelling houses are to be converted into stores. We are tempted with prices so exorbitantly high that none can resist."

During the 1830s and 1840s, Lafayette Place rivaled Bond and Bleecker Streets as the city's most fashionable address. The houses of Colonnade Row were "universally allowed to be unequalled for grandeur and effect," acclaimed the *Ladies' Companion* in 1836—they were judged to be the "most imposing and magnificent" houses in the city and were home to such luminaries as John Jacob Astor, who lived at No. 37. Fine row houses, mansions on tree-shaded grounds, and churches lined the rest of Lafayette Place.

The street's glory was sadly short-lived. Nearby Broadway's transformation from an elegant residential to a fashionable commercial street in the late 1840s and 1850s introduced unwanted nonresidential uses into the neighborhood. The first portion of the Astor Library was built across the street from the Colonnade Row in 1849–53. In the Colonnade Row itself, Israel Underhill opened 43 and 45 Lafayette Place as an elegant boardinghouse. In 1859 massive Cooper Union was completed at the Bowery and Astor Place, just to the north of the Colonnade Row. Nevertheless, unlike nearby Bond and Bleecker Streets, Lafayette Place was somewhat isolated from the rising commercial activity on Broadway and the Bowery and remained one of the city's finest streets into the 1850s.

With the 1860s, Lafayette Place surrendered its residential fashion. William B. Astor moved to a brownstone mansion on Fifth Avenue, and his splendid mansion on Lafayette Place, across the street from the Colonnade Row, became a restaurant. The five southernmost houses of Colonnade Row became part of the Colonnade Hotel, whose entrance faced Broadway. In the late 1890s, Lafayette Place was widened and extended below Great Jones Street toward City Hall. The once-patrician row houses along Lafayette Place and adjacent streets became cheap boardinghouses and tenements or were torn down for sweatshop lofts and massive warehouses.

WASHINGTON SQUARE AND GREENWICH VILLAGE

"Washington Square is another great and most effective ornament to our city," wrote the 1828 *The Picture of New-York* guidebook. "There have already been erected around it, many handsome private dwellings, and the vicinity has likewise become a most fashionable residence, although somewhat remote at present from the centre of business." Today, Washington Square retains a large measure of its original dignity. Despite changes over the years, the Greek Revival row house mansions along the north side of Washington Square Park are among the city's finest remaining nineteenth-century dwellings and, with their restrained redbrick fronts, white-marble porches, and planted front yards, recall a seemingly more pleasant and gracious New York.

Beloved Washington Square was originally marshland fed by the Minetta Brook. After 1795, it served as a paupers' burial ground and the site of the city gallows. In 1826 the city purchased several additional acres of land and converted the area into the Washington Military Parade-Ground and a public park. In the next decade, palatial row houses rose along the north, west, and south sides. In 1837, New York University completed its first building, in a Gothic Revival mode, on the east side of the park.

No. 1–13 Washington Square North (1831–33), east of Fifth Avenue, were among the finest and earliest Greek Revival row houses in the city. An 1833 real estate advertisement for the just-completed 2 Washington Square North declared that this "ELEGANT PRIVATE RESIDENCE . . . is believed to be inferior to no house in the United States, either in workmanship or convenience." Although the redbrick street fronts, rising from a rusticated white-marble basement, epitomize the severity valued by the Greek Revival style, the houses have

27

several rich and highly original ornamental features. The square basement windows recall the passing Federal style and display an elegant four-sided enframement enhanced by a keystone at the center of the top jamb and square impost blocks down the side jambs. Elegant vermiculation, a rough-surfaced, twisting, wormlike surface, decorates the keystones and impost blocks on the basement windows in some houses. Freestanding white-marble porches with handsome Doric or Ionic columns shield the front doors, and rather than the usual iron railings of the period the stoops have massive white-marble balustrades, a glance backward to the Renaissance tradition. All the houses but one retain the original iron front fences with handsome anthemia, Greek keys, and lyres.

This blockfront was one of the first monumental row house streetscapes in the city and, in the nineteenth century, was known simply as "the Row." A continuous cornice line, evenly aligned doors and windows, and a front fence several hundred feet long make for the impressive continuous vista. The freestanding doorway porches and balustraded stoops punctuate the blockfront and form a contrast to the flat and plainly detailed street fronts. The 12-foot-deep front yards, enclosed by a continuous iron fence and shaded by trees, and its location facing Washington Square impart to the Row a patrician grandeur and detachment missing in the usual New York row house built close to the sidewalk on a narrow street.

The construction of the Row was an outstanding example of private planning in nineteenth-century America. The blockfront was developed under the control of the Sailors' Snug Harbor, a home for retired sailors that owned several blocks east of Fifth Avenue and north of Washington Square. In 1831 James Boorman, John Johnston, and John Morrison leased the building lots of the Row from the Sailors' Snug Harbor for one hundred years and built up the blockfront between 1831 and 1833 in two remarkably uniform and complementary rows of houses, respectively 1–6 and 7–13 Washington Square North. Under the terms of the 1831 leases, the lessee agreed to build "a good and substantial dwelling house, of the width of said lot, three or more stories high, in brick or stone, covered with slate or metal," set back 12 feet from the front lot line, and "to be finished in such style as may be approved of by the "lessor." The lessee also had the right to build a private stable at the rear of each lot, provided it not become a "slaughter house, tallow chandlery, smith shop, forge, furnace or brass foundry, nail or other iron factory, or any manufactory . . . trade or business which may be noxious or offensive to the neighbors." The carriage houses of the Row are known today as Washington Mews, an east–west lane located behind the Row.

To the north of Washington Square, Ninth, Tenth, Eleventh, and Twelfth Streets are charming tree-lined streets whose row houses reflect all the early and mid-nineteenth-century architectural styles. The Greek Revival dwellings on the south side of West Eleventh Street, between Fifth and Sixth Avenues, built in several groups in the 1840s, form one of the finest early nineteenth-century streetscapes in the area. The flat street fronts, modest door enframements and window details, and a fairly uniform cornice line unconsciously create a unified, nearly 500-foot-long blockfront. The iron front fences and stoop railings, nearly all of which remain on these houses, add elegance and visual excitement to this remarkable vista.

Greenwich Village as a whole abounds in ordinary row houses, erected by architect-builders for the city's prosperous business and professional men. In the early nineteenth century, the differences between the houses of the rich, as seen on Washington Square North, and the houses of the merely well-to-do, as seen on West Eleventh Street, were less dramatic than they would be in the remaining decades of the nineteenth century. Though the row houses on West Eleventh Street are narrower and not built as deeply nor as tall as the mansions along Washington Square North, they are otherwise not dramatically different in appearance.

In the 1830s and 1840s, visitors to New York commented on the restrained lifestyle and handsome, but not extravagant, houses of the city's rich families. "The upper classes live in a more simple form, wanting some of the most refined improvements of high English life," wrote one Englishman in the 1840s. This situation "might be expected in a country where labor is comparatively high, and the fortunes, though great, still not often as princely as in the mother country." Few New Yorkers lived in palatial mansions until the Industrial Revolution and Civil War–induced boom piled up great fortunes and the rising tide of immigration offered ample supply of low-paid servants to run these large households. And only with these new fortunes did mansions come to line Fifth Avenue and an extravagant house become a prerequisite to an elevated social standing.

CHELSEA

By the 1840s, row house construction had swept past Fourteenth Street into the Chelsea area near the Hudson River. "The neighborhood which bears the name Chelsea is rapidly covering itself with new buildings," wrote one newspaper in 1846. "The arrangements made by the original proprietors of the land in that quarter are such that no building can be erected for any purpose which will make the neighborhood disagreeable, and it is becoming a favorite place of residence."

Chelsea was originally the eighteenth-century estate of Captain Thomas Clarke, with boundaries from the present-day Fourteenth Street to Twenty-Seventh Street and from Seventh Avenue west to the Hudson River. Clarke expected that his country estate would be his retreat in old age and, as a soldier, chose the name Chelsea from the Royal Hospital Chelsea in London, a home for old soldiers and sailors. However, soon after buying the estate, Captain Clarke died. His widow nevertheless built the estate's mansion, which once stood on Twenty-Third Street, 200 feet west of Ninth Avenue, surrounded by terraced grounds and sitting on a hill overlooking the Hudson River. Several generations later, the estate passed to Thomas Clarke's grandson, Clement Clarke Moore, a noted classical scholar, now remembered as the author of *A Visit from St. Nicholas* (although there is continued controversy about authorship). In the 1830s, Clement Clarke Moore mapped the estate into building lots and gave a full block to the General Theological Seminary.

An exceptionally fine row of Greek Revival–style houses stands at 406–418 West Twentieth Street. These houses were built by Don Alonzo Cushman, a friend of Moore's, who developed much of Chelsea. Cushman Row is noted for the nearly original street fronts, particularly the fine cast-iron wreaths encircling the small attic windows in the cornice, and for the iron stoop railings and areaway fences. At the southeast corner of Twentieth Street, at 162 Ninth Avenue, is the 1834 mansion of James N. Wells, a builder, with a doorway porch with freestanding fluted white-marble Doric columns and pedimented lintels similar to the houses of Washington Square North.

Previous pages:
Cushman Row, 406–418 West Twentieth Street, Chelsea (1839–40). Chelsea Historic District.

Left: Attic window, Cushman Row (1839–40). Chelsea Historic District.

Opposite: Doorway and ironwork, Cushman Row, 416 West Twentieth Street (1839–40). Chelsea Historic District.

Following pages:
57 Willow Street, Brooklyn Heights (ca. 1825). Though largely Federal in style, this house has Greek keys on the fascia boards of the cornice, one of the earliest surviving examples of the rising Grecian influence in New York in the 1820s. Brooklyn Heights Historic District.

57

BROOKLYN HEIGHTS

In the eighteenth century, Brooklyn was a quiet farming area at the westernmost end of Long Island just across the East River from Manhattan. Many farms were held by families to whom the land had been granted in the seventeenth century under Dutch patents, and small villages, such as Flatbush, Bedford, and Bushwick dotted the countryside. However, Brooklyn's rural seclusion lasted only into the early nineteenth century. With the start of regularly scheduled ferry service between Brooklyn and Fulton Street in Manhattan in 1814, Brooklyn began its growth as a thriving autonomous city and as a desirable residential community.

On Brooklyn Heights, poised on a bluff overlooking the East River and the city of New York (then clustered around the Battery), the several landowners there divided their farms into row house building lots. Their names today are preserved in such Brooklyn Heights street names as Joralemon, Pierrepont, and Remsen. Well-to-do merchants, many of whom worked in Manhattan, built houses on Brooklyn Heights, attracted by the easy walk to the ferry to Manhattan and its spectacular view of New York Bay. The sight of the harbor from Brooklyn Heights, wrote one visitor in the 1830s, is "one of the most stunning views imaginable—the ferry-boats passing and repassing, the shipping, the harbour and the fortified islands in the vicinity, are all seen to great advantage."

By the 1820s, wood and brick houses dotted Brooklyn Heights. "The houses in the principal streets have a particularly neat and elegant appearance," recalled one Englishman around 1830: "They are chiefly built of wood, and painted white, with green latticed blinds on the outside. . . . For the entire length of some of the streets, weeping willows are planted on each side, which, independent of being very ornamental, offered a delightful shade to the fronts of the houses, and protect the foot paths even from the noon-day sun." A few of these Federal-style houses have survived to the present day. One of the oldest and most beautiful dwellings on Brooklyn Heights is wood-framed 24 Middagh Street, at Willow Street, the former Eugene Boisselet House. Although most houses built on Brooklyn Heights in the 1820s were wood frame, as befitted the then-rural community, 155, 157, and 159 Willow Street (ca. 1825) are three brick Federal-style row houses. The houses at 155 and 157 Willow Street retain their original pitched roofs and dormers, which at 159 were replaced by a full third floor soon after the completion of the row.

Although Brooklyn's population almost doubled between 1820 and 1830 from 11,000 to 20,000 people, only Brooklyn Heights and the area around the ferry station resembled a city. In the mid-nineteenth century, George Hall, the first mayor of Brooklyn, recalled the city of 1823:

> The population of the city at that time consisted of about 20,000 persons; residing for the most part within the distance of about three quarters of a mile from Fulton Ferry. Beyond this limit no streets of any consequence were laid out, and the ground was chiefly occupied for agricultural purposes. The shores, throughout nearly their whole extent, were in their natural condition, washed by the East River and the bay. There were two ferries, by which communication was had with the city of New York, ceasing at twelve o'clock at night. . . . Of commerce and manufactures it can scarcely be said to have had any, its business consisting chiefly of that which was required for supplying the wants of its inhabitants. Sixteen of its streets were lighted with public lamps, of which thirteen had been supplied within the previous year.

In the following decades, Brooklyn grew rapidly and took on an urban character. In 1834 Brooklyn received a city charter, the jurisdiction encompassing the present-day downtown, South Brooklyn, Navy Yard, and Fort Greene area. Feverish land speculation and an almost never-ending building boom accompanied Brooklyn's growing population, which reached 48,000 in 1840 and 139,000 in 1850. "The rage for speculating in lands on Long Island is one of the bubbles of the day," wrote Philip Hone in the prosperous mid-1830s. "Men in moderate circumstances have become immensely rich merely by the good fortune of owning farms of a few acres of this chosen land. Abraham Schermerhorn has sold his farm of 170 acres at Gowanus, three miles from Brooklyn, at $600 an acre; four years ago, having got out of conceit of it as a residence, he offered it for sale at $20,000, and would have taken $18,000; to-day he pockets $102,000, and regrets that he sold it so cheap!"

By the 1830s and 1840s, handsome Greek Revival row houses filled many blocks of Brooklyn Heights. Construction first occurred in the northern portion of Brooklyn Heights, close to the ferry at the foot of Brooklyn's Fulton Street. The start of ferry service in 1836 from the foot of Atlantic Street (now Avenue) in Brooklyn to South Ferry in Manhattan spurred development of the southern portion of Brooklyn Heights and adjacent South Brooklyn.

43–49 Willow Place, Brooklyn Heights (ca. 1846). This modest colonnade row is a delightful sight on secluded, one-block-long Willow Place. Brooklyn Heights Historic District.

The Heights had its own extravagant Colonnade Row, now lost. In 1835 General Underhill built eight Greek Revival–style row houses on Columbia Heights, between Cranberry and Middagh Streets, overlooking the East River. A monumental three-story wood colonnade united the houses, which each cost $15,000 when new. Early on the morning of December 20, 1853, one of the corner houses caught fire and, according to contemporary accounts, "[B]efore the second house was on fire inside, the fire had extended the whole length of the block outside, front and rear." The much more modest 43–49 Willow Place (1846) in Brooklyn Heights is the only remaining example in Brooklyn of this daring urban form. Square wood columns support a two-story-tall wood porch that dignifies but does not hide the two-story-tall narrow brick houses to which it has been added.

In Brooklyn Heights today, these ensembles of houses together evoke the dignified streetscape of mid-nineteenth-century New York. These streets take a special charm from the casual, unforced manner in which they were built up. The cornices are of varying heights, and the house fronts are shades of red brick or pastel paints and gently step in and out. Viewed today, with trees at the curb and occasional gardens in the front yards, some Brooklyn Heights blocks have the beauty and serenity, if not complete appearance, of the city before the Civil War.

THE GREEK MANIA EXHAUSTED

The Greek Revival was the style for nearly all New York row houses from the early 1830s to the late 1840s and, on some houses, lasted into the early 1850s. The very popularity of the Greek Revival contributed to its decline—its excessive use had cheapened the impact of the style.

In James Fenimore Cooper's *Home As Found* (1838), the Effingham family takes a boat ride up the Hudson River from New York. Passing numerous Greek Revival–style country houses along the river, one character remarks that "an extraordinary taste is afflicting this country in the way of architecture . . . nothing but a Grecian temple being now deemed a suitable residence." His companion replies: "One such temple well placed in a wood, might be a pleasant object enough; but to see a river lined with them, with children trundling hoops before their doors, beef carried into their kitchens, and smoke issuing, moreover, from those unclassical objects, chimneys, is too much ever for a high taste."

In the 1840s, critics also linked the style to the "paganism" of ancient Greece and argued that it was incompatible with a Christian nation's ideals. Other Americans recalled that man's earliest democracy in ancient Greece also had been cursed with the institution of slavery—of course the predominant and divisive political issue of the era.

"We are firm in the belief that the introduction of Grecian architecture among us has been a great mistake," wrote the *North American Review* in 1844, at the peak of the style's popularity. "Its edifices belong to another climate; they are the legitimate offspring of a remote age, an antagonistic religion, an obsolete form of government, and a widely different state of society from our own."

46 Willow Place, Brooklyn Heights Historic District.

III

1850–1873
THE BROWNSTONE ERA

By the end of the 1840s, the wealth and social ambitions of many New York families exceeded the scale and architectural treatment of the traditional row house mansion in the Bond Street or Washington Square tradition. In 1848 and 1849 and in quick succession, the extravagant Thorne, Haight, Benkard, Parish, and Van Buren mansions on or near Fifth Avenue introduced impressive brownstone fronts on houses whose height, depth, and rich architectural embellishments surpassed that of all the city's earlier dwellings. The long-reigning ideal of republican simplicity all but vanished in favor of architectural flamboyance and ostentation.

Within several years nearly all of New York's large row houses were built with the fashionable brownstone front. Despite its humble background as an inexpensive local substitute for marble or limestone, brownstone came to epitomize luxury and architectural sophistication. "Brownstone has now, as all our town readers know, come to be the favorite building material for shops, churches, and residences," wrote *Putnam's* magazine in 1853. The "prevailing tint of New York is fixed."

The adoption of the brownstone front also brought with it a new style, as housebuilders adopted the Italianate palazzo mode, which featured a bracketed cornice and heavy projecting ornament, with full enframement of windows and doorways. Italianate forms had already appeared as motifs on otherwise Greek Revival–style row houses in the city, such as 16 East Tenth Street (1846) and its neighbor 20 East Tenth Street (1848). Those houses were part of a block on the south side of East Tenth Street east of Fifth Avenue constructed by various builders in the 1840s with brick fronts of similar scale but diverse revival architectural embellishments. Two other nearby houses, No. 4 (1848) and No. 18 (1847), featured Gothic Revival doorways and hood moldings above windows, joining neighboring houses at No. 6 (1848) and Nos. 8–14 (1839–42) that were all constructed in a relatively pure Greek Revival form. To some critics, the mixing of revival styles on a single house as well as on a block of houses represented architectural confusion, and the Italianate style presented an avenue toward stylistic unity. "The present age

131 and 135 Hicks Street, Brooklyn Heights (1847–48). Gothic Revival row houses with brownstone fronts. Though relatively few row houses in the Gothic Revival mode were constructed in the 1840s and 1850s, they introduced the full brownstone front to New York's houses. In the mid-nineteenth century, brownstone-front houses were built in such large numbers that they a provided a lasting name for all New York's row houses—the brownstone. Brooklyn Heights Historic District.

is distinguished," wrote Marriott Field in his 1853 *City Architecture* "by too cosmopolitan a taste for variety of styles, with a view to the production of novelty and picturesqueness." Field advised adherence to a single classical style instead: "We should eschew all unpure, mixed, and transition styles, and for city architecture should adopt the Italian." This advice was largely heeded by the city's builders, as the brownstone-front Italianate row house brought a stylistic uniformity for New York row houses that would reign for the next two decades.

NEW YORK'S AFFLUENCE AND MACHINE-MADE GRANDEUR

The scale and elaborate ornament of New York's houses mirrored the growing affluence of America's most prosperous city, long the unquestioned leader of American trade. Along the East River, swift clippers and international packet ships cast anchor and embarked; dry goods and foodstuffs filled merchants' warehouses and often overflowed onto the sidewalks; and the renowned East River shipyards built some of the finest ships in the world. "One needs to come down to the river quays to see the greatness of New York City," wrote Scottish visitor William Ferguson in 1855. By 1860, more than one-third of the nation's exports and more than two-thirds of its imports, as measured by value, passed through New York.

The city also became the nation's uncontested financial and business center in the 1850s and 1860s as banks and insurance companies proliferated in size, assets, and numbers. British businessman James Robertson in 1855 described New York as "now the largest—indeed *the* money market of the States." In turn, the city's array of financial services strengthened its trade position because, he noted, its market offered "facilities to merchants" that "cannot be afforded by any other city." At the same time, this activity attracted the main offices of the nation's corporations, paving the way for the city's concentration of corporate headquarters in later years.

New York had also become a leading manufacturing center in the mid-nineteenth century. The city's rail and water transport routes offered easy connections to raw materials as well as to markets for the finished goods, and a rising tide of immigrants provided ample cheap labor. In these decades of unparalleled prosperity, New York's population tripled in just thirty years—from 313,000 in 1840, to 515,000 in 1850, to 814,000 in 1860, and to 942,000 in 1870.

These thriving trade, financial, and manufacturing activities brought great wealth to many families. Reveling in newly won riches, these families flaunted their prosperity and sought concomitant social recognition from the city's longer-established families, imitating them as best they could in houses, carriages, parties, and clothing. Although visitors to New York pointed out its showy social scene as early as the 1820s, the mid-nineteenth century brought an unmatched extravagance and competition to the game.

New York's social life was "in a state of constant fluctuation, in accordance with the fluctuating fortunes of commercial life," wrote

Rhinelander Gardens, 102–116 West Eleventh Street, Greenwich Village, architect James Renwick Jr. (ca. 1854), photographed in 1936. Deep front yards and dazzling Gothic Revival cast-iron porches made this row of ordinary brick houses one of Greenwich Village's visual treats. Demolished.

Scottish journalist Alexander Mackay in the late 1840s. "Its doors are guarded, but they never seem to be closed, and you have a constant stream flowing in and out." Two decades later, in 1868, *Putnam's* magazine lamented that New York "'Society' is constantly shifting—it is a kaleidoscope. Few, if any, of the leaders of ten years ago remain; all are gone—gone, and none know whither, or care. 'Society' is too eager, too busy, to stop and shed a tear upon ruined fortunes or blasted hopes."

In such an extravagant and frantic social setting, the tastefulness of one's dwelling was an object of great concern. Although only a few families were prosperous enough to afford freestanding mansions on Fifth Avenue or splendid 25- or 30-foot-wide houses, many thousands of families lived in brownstone-front row houses throughout the city that aspired to a similar grandeur of scale and embellishment.

Sophisticated machine technology offered the means by which the city's brownstone-front row houses could be built in wide numbers and approach the grandeur of mansions but with far less cost. With the improved capabilities and economies of machine manufacture available by the 1850s, showy materials and elaborate ornament began to appear in the houses of the city's merely well-to-do upper middle class and, despite the savings in cost, retained the status connotations of hand-labor days.

Women's magazines, led by *Godey's Lady's Book*, and books purporting to be guides to good taste in interior decoration also first appeared in the 1850s, a signal of the era's aspirational values. Philadelphia architect Samuel Sloan, author of several vastly influential books on city- and country-house architecture in the era, was among the most canny observers (and exploiters) of the appetite for conspicuous display of wealth and taste at home. In the 1852 volume *Model Architecture*, Sloan wrote: "A man's dwelling at the present day, is not only an index of his wealth, but also of his character. The moment he begins to build, his tact for arrangement, his private feelings, the refinement of his taste and the peculiarities of his judgment are all laid bare for public inspection and criticism. And the public makes free use of this prerogative. It expects an effort to be made, and forms opinions upon the result."

THE FASHION FOR BROWNSTONE AND THE GOTHIC REVIVAL

Local brownstone was a regular building material in New York and its environs long before it achieved overwhelming popularity and fashion in the 1850s. Half a mile north of the Battery, at the intersection of Broadway and Fulton Street, is St. Paul's Chapel (1766), the oldest church on Manhattan Island, which is constructed of Manhattan schist and brownstone. As noted previously, brownstone had long served as an inexpensive substitute building material for marble, granite, and limestone on the city's houses. Brownstone's rise to fashion for house fronts, however, came with the Gothic Revival in the 1840s, when the brownstone front was transposed from the city's architecturally influential churches to its homes.

Trinity Church (1839–46) at Broadway and Wall Street, designed by Richard Upjohn, was one of the earliest Gothic Revival churches in New York and also one of the most noteworthy buildings completed in the United States in the 1840s. "There are few things in architecture, that could hold out less promise of excellence" than the Gothic mode, wrote architect Arthur D. Gilman in the *North American Review* in 1844, and it was "evident" that a "rapid advance" had "been made in an acquaintance with the true principles of the Gothic style" at Trinity and other Gothic Revival churches in Manhattan and Brooklyn.

Trinity was also one of the first of the major buildings in New York to feature a full brownstone facade. As the city's wealthiest congregation as well as its most fashionable, Trinity was a bellwether of ecclesiastical architecture, and congregations soon followed Trinity's lead by selecting brownstone for their Gothic Revival churches. By the 1850s, brownstone was nearly a mandatory building material for wealthy city churches in New York and nationwide. James Renwick Jr.'s much-acclaimed white marble Grace Church on Broadway, completed in 1846, was a decade later subtly panned by *New-York Quarterly* magazine as a "very showy building, very florid, and of had white marble"—"had" as in out of fashion.

Brownstone, unlike brick or marble or limestone, was viewed as a Picturesque shade that complemented nature and thus appropriate to the medieval roots of the Gothic in Europe. "The practical rule" was "to avoid all those colors which nature avoids," wrote Andrew Jackson Downing in his 1850 *Architecture of Country Houses*. That rule applied to residential architecture as well as churches: "In building we should copy those that she offers chiefly to the eye—such as those of soil, rocks, wood, and the bark of trees—the materials of which houses are built."

The first Gothic Revival dwellings in New York were the rectories of these costly churches built in the 1840s. The splendid 7 West Tenth Street (1839–41), the rectory of the Church of the Ascension around the corner on Fifth Avenue, features asymmetrical massing as well as applied medieval ornament of handsome drip moldings above the door and windows. The house is also significant as perhaps the first full brownstone-front row house in the city, a startling innovation at the time of its construction. Here, the brownstone was set in roughly textured blocks, different from smooth-surfaced brownstone fronts typical in succeeding decades.

Apart from rectories, many other early surviving brownstone-front houses in New York are in the Gothic Revival style, among them 16 Gramercy Park South (1844–45), an unusually wide Gothic Revival–style row house, later remodeled in 1888 by Stanford White for the Players, a private club; 28 East Twentieth Street, now known as the Theodore Roosevelt House (1847–48); 10 Fifth Avenue (1848–49) at the northwest corner of West Eighth Street; and, in Brooklyn Heights, Nos. 131 and 135 Hicks Street (1847–48), the last two arguably the most fully realized Gothic Revival row houses in the city.

The Gothic Revival style, however, was far more commonly manifested as select brownstone decorative features of an otherwise typical brick house front. The simplest treatment was a rectangular doorway topped with a hood mold, a horizontal form with rectangular drip molds at each end. Downing significantly favored the square-headed door or window surmounted by the horizontal hood mold rather than the Tudor arch. Wrote Downing, "To our own feeling, there is more *domesticity* in the square-headed window, and we would therefore, only introduce the arch in doors and windows of private houses, in particular cases, when the stronger indication of style is needed to give spirit to the composition."

Gothic Revival forms were most popular in ironwork, which was easier and far less expensive to adapt to complicated Gothic forms than stone. Cast-iron stoop railings, front fences, parlor-window balconies, and verandas displayed elaborate Gothic details, but almost nothing of it survives in New York save occasional railings and fences. Before their demolition in 1955, the spectacular three-story-tall porches of the Rhinelander Gardens, at Nos. 102–116 West Eleventh Street, displayed the finest Gothic Revival–style ironwork in the city.

For the most part, the Gothic Revival was quite rare as a fully realized style on New York row houses. Narrow city lots prevented the asymmetrical massing and gabled roofline favored on country houses of the same style. Besides, a style so strongly associated with untamed nature seemed inherently unsuited for the town houses of bustling mid-nineteenth-century New York. Its real legacy in the city's domestic architecture was in pioneering the full brownstone front, which would flourish with the Italianate style.

THE BACKGROUND OF THE ITALIANATE STYLE

The inspiration for the Italianate style in New York row houses was the fifteenth-century Italian city palace, or palazzo. In 1829 the British architect Sir Charles Barry probably made the first use of the palazzo or cinquecento mode for the Travellers Club (1829–31) on London's Pall Mall. Barry again employed the richly decorated palazzo mode for the Reform Club (1841), and later for government offices in the Whitehall area. About the same time, graduates of the famed École des Beaux-Arts in Paris adopted the palazzo mode for government buildings there, because its monumental scale and rich classical ornament were deemed suitable to express the dignity of the French state. Designs for large public buildings in Berlin, Vienna, and other European capitals soon reflected this mode.

In the United States, architect Arthur D. Gilman was probably the first American to recommend the palazzo mode as an alternative to the Greek Revival style, in an 1844 article in the *North American Review*. In the following years, occasional buildings in the Renaissance palazzo mode began to appear in American cities. The Athenaeum of Philadelphia (1845–47), designed by John Notman, was one of the first palazzo-mode buildings in the United States and still stands on the east side of that city's Washington Square. In her *History of Architecture, from the Earliest Times; Its Condition in Europe and the United States* (1848), Louisa Caroline Tuthill mentioned the Athenaeum and expressed the rising concern for the architectural treatment of

Opposite:
Top: Athenaeum of Philadelphia (1845–47), one of the first palazzo-inspired buildings in the United States. This engraving of the building was published in Louisa Caroline Tuthill's 1848 *History of Architecture, from the Earliest Times*. Tuthill deemed the building a "beautiful specimen of street architecture."

Bottom: A. T. Stewart Store, east side of Broadway, between Chambers and Reade Streets (1845–46), photographed in the 1870s. One of the most important buildings ever constructed in New York, it was the city's first Italian palazzo–inspired building and one of the first department stores in the world.

Right: Brooklyn Savings Bank, Fulton and Concord Streets, Brooklyn, architect Minard Lafever (1846–47). One of the first palazzo-mode buildings in New York. Demolished.

the city streetscape. "This building is a beautiful specimen of street architecture. Where the space for an edifice in the city is necessarily very limited, the best possible way of rendering it ornamental, is to decorate the doors and windows, the cornice and balustrade."

Another equally early—and consequential—building in this mode was the A. T. Stewart Store (1845–46) in New York at Broadway and Chambers Street, one of the first department stores in the world. It was a "splendid edifice," wrote Philip Hone in 1846. "There is nothing in Paris or London to compare with this dry goods palace," Hone declared, a sentiment widely shared in the city. The A. T. Stewart Store became a landmark on Broadway, then New York's street of fashionable shops and hotels, and was instrumental in popularizing Italianate forms. *Harper's* wrote in 1854:

> A few years ago, when a man returned from Europe, his eye being full of the lofty buildings of the Continent, our cities seemed insignificant and mean. . . . But the moment Stewart's fine building was erected, the difficulty appeared. That tyrannized over the rest of the street—that was a key-note, a model. There had been other high buildings, but none so stately and simple. And even now there is, in its way, no finer street effect than the view of Stewart's building seen on a clear, blue, brilliant day, from a point as low on Broadway as . . . Trinity Church. It rises out of the sea of green foliage in the [City Hall] Park, a white marble cliff, sharply drawn against the sky.

The article concluded that we "will look up to the beautiful buildings in Broadway and long not for Italy and an Italian beauty, but be gratefully contented for what we are." Even with various additions and alterations over the years, the A. T. Stewart Store building is still recognizable today and serves as the Manhattan Department of Buildings.

Across the East River, Minard Lafever's Brooklyn Savings Bank (1846–47) at Fulton and Concord Streets displayed the palazzo mode tempered with some Greek Revival details. Although the bank was demolished in 1936 for Cadman Plaza park at the foot of the Brooklyn Bridge, a print in Lafever's *The Architectural Instructor* (1856) shows that, as originally built, it exhibited many Renaissance palazzo motifs later to be seen in New York's Italianate-style row houses. In *The Architectural Instructor*, Lafever described the Brooklyn Savings Bank as in the "Italian style" and noted that the fronts of the adjoining dwelling houses were designed to harmonize with the bank.

THE APPEARANCE OF THE PALAZZO MODE ON NEW YORK DWELLINGS

The palazzo mode won immediate acclaim in New York and throughout the United States for commercial and public buildings, and by the late 1840s daring mansions and row houses in the city occasionally employed its domestic offshoot, the Italianate style. By 1854, *Putnam's* magazine stated that "the Grecian taste . . . has within the last few years been succeeded and almost entirely superseded, both here and in England, by the revival of the Italian style."

Herman Thorne Residence, south side of West Sixteenth Street, just off Fifth Avenue, architects Trench and Snook (1846–48). The Thorne residence was probably the first Italianate-style dwelling house in New York. Demolished.

The first Italianate-style dwelling in New York was very likely the Herman Thorne mansion (1846–48) on the south side of West Sixteenth Street, just off Fifth Avenue. Designed by the firm of Trench and Snook, the Thorne residence featured a brownstone front, a fully enframed and boldly ornamented front doorway and windows, and a prominent cornice. In 1847, the *United States Magazine and Democratic Review* described the then-unfinished Thorne Mansion as "unquestionably the finest private dwelling in the country . . . it has an air of unostentatious magnificence that no town house in the Union can pretend to." The article heralded the significance of the mansion's brownstone front and Italianate style to the architecture of the ordinary house, declaring that "we are glad for the sake of our domestic architecture, that Col. Thorn [*sic*] has erected a noble mansion in 16th street. It will help vastly to ornament our growing town and to improve the taste and knowledge of our builders." The Thorne mansion "has the advantage of standing back in an inclosed fore-court, with double gates and a carriage-drive

Van Buren residence, north side of Fourteenth Street between Fifth and Sixth Avenues, (1849–50). Demolished. By the mid-1850s, lower Fifth Avenue north of Washington Square was lined with similar grand Italianate mansions, some of them freestanding with grounds. Today, 47 Fifth Avenue, now the Salmagundi Club, is the only survivor from the era.

sweeping under a portico, of the Tuscan order," noted *Putnam's* in an 1854 survey of New York's private residences. "On each side of the entrance door is a niche, with a bronzed figure of a Mercury, holding a lamp; there are also two recumbent figures of dogs on the landing before the door. A pretty white marble basin and fountain stand in front of the portico."

Another early mansion to introduce the palazzo mode to New York was the Richard K. Haight residence (1848–49) at the southeast corner of Fifth Avenue and Fifteenth Street, also designed by Trench and Snook. Engravings and photographs show a freestanding brownstone mansion of plain Italianate style with a rusticated basement, impressive stoop and doorway, fully enframed windows, and a classical balustrade at the roofline. The Haight mansion was "Palladian" in style, according to the same *Putnam's* survey, and "though it may have been since exceeded in richness of decoration, we doubt if it has been in good proportion, and purity of design." In 1855, *New-York Quarterly* magazine praised the "chaste and elegant house of Mr. Haight" and found that "if it has a fault, it is its over-refinement. Every window and doorway indicates a careful study, which is refreshing after the hurried and careless treatment which is stamped on almost all our architecture. It is a pure specimen of Italian architecture."

The sumptuous parlors of the Haight mansion more than compensated for any simplicity in its street-front appearance. In New York, "the house most elegantly fitted up is unquestionably that of Mr. Haight," wrote Hungarian visitors Ferenc and Theresa Pulszky in 1853, "with an Italian winter garden, playing fountains, large saloons in the Parisian fashion, a drawing room in the style of the Taj Mahal at Agra, a splendid library, &c., &c. You perceive at once that the owner of the house has travelled all over Europe, and likes to be surrounded with the recollections of everything he has seen abroad."

One of the largest and showiest mansions of this period was the Henry Parish residence at 26 East Seventeenth Street, near Fifth Avenue on fashionable Union Square, where it neighbored the C. V. S. Roosevelt, Samuel B. Ruggles, James F. Penniman mansions, as well as those of the Goelet brothers, Robert and Ogden. The British visitor Isabella Lucy Bird visited the Henry Parish mansion and described its sumptuous interior in considerable detail in 1856:

> At one house which I visited . . . about the largest private residence in the city, and one which is considered to combine the greatest splendour with the greatest taste, we entered a spacious marble hall, leading to a circular stone staircase of great width, the balustrades being figures elaborately cast in bronze. About this staircase was a lofty dome, decorated with paintings in fresco of eastern scenes. There were niches in the walls, some containing Italian statuary, and others small jets of water pouring over artificial moss.
>
> There were six or eight magnificent reception-rooms, furnished in various styles—the Mediaeval, the Elizabethan, the Italian, the Persian, the modern English, &c. There were fountains of fairy workmanship, pictures from old masters, statues from Italy . . . porcelain from China and Sèvres; damasks, cloth of gold, and bijoux from the East; Gobelin tapestry, tables of malachite and agate, and 'knick-knacks' of every description. . . . I saw one table the value of which might be about 2000 guineas.

The twenty-three-year-old Miss Bird wrote that on the second floor "the bedrooms were scarcely less magnificently furnished than the reception-rooms." Although she felt that such Fifth Avenue mansions as the Parish residence "were rather at variance with my ideas of republican simplicity," she nonetheless wrote of the Parish mansion that "there was nothing gaudy, profuse, or prominent in the decorations or furniture; everything had evidently been selected by a person of very refined taste."

These mansions together introduced an unparalleled grandeur of scale and richness of ornament to the city's houses, one that more modest Italianate-style row houses and their owners would quickly imitate. By comparison, the city's late eighteenth- and early nineteenth-century-style row houses indeed were plain in appearance and severely out of fashion. "The old three story brick dwelling houses," observed the *United States Magazine and Democratic Review* in 1847, "although spacious and comfortable in their construction, were entirely destitute of all architectural embellishments; they had no dressings to their windows, and the fan-light over the door, and sometimes a fantastic wood pillar, of no particular order or character, were all that our best houses could boast of in the way of external ornament. Now, the humblest of our city dwellings, however, make a gratifying display of knowledge and taste in their frontage."

Above: Marriott Field, design for an Italian palazzo–inspired New York row house, from his 1853 book, *City Architecture*. His design for an individual house more closely hews to the palazzo mode than the typical brownstone-front Italianate row house produced in large numbers ever would.

Opposite: 210 Columbia Heights, Brooklyn Heights (1852). A doorway porch with freestanding columns was found only on the finest Italianate-style houses. Brooklyn Heights Historic District.

THE ITALIANATE ROW HOUSE FRONT

New York builders readily adopted a variation of the Italian palazzo form of these mansions to the narrower confines of the row house. The same forms of the prominent cornice, elaborate projecting ornament, and brownstone front were easily adapted from large freestanding houses to the row house front, especially when built side by side with many effectively identical houses.

The "curved and flowing lines and a profusion of delicate ornament in relief" on an Italianate-style dwelling produced "a very ornate and elegant effect," wrote Andrew Jackson Downing in *The Architecture of Country Houses*. Likewise, Samuel Sloan found that such ornament was a key indicator of the character of the house dweller; in his words, "[F]ashion in all its gaudy glare of ornament kept exclusive ability to astonish and confound the luckless lookers-on at all this palatial effort of accumulated wealth, to let its bursting pride be seen and felt." Some even considered a showy house a moral as well as an architectural imperative. "Nothing denotes more greatly a nation's advancement in civilization than the ornate and improved styles of its architecture, and the erection of palatial private residences," wrote the *New-York Times* in 1869.

Reveling in these new architectural ideals after decades of simplicity and restraint, some New York builders decorated the brownstone-front row houses with excessive carved ornament, often poorly composed. Sloan, despite his effusive praise for conspicuous adornment, still recommended that "ornamentation should be given rather to display some portion of the design than to hide it"—advice that was often not heeded.

Doorway. The front doorway was the most striking feature of the Italianate row house facade. On a fine brownstone front, rounded consoles, faced with acanthus leaves, supported a heavy and protruding door hood or door cover, usually a modestly rounded form but sometimes flatheaded or with a triangular pediment. On either side of the deeply recessed doorway, pilasters decorated with recessed panels and circles for the full length rose to the consoles and the door hood. Roundheaded double doors, with heavily molded panels of circular forms at the lower part of each door and windows at the upper half to light the foyer and stair hallway, replaced the traditional single front door with two sidelights and a toplight.

On large dwellings, a stone arch below the console-supported door hood and above the double doors repeated the form of the roundheaded double doors and introduced another arch to the doorway. For additional richness, an elaborately detailed keystone marked the top of this arch, and small consoles with their scrolled sides facing the street supported each end as it sprang from the doorjamb. The deeply recessed doorway introduced a mysterious shadowed volume to the facade, presenting, in the words of one magazine, an "opportunity for the greatest beauty and grandeur of light and shade."

The elaborate ornament of such a doorway treatment was too costly and of too large a scale for the modest, often brick-front, middle-class row houses of the period. Instead, on these houses, the door hoods often were a modest projecting rectangular form, supported on unornamented brackets or modestly embellished consoles. Front double doors on such modest houses usually were flatheaded rather than the costly roundheaded form but were nevertheless embellished with circular panels.

The profusion of arched and rounded consoles on the Italianate doorway reflected the newly fashionable love of circular forms so evident in the row house fronts and interiors of the period. "The new element of beauty . . . is the use of the circle, subordinate to, and contrasting with, the horizontal or straight line. This is seen chiefly, in the round arch, which appears in doors and windows," observed Downing. The circle, he wrote, "addresses itself more to the feelings and the sense, and less to the reason and judgment."

A grander doorway porch, with two freestanding columns supporting a triangular pediment or rectangular entablature, appeared on some of the city's finest brownstone fronts. Because a freestanding doorway porch cast even greater shadows than did a console-supported hood, it often was considered aesthetically superior to the usual doorway hood. "The portico," wrote one magazine, "yields the greatest scope for design and decorative effect, as it produces the broadest and deepest shadow, while the cylindrical surface of the columns gives the highest lights." A freestanding porch also was closer to the Renaissance palazzo inspiration of the Italianate-style row house than the usual rounded doorway hood. To enhance this Renaissance feeling, builders occasionally added rustication blocks around the round arch over the doors beneath the porch. The freestanding doorway porch was more difficult to construct than the rounded doorway hood and, consequently, was found only on the most expensive dwellings in the city. Nineteenth-century photographs of long-gone Italianate brownstone-front dwellings along Fifth Avenue show doorway porches that stand two or three feet from the facade.

Stoop and Railings. The stoop of an Italianate row house was several feet higher and wider than that of a similar row house of preceding years. The stoop was an "important accessory, worthy in all respects, the best efforts of the architect," wrote architect David H. Arnot in 1850, because it offered an "imposing mode of access" and "a degree of stateliness" to "the principal floor by an adequate ascendency over the sidewalk and its daily crowds." And from a practical standpoint, the higher ceilings of the basement floor forced the stoop's increased height. In an unexpected benefit, these large stoops set the row house back several feet farther from the street than in earlier years. Very often the areaways in front were planted with shrubs and flowers or wisteria that climbed up guide wires just in front of the facade to the cornice.

Above: Console or scrolled brackets supporting arched doorway hood, 194 Columbia Heights, Brooklyn Heights (ca. 1860). Brooklyn Heights Historic District.

Opposite: Doorway, 212 Columbia Heights, Brooklyn Heights (ca. 1860). A heavy door hood supported by consoles is the usual doorway style on Italianate-mode dwelling houses in New York. Brooklyn Heights Historic District.

The cast-iron stoop railing was one of the first elements of the New York row house to evidence the emerging Italianate style. As early as 1846 and 1847, the stoop railings, front fences, and window balconies of otherwise Greek Revival row houses had shown an Italianate inspiration in simple oblong forms with rounded ends. Several years later, the elliptical loop ironwork often looked like a twisting rope or

290
292

appeared with its center adorned with other circle-inspired or foliate forms. The ironwork "of lofty size and excellent workmanship" on fine New York row houses excited "much surprise" in one Englishman in the 1850s. The elaborate stoop railings and front fences, marble or brownstone "flight of steps . . . marble pillars and facade, and lamps of bronze and plate glass, make a very imposing entrance to the house of a *republican aristocrat*."

By the mid-1850s, the stoop railings and areaway fences of large brownstone fronts were composed of thick handrails and round balustrades more in keeping with the style's inspiration in Renaissance Italy. On some row houses, they were cast iron finished to appear as brownstone. The balustrade motif sometimes appeared on row house fronts cut into the stone under parlor-floor windows.

In the 1850s and 1860s, the city's modest brick-front row houses rarely employed the balustrade for stoop railings and areaway fences, because it was too expensive a feature and of too large a scale for these small dwellings. Instead, these houses employed oblong loop ironwork, which now provides an important clue to identifying them as Italianate style. Just as these houses employed an ordinary brick front rather than expensive brownstone, they eliminated such costly ornament as the console-supported rounded door hood and massive cornice.

Cornice. A striking feature on the Italianate row house was a protruding cornice supported by rectangular brackets or the familiar rounded consoles. A projecting roofline was "one of the simplest, cheapest, and most effective modes of giving force and spirit to any building," wrote Downing. The cornice cast deep shadows on the facade and set a definite upward limit on the house necessary to good proportion. On New York row houses, cornices were many pieces of wood, a single piece of pressed metal, or occasionally stone. As one of the easiest parts of a row house front to replace, Italianate-style cornices were often added to earlier houses to bring them closer to current fashion, without altering the rest of the house front below.

Windows. The street-front windows enhanced the monumentality and elegance of the row house. Windows were longer and often wider than in preceding years, and continuing the precedent of the Greek Revival, the front-parlor windows usually dropped to the floor. "The nearer a window-sill approaches the floor," wrote one magazine in 1850, "the more cheerful a room will look: placing the sill even with the floor, seems almost essential to the elegance of a drawing room; while the opposite treatment gives the appearance of confinement and gloom."

290 West Fourth Street, Greenwich Village (1860). Apart from the painted facade, which masks the masonry front and brownstone trim beneath, this house is a completely intact example of the brick-front Italianate row house. Note the segmental lintels above the doorway and parlor-floor windows with original cast-iron grilles. The stoop ironwork, newel posts, and areaway fence are all also original to the house. Greenwich Village Historic District.

During the 1850s, several-foot-high, cast-iron guard railings or a low parlor-window balcony shielded the parlor from the view of passersby. By the 1860s, most brownstone-front row houses abandoned ornamental guard railings and balconies and relied instead on wood interior shutters to shield the parlor from view. The windowsill often became a one-to-two-foot-deep shelf supported on stone or cast-iron consoles with a foot high balustrade around its edges.

Window surrounds were another of the early elements of the row house front to show the influence of the emerging Italianate style in the 1840s. On some Greek Revival row houses of the period, the window lintels and sills protruded several inches from the previously planar facade and often rested on modest brackets. As early as 1836, the *North American Review* lamented row house fronts "which are generally so plain as to be painful to the eye" and recommended "the appropriate ornament of windows, a rich heavy cornice above them and a moulding extending sometimes down their sides. This contributes very greatly to relieve the plain surface, and give it a finished and elegant air." With the triumph of the Italianate style in the late 1840s, windows gained projecting lintels and sills and, in some cases, vertical side jambs for a full enframement on all four sides, which cast even greater shadow on the brownstone front. Unlike earlier houses, shutters appeared on the fine Italianate-style row houses only when the family was away for the summer in the country or the house otherwise was empty.

In the late 1840s and 1850s, advancing technology permitted ever larger panes of glass in the windows themselves. In the early nineteenth century, houses had small-size windowpanes in a six-over-six configuration. By the late 1840s, the windows in fine row houses featured large panes of glass, about 15 inches wide and 30 inches

Opposite: 137 and 139 St. James Place, Clinton Hill, Brooklyn. The brick-front No. 137 was constructed in 1860, while No. 139, its brownstone-front neighbor, was constructed in 1871. Many brick-front Italianate houses were constructed in Brooklyn through the 1860s, unlike in Manhattan, where brownstone fronts were de rigueur for fashionable houses by the late 1850s. Clinton Hill Historic District.

Right: 101 St. James Place, Clinton Hill, Brooklyn (1865). The segmental archway over the doorway, console brackets, and doors are all intact. Clinton Hill Historic District.

long, in ordinary double-hung windows or, occasionally, with genuine outward-opening casement windows. By the mid-1850s, plate glass allowed a huge undivided sheet of glass in a window sash without any intervening muntin.

THE MONUMENTAL STREETSCAPE

By the late 1840s, the term *street architecture* commonly appeared in architectural literature, and the creation of monumental streetscapes became an important consideration in the design of city dwellings. Likewise, during the brownstone era, streetscapes formed by a nearly uniform house row of virtually identical fronts became commonplace. However, despite the unified appearance as a single block, one builder did not typically construct all the houses on one side of the street as part of a single composition, as in English house terraces or at New York's own Colonnade Row.

Instead, a block was typically filled in by various builders, a few houses at a time, over a period of years. House facades were built at a uniform distance from the street to form a continuous plane. To gain the monumentality of a continuous front elevation and uniform or nearly uniform cornice, each builder consciously maintained the street-front design fixed by the earlier row houses on the block. When lined up, cornices, doorway porches, and stoops led the eye down a sweeping vista.

A "range" of mid-nineteenth-century brownstone fronts, 322–350 West Forty-Sixth Street, Manhattan, photographed about 1900. Demolished. In the mid-nineteenth century, the monumental streetscape was a design ideal. Here, the uniform wall of houses recedes to a vanishing point in an almost comical fashion.

The projecting ornament of the Italianate style was well suited to such monumental streetscapes. Because houses were typically viewed at an angle from the sidewalk or street and as part of the blockfront, architectural writer Marriott Field in his 1853 *City Architecture* recommended that architectural plans and "views of street buildings should always be taken *obliquely*, and show the neighbouring houses as well, because they in fact assist to support them, and form part of the general effect." According to Samuel Sloan's 1859 *City and Suburban Architecture*, only ornament heavily projecting from the street front could be seen clearly from such an angle, and the building thereby avoided "the meagerness presented by naked walls and unbroken surfaces."

The monumental quality of a block of Italianate houses was magnified by the height of the houses, now typically a full floor taller than houses of the previous era. The reason for this additional height, however, was economic, not aesthetic. A sharp increase in the price of lots convenient to downtown Manhattan beginning in the 1850s forced builders to construct row houses several feet narrower in width than in previous decades. Whereas the luxurious row houses of the 1820s and 1830s on Bond Street or around St. John's Park were 27, 29, or even 30 feet wide, the fashionable brownstone fronts of the 1850s in the Fifth Avenue and Madison Square district rarely exceeded the standard 25-foot lot width. The row houses of middle-class families shrank from the comfortable 25 feet of the early nineteenth century to 20 and 18 feet. Some of the lost volume was made up for in higher ceilings, and the lost square footage was regained with greater depth and an additional floor.

ONE WAY
ONE WAY

As the width of row houses decreased and their height increased simultaneously, the awkward proportions of the individual house front presented a serious architectural problem. On the eve of the Civil War, costly New York row houses were 22 to 25 feet wide and 50 to 60 feet tall—a height twice or more than their width. In the 16- and 18-foot-wide row houses, the proportions of the individual 50- or 60-foot-tall houses were even more awkward—often a height two and a half or three times its width.

Field devoted several pages of *City Architecture* to the means of "creating harmonious proportions in the elevations of city buildings, which, from economy of ground plot, are necessarily too narrow for a good proportion, and would appear likely to fall unless propped up by their neighbours." Field recommended stringcourses, 6-or-so-inch-wide bands across the street fronts between some floors, in order to introduce a strong horizontal line to the facade and to divide it into reasonably square portions so as to "counteract the excessive height of numerous stories." Since the late eighteenth century, the city's row houses commonly had a white-marble or brownstone stringcourse between the basement and first floor, but for the exceptionally tall and narrow mid-nineteenth-century row house Field suggested a "three-fold" division of the facade, consisting of a stringcourse between the rusticated basement and first floor and another between the top floor and the next-to-top floor. The latter additional measure was never adopted on New York's Italianate house rows.

Field recommended that "the corner houses of the block may be higher and more decorated than the rest." In the 1850s, such ornamental treatment was limited to quoins, a vertical row of rustication blocks, at the corner from the basement floor to the roofline. An unusually rich architectural feature in the Renaissance tradition, quoins turned the eye inward to the center of the blockfront and emphasized its horizontality. With the appearance of the Second Empire style in the 1860s, corner houses often gained a steep mansard roof, much in the manner of corner pavilions.

THE BROWNSTONE FRONT

Nineteenth-century New Yorkers accurately referred to the city's brownstone row houses as brownstone fronts, for they actually are brick houses whose street front has a 4-to-6-inch-thick brownstone facing or veneer. The rear walls of a brownstone-front row house are ordinary brick. The architectural deception of the brownstone front clearly appears on corner houses, where the narrow 20-to-25-foot-wide street front has brownstone facing, and the 50-foot-long side wall around the corner is brick.

Advancing technology was partly responsible for the widespread popularity of brownstone for New York row houses, as the invention of steam-channeling or steam-cutting processes lowered the cost of cut stone and brought fashionable brownstone within the reach of even middle-class row house owners. Brownstone quarries were located close to New York, and water routes offered a quick and relatively inexpensive

77 Willow Street, Brooklyn Heights. Brownstones were originally referred to as brownstone fronts, a more accurate term, since brownstone was only a veneer on the building's front, with the house still constructed from masonry behind. Here, on a corner house, the contrast between brownstone front and brick side is clearly visible. The corner quoining, here in offset blocks, is an elegant treatment to connect the two sides. Brooklyn Heights Historic District.

194 Columbia Heights, Brooklyn Heights (ca. 1860). Brooklyn Heights Historic District.

transport to the city. The brownstone most often used in New York came from a belt about 20 miles long centered at Portland, Connecticut, a town named for the famous British quarry town. Barges carried the stone down the Connecticut River to Long Island Sound and then to New York. The other major brownstone quarries were near Little Falls, New Jersey, on the Passaic River close to Paterson. The brownstone for Trinity Church in New York came from these New Jersey quarries, whose stone had a lighter shade than the Connecticut variety.

Stone was considered a more dignified building material than brick or wood, and brownstone's smooth surface visually united the houses along the street and called attention to the elaborate doorway and window ornament. New York builders minimized the seams between slabs of brownstone much in the way that builders of Greek Revival–style row houses put lampblack in the mortar to minimize its whiteness between the bricks. Builders used slabs of brownstone as large "as could be procured, and the joints narrowed till they were as nearly as possible imperceptible, the assumption of the builder apparently being that the whole brownstone veneer should seem to be a single sheet," wrote Montgomery Schuyler in the 1890s, looking backward. "In the later works of the brown-stone period, this assumption comes so near being made good that in the first floor there are no joints visible, great slabs of veneer stretching from opening to opening and one or two joints that could not be obviated being concealed by mouldings tacked on."

Brownstone is a soft, close-grained Triassic sandstone or freestone. When first cut the stone is pink, but it soon weathers to an even, rich, chocolate brown because of the presence of hematite iron ore. Apart from this expected weathering, the material's durability has long been a problem on New York buildings. On the brownstone-front north side of City Hall, wrote the *Crayon* in 1856, "decay is visible in almost every part, and many of the stones are miserably peeled and mutilated" after less than half a century. The article wondered if New York's architects and builders ever examined brownstone and other building materials with regard to their "absolute or comparative fitness and durability." In the mid-nineteenth century, several purportedly scientific articles recommended various treatments to preserve brownstone fronts, among them a yearly oiling with linseed, to prevent the stone from "drying out" and to keep out harmful moisture. Over the years, the brownstone fronts of some row houses have spalled badly, and the elaborately carved doorways and window details have crumbled and occasionally entirely fallen off. Many surviving brownstone-front houses in New York have been resurfaced with a brownstone-colored textured stucco, itself of highly varying durability and often atrocious quality. Indeed, the resurfacing of many houses, including significant numbers of them in historic districts, has eliminated many original Italianate details for crude smoothed-over versions.

Nevertheless, brownstone, when properly cut and laid, should not deteriorate any more than any other building stone. The brownstone facade of Trinity Church, for instance, remains in good condition today. However, to last brownstone must be cut across the grain and laid ashlar, i.e., with the grain running perpendicular to the building facade. Still, even with the aid of steam-channeling equipment, New York builders often ignored these time-consuming quarrying and construction methods. Although this distinction about the grain of the stone, in the words of *Putnam's* in 1853, "seems to the careless reader a merely whimsical objection," it "is in truth a very important matter, as any upright and well-informed builder will confess." When cut and laid with the grain, brownstone crumbles and scales, because water seeps into the exposed pores of the thin brownstone blocks and, upon freezing, expands and splits the stone into large, thin sheets. Had the stone been cut and laid across the grain in the first place, the deterioration of most brownstone fronts, then and now, would be minimal.

BRICK AND MARBLE FRONTS

Ordinary brick remained an acceptable material for row house fronts until the eve of the Civil War. After that, the plain brick front was relegated to the modest middle-class and working-class dwellings, which have disappeared largely from Manhattan but remain in sizable numbers in Brooklyn. "Houses built of stone, or having stone fronts, are the only kind which meet with favor from the moneyed portion of our community," wrote one newspaper in the 1860s. "Brick is getting too common for first-class fashionable circles, and [. . .] left to be occupied by the more humble of the people."

The only exception to the brownstone hegemony was costly, pressed brick, known as Philadelphia brick, which had a smooth surface, much like that of stone, and a uniform dark red color. In the manufacture of pressed brick, clay was ground into fine particles and

14
13
15
11
8
A. J. DAVIS.
Elevation of the Principal front.
Phillips & Tabor. 12th st. N. Y.
0
10
20
30
40

put into molds whose sides first had been dampened. Enormous pressure acted on the molds and compacted the clay into a solid brick, which then was fired in a kiln. The pressed brick was longer and narrower in size than the usual brick, and, according to one architectural journal, the usual dimensions were 8½ inches long, 4¼ inches broad, and 2½ inches thick. During the 1850s and 1860s, a veneer of pressed brick on a row house front apparently cost as much as brownstone—or four times the cost of the ordinary rough-surfaced brick front. It was popular on Anglo-Italianate house fronts, as described below.

During the rage for brownstone fronts, occasional white-marble-front dwellings were also still built in New York, the most famous being the A. T. Stewart mansion at Fifth Avenue and Thirty-Fourth Street. Another marble-faced dwelling of the period was the John Taylor Johnston residence (1856), a basement-and-four-story-tall row house in a simple, but impressive, Italianate style, which stood at 8 Fifth Avenue, at the southwest corner of Eighth Street. However, white marble never was a popular facade material in the era. Besides its high cost, marble was too hard to take the elaborate foliate carving that so delighted New Yorkers in the mid-nineteenth century.

THE ANGLO-ITALIANATE CONFIGURATION

As the Italianate style emerged in New York in the late 1840s, occasional row houses adopted the handsome and practical Anglo-Italianate configuration. The Anglo-Italianate, or English basement–style Italianate row house, had a two- or three-step stoop at the front doorway rather than the immense ten- to twelve-step stoop popular at the time. This low stoop placed the first floor of the building almost at street level, with the second floor becoming the parlor floor of the house.

Inside, this configuration allowed an unusual floor plan that better handled the problem of rising land costs and increasingly narrow building lots. The ground-level entrance led down a hallway to an elliptical stairway occupying the center of the house. By removing the need for a long stair run on the upper stories of the house, the stairway both took advantage of the poorly lit and ventilated center of the house, and, more importantly, allowed the front and back rooms to fill the full width of the house. "It has been found that quite as spacious rooms may be had in a house of twenty feet front, as in the old style of houses built on a full sized [25-foot-wide] lot," observed *Putnam's* in 1854, several years after the configuration's appearance.

With this new floor plan, room use in the Anglo-Italianate row house differed significantly from the typical row house. The basement was far deeper than that of a high-stooped house, and was used for the kitchen and storage only, not dining. On the first floor of grander houses, the small room at one side of the front door hallway was an office or waiting room for guests, and the back room overlooking the garden likely was the formal dining room. On the first floor of more modest Anglo-Italianate houses, the dining room was located on the first floor facing the street, with the rear room facing the garden serving as the kitchen, with the deep basement floor serving only as storage.

12–14 West Twelfth Street, Greenwich Village, architect Alexander Jackson Davis (1848–49). Possibly the first Anglo-Italianate, or English basement, row houses built in New York. Demolished

On the second floor of grand houses, the front and back rooms, occupying the full width of the house, were twin parlors with an anteroom and stairway in the center, making "a suite of three handsome rooms when the sliding doors are thrown open," according to a contemporary description. The parents' and children's bedrooms and servants' quarters occupied the upper floors. In more modest homes, only the front room served as a parlor, with the rear room serving as a bedroom, and the central anteroom was replaced by closets.

Dwellings of this style were typically a basement and four stories tall and 16 to 18 feet wide, though smaller dwellings of three stories were also occasionally constructed. The basement and first story were faced with the familiar rusticated brownstone, and the doorway and single window at the side were roundheaded and often enframed by a molding. Above the basement and first story, the street front was smooth brownstone or a dark red Philadelphia pressed brick with window details in handsomely contrasting brownstone. The windows of the second-floor parlors dropped to the floor and often opened onto a cast-iron balcony that, along with the roofline cornice, helped to unify the row visually.

The first Anglo-Italianate dwellings in New York were very likely Nos. 12–14 West Twelfth Street (1848–49), designed by Alexander Jackson Davis, an antagonist of the ubiquitous stoop, which were demolished in 1958 for the construction of the Church House of the First Presbyterian Church. Today, the few other surviving Anglo-Italianate row houses are found on West Ninth, Tenth, and Twelfth Streets off lower Fifth Avenue in Greenwich Village, on several handsome blocks of Chelsea, and in the spectacular houses of the Triangle on Stuyvesant Street. Anglo-Italianate row houses were less commonly built in Brooklyn, as full-sized building lots were much cheaper than in Manhattan. Rare surviving intact Brooklyn examples are the handsome trio of Nos. 230–234 Carlton Avenue in Fort Greene.

Although the Anglo-Italianate dwelling offered an imaginative solution to the problem of costly city land in the 1850s, it never neared the popularity of the high-stooped brownstone front, and it was not until the emergence of American and English basement plans in the 1890s that alternatives again emerged to the prototypical row house plan.

Above: 301 Hicks Street, Brooklyn Heights (ca. 1862), photographed in the late nineteenth century. A pleasant brownstone front in the typical high-stoop configuration, with the entry hallway and parlor located on the first floor at the top of the stoop stairs.

Opposite: 230–234 Carlton Avenue, Fort Greene, Brooklyn (ca. 1865). By contrast, this handsome trio of houses shows the low-stoop Anglo-Italianate configuration. The entry stairs on the first floor lead to a vestibule and central interior staircase, with the main parlor on the second floor stretching the full width of the house—ideal for narrow building lots like these. Fort Greene Historic District.

MANSARD ROOFS: THE SECOND EMPIRE STYLE

Another variation on the Italianate style for the New York row house was the Second Empire or mansard-roof style. Inspired by the Paris of Emperor Napoleon III (Charles-Louis Napoléon Bonaparte) and Baron Haussmann, the style epitomized elegance and sophistication and was the national rage in the United States in the late 1860s and early 1870s. So complete was its conquest of American architecture that, in 1868, Samuel Sloan confidently stated that the "French Roof—or, as it is often called, the Mansard—was and is in great request. Public and private dwellings, and even stables, are covered, with this new roof; and no man who wants a fashionable house, will be without it."

The Second Empire style did not reach American architects directly from Paris but apparently came indirectly from the Parisian-inspired hotels built in London in the mid-1850s. Although Americans had little contact with French architectural developments in the 1850s, a number of British architectural publications, widely read in the United States, kept American architects fully informed of events in England. After the Civil War, it attained its full popularity in New York. "We see this wonderful power of fashion in the sudden and universal application of the mansard roof among us," wrote *The Architects' and Builders' Guide* in 1868. "A very short time ago nobody seemed to know that buildings had roofs, and that roofs were not necessarily a thing to hide but to be seen and ornamented. . . . Suddenly, however, a sort of roof epidemic seemed to seize us; and now no building, great or small, can be a building without its 'French roof.'"

The salient feature of the Second Empire row house was the steeply sloped mansard roof, pierced by two or three dormer windows and decorated with a cast-iron railing known as a cresting at the street-front edge of the roof. Indeed, on the New York row house, the Second Empire style usually involved only the addition of a mansard roof above the cornice of an otherwise Italianate dwelling. At a time when high ceilings and a usual fifth floor gave fine New York brownstone fronts awkwardly narrow proportions, the mansard roof gave the roofline a Picturesque look and offered the space of another floor without the excessively vertical elevation of a basement-and-four-story-tall facade.

The mansard roof makes the Second Empire a simple style to identify, for it was difficult and economically foolhardy to remove in later renovations. But the presence of a mansard roof on a row house does not necessarily mean Second Empire. In the 1860s, these French roofs were added to many Federal and Greek Revival row houses to modernize them and add another floor in a city of always scarce housing and high rents. These modernizations are usually easy to detect because the builder rarely updated the plain Federal or Greek Revival doorway, window lintels, or cornice. Throughout Greenwich Village and Brooklyn Heights, the trained eye picks out mansard roofs over Flemish-bond brick fronts, a dentiled cornice, or a Greek Revival doorway.

Opposite: 97–99 St. Marks Avenue, Prospect Heights, Brooklyn (early 1870s). Brownstone-front houses with Second Empire–style mansard roofs. Prospect Heights Historic District.

Following pages: 292–302 Washington Avenue, Clinton Hill, Brooklyn (1876). A typical row of brownstone-front dwellings, the right two with mansard roofs. In Brooklyn, large numbers of brownstone-front dwellings survive, unlike in Manhattan, where almost no unaltered rows are left. Clinton Hill Historic District.

SAINT
ANGELA
HALL

Above: 17 East 128th Street, East Harlem (ca. 1865). Frame houses were constructed beyond the northern limits of the built-up city, and this Second Empire–style house is a rare survivor from before row house construction began in earnest in Harlem in the 1870s. New York City Landmark.

Opposite: 19 Cranberry Street, Brooklyn Heights. A Federal house (ca. 1834), with a mansard roof addition in the Second Empire style added some four decades later to update the house to contemporary fashion—and to add another usable floor. Brooklyn Heights Historic District.

The Second Empire mansard roof quickly lost popularity for New York row houses after several years of frenzied fashion. "The very name is now more appropriately the absurd roof," wrote Samuel Sloan. "Fashion begins to look coldly upon her recent favorite . . . and it is doomed."

ROW HOUSE FLOOR PLANS IN THE 1850s AND 1860s

Early Italianate New York row houses continued the same basic interior plan as earlier row houses (with the exception of those constructed in the Anglo-Italianate configuration built without a high stoop, as discussed above). The first (or parlor) floor consisted of identical front and back parlors, separated by sliding double doors, an open archway or a screen of Corinthian columns, and an 8-to-10-foot-deep tearoom across the back of the house overlooking the yard. The tearoom usually was a wood extension on the basement and first floors only, and it did not reach to the second and third floors.

By the mid-1850s, large brownstone fronts adopted a new floor plan whose grandeur reflected the increasing wealth and social aspirations of New York families. A full-sized third room, 15 to 20 feet deep and a regular part of the house structure, replaced the 8-foot-deep tearoom extension. This third room served as the dining room, a function made practical only after the invention of the dumbwaiter in about 1850. No longer did the servants have to carry plates and food up and down the narrow stairway between the kitchen in the basement and the dining room on the first floor. A small butler's pantry with the dumbwaiter occupied the space behind the stairway and near the dining room.

Under this elongated floor plan, the former back parlor, which had looked into the tearoom or an open back porch, became a center room without its own windows. Because sliding doors separated this center room from the back dining room, it effectively became a part of the front parlor. To enhance this impressive union of the front and back parlors and increase the light and ventilation in the center room, only a shallow arch at the ceiling or a screen of Corinthian columns rather than solid parlor doors separated the two rooms. The front and middle rooms thus functioned as a single 35-to-40-foot-deep parlor, but they still had separate fireplaces, two sets of ceiling centerpieces and moldings, and separate doorways on the side hallway in each room, maintaining the distinction of front and back parlors.

The fine brownstone fronts of the Fourteenth Street and Madison Square areas in the 1850s and 1860s thus attained truly monumental dimensions: 22, 25, or 30 feet wide, a basement and four stories tall, and 60 or 65 feet deep. Fourteen-foot-tall ceilings and elaborate architectural ornament in the parlors complemented these patrician dimensions. Because the third room on the parlor floor was a regular part of the house structure and not merely an extension of the basement and first floor, the bedrooms on the upper floors were correspondingly deeper, and identical pairs of washrooms and storage closets for each bedroom occupied the center 10 feet of these floors.

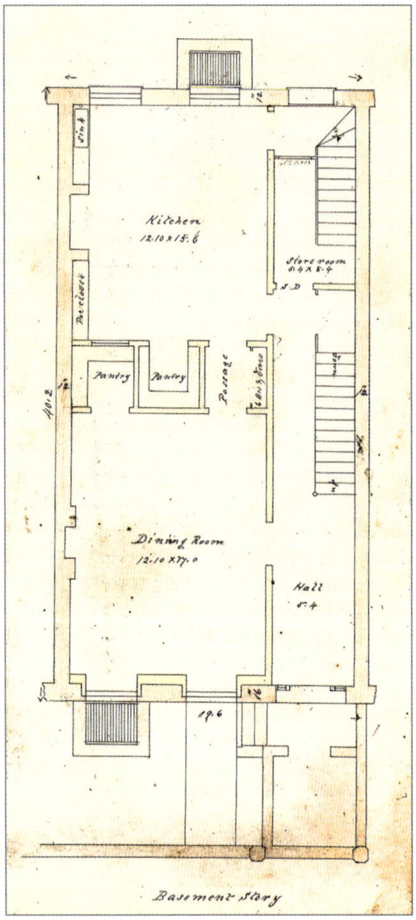

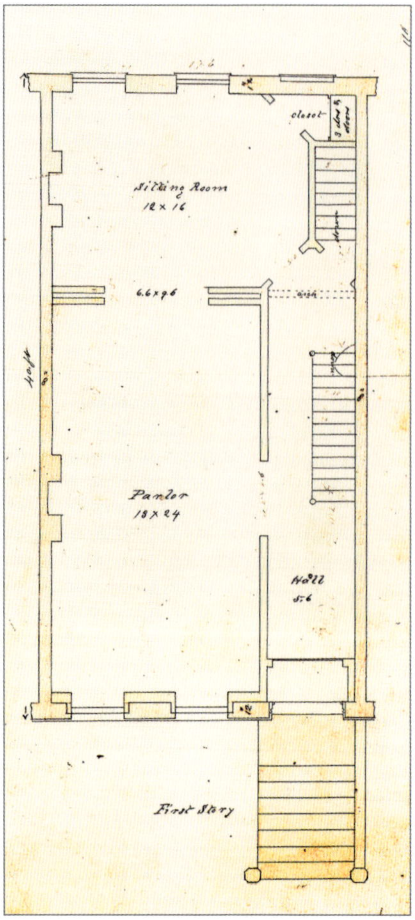

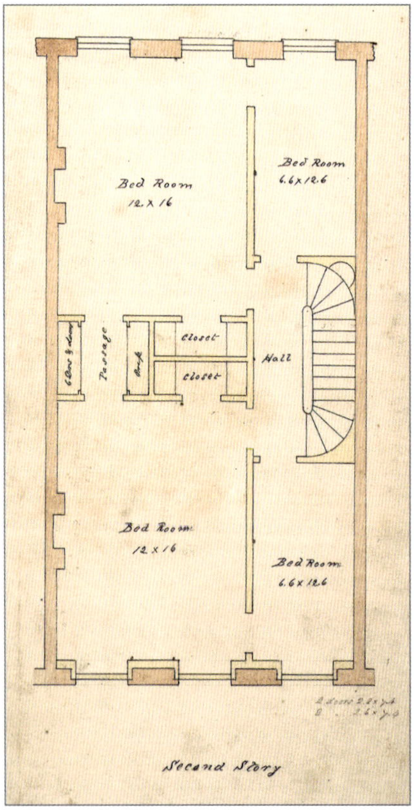

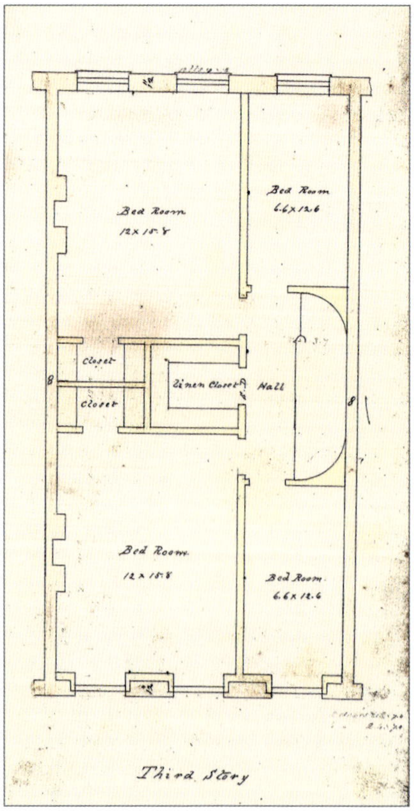

Below: Triple-parlor house plans, likely Brooklyn Heights, London-born American architect-builder, James W. Martens (1850s or 1860s). The demand for showy, ostentatious houses in the brownstone era led to progressively deeper house plans, with three instead of two parlors, which covered much of a building lot. In this particularly grand plan, there are front and middle parlors, a rear dining room, and a tea porch, with a butler's pantry to the side. The middle parlors in such houses were notoriously dark, with the only sunlight coming from the adjacent front and rear rooms. Many similar houses were constructed on Fifth Avenue and adjacent streets in Manhattan, though nearly all of them have been demolished or so reconfigured that they are unrecognizable.

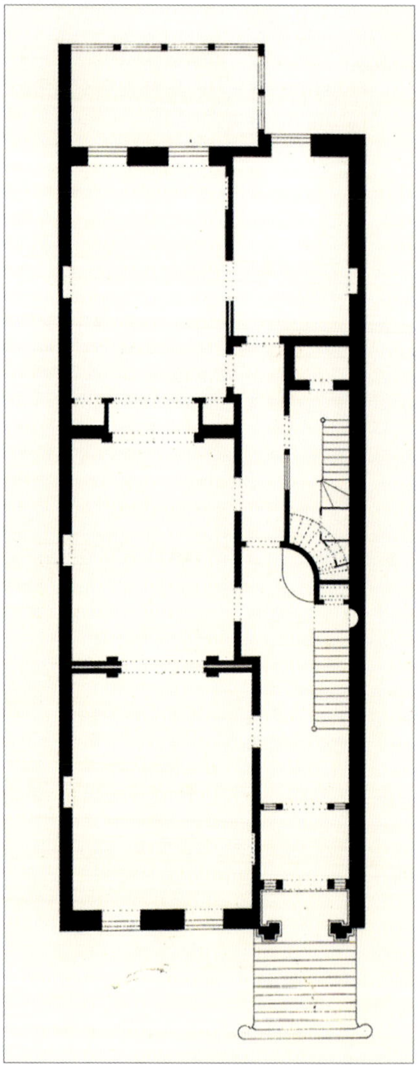

Left, top and bottom: House in Brooklyn, architect-builder James W. Martens, 1850s. This house features a service stairway between the kitchen and rear parlor above (identified in the drawing as a "sitting room"). Otherwise, this plan continues the basic New York row house plan established decades before.

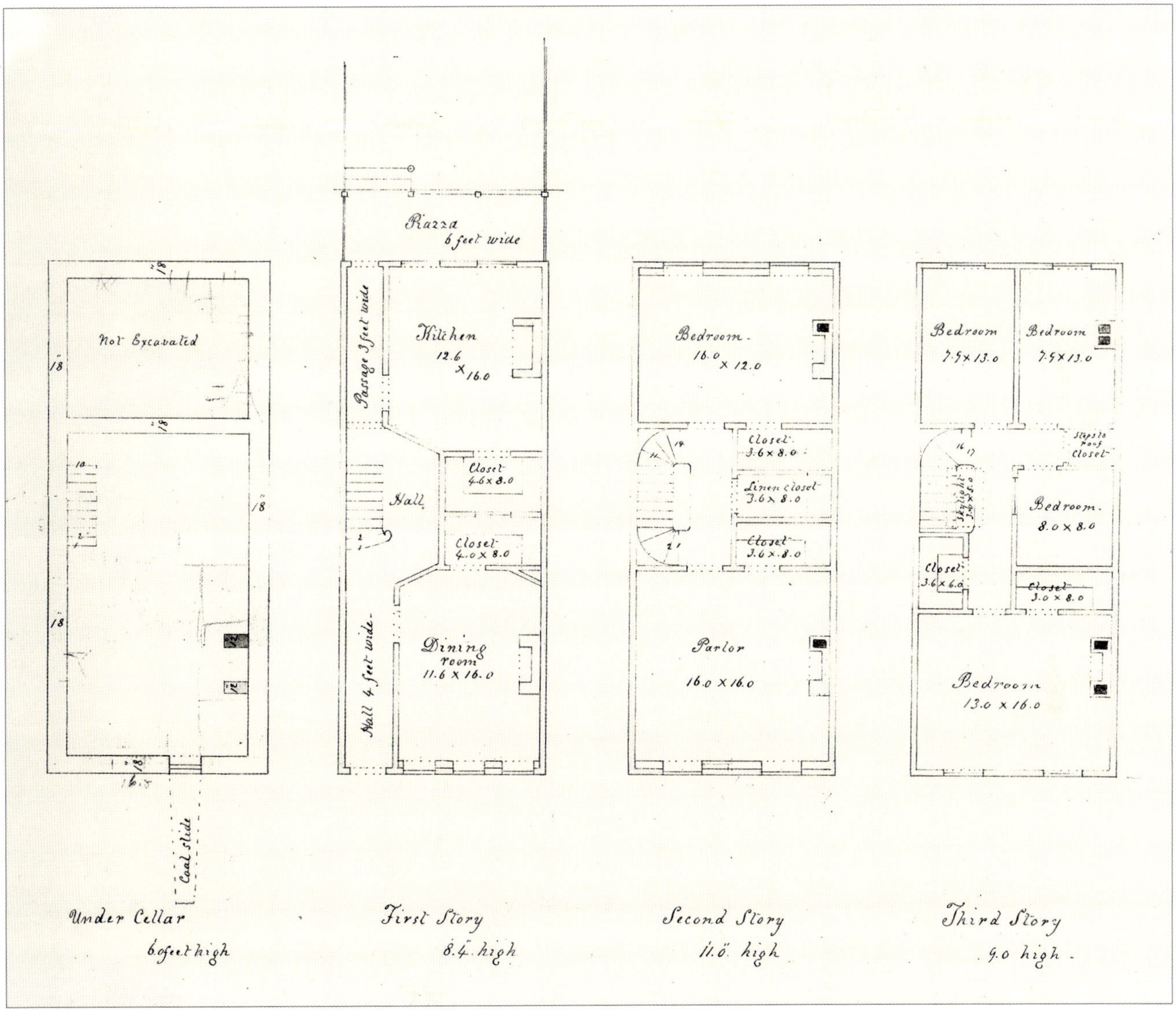

Above: Three-story Anglo-Italianate plans for a Brooklyn house, James W. Martens (1850s). Unlike a typical high-stooped house, the main entrance to an Anglo-Italianate house was only several steps above the street, with a central stair allowing the front parlor, located on the second floor, to stretch the entire width of the house. In this modest plan, the front parlor and main bedroom on the second floor are separated by closets. In grander houses, an anteroom with sliding doors replaced the closets, allowing the full length and width of the house to form one contiguous space.

The first-floor parlors of these houses, though impressive for occasional entertaining, were poorly lit and ventilated from the front and back windows. As the price of land in a fashionable neighborhood convenient to downtown Manhattan continued to rise, only the most expensive row houses could be built with the 25-foot width necessary for the proper scale, lighting, and ventilation of a 60-foot-deep dwelling.

In response, by the 1860s, many builders replaced double parlors with a single large parlor with one fireplace and marble mantel in the center of one long wall and a large double doorway opposite, which opened onto the side hallway. With a single 30-to-35-foot-deep parlor at the front and a dining room at the rear overlooking the backyard, the depth of such fine row houses could be scaled back from 60 feet to a more reasonable 50 or so. Under this floor plan, the butler's pantry sometimes moved from behind the stairway and became a small extension on the back of the house.

Despite the variation in parlor-floor design, the basement and uppermost floors remained largely similar to those of the houses of previous eras, except that they incorporated the recent advances in heating and indoor plumbing. On the second floor of large houses, however, the front room often took the full width of the house and was a family sitting room or library. The back room, separated from the front room by closets and dressing alcoves with washbasins, was the parents' bedroom and had a bathroom with toilet, tub, and shower. The third and fourth floors included children's bedrooms and several small servants' rooms.

In an era of large families and several live-in servants, the sixteen-room, five-story-tall brownstone front combined grand parlors for entertaining and spacious living quarters for the family, and, with its many floors, offered privacy for parents, children, and servants. Different ceiling heights throughout a row house of the period reflected the importance attached to the various floors. In a basement-and-four-story-tall dwelling, basement ceilings typically were 9 feet high, the first floor an imposing 14 feet high, the second floor 11 feet, the third floor 10 feet, and the fourth floor 9 feet.

The full five floors with high ceilings were problems in themselves, and in 1874 *Scribner's* complained that a town house was "little else but a string of stairs, with more or less extended landings. . . . Up and down, up and down, the women folk are perpetually toiling as in a treadmill . . . in the fruitless and health-destroying labor of carrying themselves from floor to floor."

INTERIOR DESIGN IN THE BROWNSTONE ERA

Although Italianate brownstone-front row houses boasted a street presence of unparalleled richness, it was in their parlors and dining rooms that these houses fully expressed the lavish ornament inherent in the style. "We must peep within the palaces if we would comprehend the full extent of their splendor. Their lavish adornment is a marvel even to traveled eyes," wrote *Appleton's* in 1869 describing the dwellings rising on Fifth Avenue after the Civil War.

The front parlor epitomized the family's roots, refinement, and social position—real or imagined. "Was there ever an American woman who, furnishing a house, did not first lay aside the money for the parlor?" asked one housekeeping book in the 1870s. "A parlor must be, even if after it there comes the deluge." Parlors of New York brownstone fronts were renowned for Brussels carpets, stamped-leather or velvet wallpaper, overstuffed sofas and chairs, and gilt mirrors in profusion. British visitor Charles Lyell, writing in 1849, signaled the extravagance of the brownstone era, in contrast to the more restrained earlier decades of New York decoration: "It is said in France that no orders sent to Lyons for the furnishing of private mansions are on so grand a scale as those from New York."

In the 1860s, the press often lampooned the many New York families who spent one-third of their income to rent a house at a fashionable address, bought showy furniture for the parlor and dining room, and then occupied the basement and several bedroom floors, which guests never saw, in genteel squalor. Fine furnishings for the parlors were breathtakingly expensive. In the 1870s, *Goodholme's Domestic Cyclopedia* advised its readers that parlor furnishings in a $5,000 to $6,000 house should cost about $600. At that ratio, the parlor furnishings for a $25,000 brownstone—a good, but not exceptional, house in Manhattan—cost about $3,000, or more than the value of some workingmen's dwellings.

During the daytime, mahogany shutters and heavy draperies in the parlors were closed lest the sun fade the furniture, and some women "were always uneasy when their visitors sat down on a sofa or an ottoman, and could not forbear inviting them to change their seats and take chairs," according to *Miss Leslie's Behavior Book*. After all, "the more the damask-covered seats were used, the sooner they would wear out."

Despite its grand architectural features and expensive furnishings, the parlor was silent and empty except for such formal moments as the morning calls, an evening party, or the fifteen minutes while guests gathered before a dinner party. Theodore Roosevelt remembered the parlor of his boyhood home, an 1848 brownstone front near Gramercy Park, as a "room of much splendor . . . open for general use only on Sunday evening or on rare occasions when there were parties."

Mantel. Fireplace mantels remained the most important decorative feature of the showy parlors and dining rooms, even as wood-burning and coal-burning fireplaces themselves were increasingly obsolescent. In the late 1840s, the basically rectangular mantels of the Greek Revival style, with flat pilasters and horizontal entablature, took on carved Rococo Revival features and appeared in some of the city's late Greek Revival and early Italianate-style dwellings. At the same time, elaborately ornamented, white-marble Italianate- or Renaissance-inspired mantels, with round-arched fireplace openings, appeared in row house parlors and remained the overwhelming fashion into the 1870s.

Italianate mantelshelves had a scalloped edge and, in large houses, were supported by an acanthus- or oak-leaf-faced console at each end. During the 1850s, the parlors of the finest dwellings had statuary mantels—that is, maidens standing on each side of the mantel carrying the shelf on top of their heads like the ancient caryatids. A handsome rope molding, like that found around the front doorway or on ironwork, edged the round-arched fireplace opening. An ornamental keystone marked the top of the arch, and aside from stylized round forms, popular designs included the Renaissance-inspired scallop shell, large pieces or baskets of fruit, shields, and the heads of beautiful women. In the 1850s and 1860s, richly carved leaves and fruit filled the spandrel or triangular area at each side of the arched fireplace opening. Architectural taste changed after the Civil War, and mantels thereafter rarely carried elaborately carved foliate forms. Then, the keystone often consisted of stylized round forms, and the spandrels had several layers of triangular moldings.

The parlor mantels were the largest and most elaborately detailed in a New York row house, and the others were of a simpler design, of a cheaper marble, and, for several years after the emergence of a new architectural style, of the passing and therefore cheaper style. As the Italianate mode emerged in New York in the late 1840s and early 1850s, the mantels on the upper floors continued to be done in a Greek Revival style—the outmoded mantels were presumably far cheaper and would never be seen by discerning visitors. By the 1860s, the Italianate style was firmly established in New York, and the mantels on the upper floors were a simple Italianate style but with modest forms and ornament. Although nearly all parlor mantels then followed the round-arched-opening Italianate style, they varied greatly in the quality of the carved ornament and marble. Elaborate carved ornament did not necessarily indicate a good mantel; the foliate or stylized forms often were cut shallow and, therefore, were somewhat indistinct in form and detail.

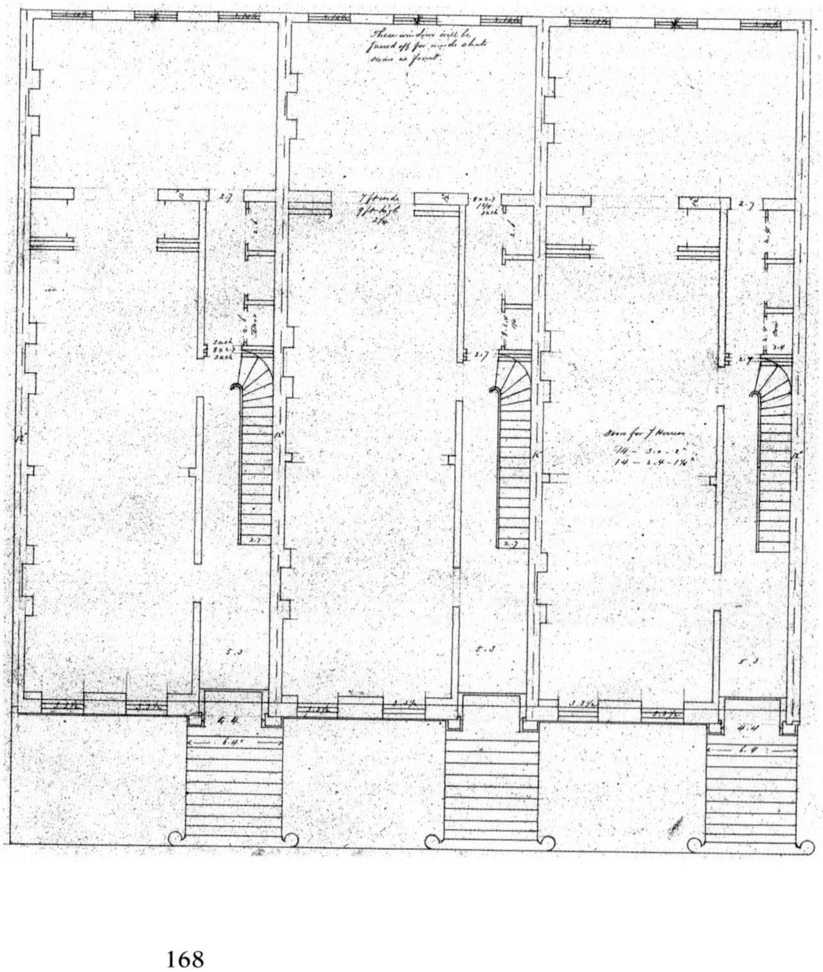

Above and right: Section, elevation, and plan for a row of three Italianate houses, likely 1860s. The section shows the gradually decreasing floor heights, from 12 feet on the parlor floor, to 10 feet on the second floor and 9½ feet on the top floor, with the basement floor only 8 feet tall. On the parlor floor, these houses feature a large front parlor, apparently separated by a decorative archway, and a rear parlor or dining room across the entire width of the house. Often, the two parlor mantels drawn here were replaced by a single central mantel directly across the doors from the entry hallway, which created an impressively deep front parlor but still allowed the house to cover less of the building lot, allowing more light into the interior spaces than deeper triple-parlor houses.

Overmantel Mirror. A large overmantel mirror in a wide gilt frame filled the width of the protruding chimney breast and climbed five, six, and even eight feet from the mantelshelf to the cornice at the ceiling. Although overmantel mirrors and the accompanying pier mirrors between the two street-front windows appeared in some parlors during the early nineteenth century, they were a part of nearly all parlors by the 1850s. "The use of large mirrors have [*sic*] become much more fashionable among us; and, in fact, there is no finer decoration for our saloons [parlors]," wrote one newspaper in 1851. Not only did the gilt-framed overmantel mirror provide another showy touch for parlors, but it also made the somewhat narrow rooms appear to be wider than they were. A large marble or bronze clock customarily was placed on the center of the mantelshelf along with other decorative objects to be reflected in the mirror.

Ceilings. "The beautiful hard-finish ceilings of a house in the city, which have thus far satisfied the most fastidious taste have been spurned, and the parlors are now finished in Papier-Mâché of the most costly and beautiful description," observed one New Yorker in the 1840s. In large row houses, a several-foot-wide centerpiece or rosette, often vaguely Baroque or Rococo in feeling and relying on vigorous foliate forms, adorned the center of the ceiling. Made of plaster or papier-mâché, these centerpieces weighed more than 100 pounds and often served a functional as well as decorative purpose. The gaslight that hung from the rosette gave off an unpleasant odor of gas combustion, so small holes were worked into the centerpiece to trap part of the rising fumes and carry them into the chimney flue and out-of-doors.

A cornice of several-inch-wide moldings and occasional foliate forms ornamented the corners where the walls met the ceiling. Like the centerpiece, the plaster or papier-mâché cornice was purchased at a factory by the linear foot and glued into place at the house. Only the simplest coved moldings in the bedroom floors were run by hand in wet plaster. Inch-thick moldings, which divided the ceiling into several panels, cast small shadows on the ceiling and broke up its vast expanse. Often they were gilded to stand out from the white-painted or frescoed ceiling. In the heady post–Civil War years, Samuel Sloan warned that "when gilding is employed, it should be used sparingly; for, if overdone, that which would have been elegant will become gaudy and vulgar."

Vernacular Parlor Interiors. The interior design of small brick-front row houses was more modest than that of fashionable brownstone fronts. These houses continued the classical tradition of architectural simplicity into the 1850s, and their parlor ceilings employed the relatively simple plaster centerpiece and cove-form cornice. Their marble mantels reflected a simple Italianate mode, but the parlor-floor doors remained rectangular with simple moldings, often with the Greek ear. Because the elaborate parlor mantels and arched parlor doors were of too large a scale or too costly for these small row houses, builders looked for other ways to ornament parlors in the late 1850s and 1860s. Relatively inexpensive machine-made plaster or papier-mâché ornament offered one way, and an elaborate but nevertheless cost-effective foliate screen, for instance, often replaced the previous simple coved form for cornices.

Doors and Woodwork. In the 1850s and 1860s, the sliding parlor doors of large and small New York row houses had frosted-glass windows with intricate etched foliate designs. Doorknobs throughout the house usually were white porcelain, but in some large brownstone-front dwellings doorknobs on the parlor floor were white porcelain with painted flowers, glass with silver granules blown in, silver plate over brass, or an extravagant solid silver.

Heavy wood moldings framed all doors in a house. The Italianate style's fascination with circular forms appeared as shallow, arched doorways or an elegant half-circle doorway arch in first-floor parlors. Only costly dwellings had an arched doorway, which was more difficult to execute than the flatheaded rectangular doorway found on the less important bedroom floors of these row houses. In the mid-nineteenth century, mahogany, black walnut, and rosewood replaced the light-colored mahogany, oak, and satinwood for parlor woodwork in fine dwellings. Only these dark woods effectively contrasted with the thick doorway and window moldings, richly decorated ceilings, and the bright colors then popular for wallpaper and carpets. Black walnut was the most popular wood of the era for its deep color, ease of taking elaborate carving, and resistance to wear. In the parlors with mahogany or black-walnut woodwork, the doors emphasized the fine finish of the wood with large, simply molded,rectangular or circular panels or a juxtaposition of different woods or stains in the same place. But the parlors of most row houses in the mid-nineteenth century had pine woodwork, which was painted a light color or given the imitation graining of a more costly wood.

Floors. The near-universal fashion for wall-to-wall carpets in Italianate row houses meant that floors were rarely treated as extravagantly as their other details, since they were not meant to be seen. Row house floors were typically 4-to-6-inch-wide pine planks, occasionally laid over an even cheaper subflooring. Before the mid-nineteenth century, carpets had been handmade and available only to the wealthy. In 1844 Erastus Bigelow invented a machine that wove ingrain carpets, and in 1848 a power loom for Brussels and tapestry carpets. Carpets dropped dramatically in price but still retained their earlier status connotations. By the 1850s nearly every middle-class family proudly put a thick floral-patterned carpet in the parlor. However, a carpet was something of a problem. It rested on a pad of woven grass called China matting, which gave off an unpleasant musty odor in damp weather. Carpets also had to be taken up once or twice a year to be cleaned. To cut down on soil and postpone this cleaning, a linen cloth usually was placed beneath the dining-room table to catch bits of food, hence the popular names "crumbcloth" or "drugget." The maid swept off or shook out the crumbcloth after each meal.

Hardwood floors in New York row houses of the 1850s and 1860s usually date from the late nineteenth or early twentieth century, when softwood floors and wall-to-wall carpets lost favor. In the mid-nineteenth century, only an occasional row house was built with hardwood floors, but stairways always were hardwood for practical reasons.

Entrance Hall. The small foyer between the two sets of round-arched double doors shrank from the comfortable 5-to-6-foot length of earlier decades to an awkward few feet where guests merely might receive shelter from bad weather. The foyer floor usually was either all white marble, a pattern of black and white rectangular tiles, or occasionally encaustic tiles, with a dull-finish tile in an elaborate pattern, usually a dark red, yellow, or black, and imported from England. A floor of highly decorated encaustic tiles often cost more than one of marble, and, according to Samuel Sloan, "for stores, vestibules, entries, outside verandahs, green houses, churches, and in fact every place where beauty, taste and economy are objects to be attained, there is nothing that can be more suitable than the Encaustic Tiles."

The long stair hallway on the first floor usually had a softwood floor, covered by carpet, white and black marble, or the encaustic tiles of the foyer. As late as the 1860s, the stairs in New York's brownstone fronts curved gracefully at the top and bottom, and in an era of hand labor, this handsome sweeping stairway, with statue niches and a mahogany handrail emphasizing its curved form, could be afforded in the ordinary row houses. After the Civil War, the straight flight of stairs with right-angled corners was considerably cheaper to construct, and the large brownstone fronts of the 1860s were the first houses in the city to include stairs that went straight up to the second floor with only a superficial curve at the various turns of the handrail.

The huge newel post at the foot of the stairway usually was an elaborate polygonal or a Renaissance-inspired baluster. The newel post, like the simpler balusters of the handrailings, usually continued the mahogany or black walnut of the parlor doorway moldings. For a particularly lavish effect, newel posts sometimes combined inlays of rosewood or butternut with black walnut or an ebony inlay with mahogany. A round or rectangular skylight, often of stained glass, partly lit the stairwell.

Kitchen. In the mid-nineteenth century, the kitchen of a New York row house included many of the appliances of a modern kitchen, though in a far simpler form. In the 1840s, a coal- or wood-burning stove replaced the hearth for cooking, and by the 1860s, kitchens included ovens, broilers, and storage space, as well as the elaborate floral ornament that denoted modernity and good taste to the era. The stove, which sat in a large brick hearth along the wall, nevertheless had to be fed by hand, banked at night, and emptied of ashes several times a day. As early as the 1840s, iceboxes appeared in New York dwelling houses and were described as "large wooden boxes, standing on feet, and lined with tin or zinc, being generally inter-lined with charcoal, and having at the bottom a receptacle for ice, and a drain to carry off the water that drops from it as it melts; a vessel being always set underneath to catch the droppings." The icebox indeed lessened the problem of food preservation, but the servants had to empty the water pan every day and keep the drainpipe to the floor pan free of the sawdust in which the iceman packed the ice. By the 1870s, iceboxes often were fine pieces of furniture with mahogany cabinets and brass or silver-plated hardware, and in occasional row houses a water pipe passed through the icebox and provided cool water in the summer.

The kitchen also was the sitting room for the servants, and a thoughtful lady of the house provided a table, a rug or piece of carpet, some magazines and books, and a good light. In mid-nineteenth-century New York, wealthy families hired six or

Above: Parlor, 9 West Sixteenth Street (1844–45). "The fashion of French furniture has come in lately, with a rush," wrote Nathaniel Parker Willis in the late 1840s, "and the nabobs are selling out from sideboard to broom, and furnishing anew à la Française, from skylight to basement." Architect Richard Upjohn reputedly designed much of the interior woodwork in the house. This photograph was taken in 1915, with all the original furniture and decoration still in place.

Right: Parlor, 61 University Place, Manhattan. Drawing room photographed in 1895 with original furniture.

seven servants—a cook, waiter, parlormaid, upstairs maid, laundress, houseman, and likely a coachman. Middle-class families had to make do with only three servants—a cook, waiter, and maid. The servants worked six days a week and received several dollars a week, plus room and board, for work that began an hour before the family awoke and ended after its members were asleep.

Bedroom and Servant Floors. While lacking the impressive mantels, woodwork, and ceiling height of the parlor and dining room, the bedrooms on the upper floors of a brownstone front epitomized the comfortable lives of wealthy New York families. In the second-floor parents' bedroom, the furnishings included a double bed, bureaus with mirrors, a dressing table, several chairs, a wall-to-wall carpet, and usually the desk where the lady of the house wrote notes, paid bills, and gave the cook instructions for the day's meals. By the 1860s, bedrooms in fine New York dwellings had large closets instead of wardrobes and elegant marble and mahogany washbasins with hot and cold running water set into alcoves instead of the old-fashioned washstand with basin and pitcher. Each family bedroom floor also included a fully equipped bathroom.

Dining room, 26 West Tenth Street, part of the Anglo-Italianate row from 20–38 West Tenth Street designed by James Renwick Jr., completed in 1856. Taken at the turn of the twentieth century, this photograph captures the still-intact original furniture and decoration of the dining room, which was located at the rear of the house.

The renowned comfort of a New York brownstone front did not extend to the servants' quarters on the top floor. In winter, a coal grate was the only source of heat, and instead of a bathroom, the servants used the washstand with water pitcher, basin, and chamber pot. The complaints about unwashed, even malodorous, servants probably were accurate, because they typically washed in a tub or sink in the kitchen about once a week.

BATHROOMS AND PLUMBING

In the mid-nineteenth century, advancing technology dramatically increased the comfort of New Yorkers living in fine row houses. "Within the past few years, more regard than formerly has been paid to domestic conveniences," wrote Minard Lafever in *The Architectural Instructor* in 1856, "and many valuable improvements have been introduced, which are beginning to be considered indispensable, even in ordinary dwellings. Among these the supplying of water to the several stories, the various modes of warming, and also of ventilating."

An 1846 advertisement for a "desirable dwelling house in East Sixteenth-st. near Union-square" boasted an entire range of conveniences, none of which had been available in a typical house two decades before: "Croton water, range, boiler, bath, water closets, double flight of stairs, furnace, dumb waiter from basement to attic, gas, and every other improvement introduced into modern built houses of the first class."

Hatch family parlor, 49 Park Avenue, northeast corner of Thirty-Ninth Street, painted by Eastman Johnson, 1871. Hatch was a prominent Wall Street broker and a president of the New York Stock Exchange. Here, the painting shows the typical interior decoration of the era, including dark wood trim, wall-to-wall carpets, and heavy curtains. Though depicted here with three generations of the family present, these showy front parlors were rarely used in daily life. Instead, they were often left shut, with the curtains drawn to protect furniture from the sun, and opened only for special occasions to show off the wealth and splendor of their inhabitants, often of new fortunes.

RICHARD SERRA DRAWING
RICHARD SERRA
THE PHOTOGRAPHS

The opening of the Croton reservoir system in 1842 guaranteed a constant supply of wholesome water to New York and for the first time made possible indoor plumbing for the city's dwelling houses. Before the availability of Croton water, most New Yorkers drank a hard and brackish water drawn from city pumps, known as tea water pumps, at most street intersections. In a growing city, where construction constantly disturbed the ground and subsoil, the water from city pumps was unpleasant-tasting, often polluted, and scarce during summer droughts. Graveyards posed a particular threat to New York's water supply, and in 1829 the city banned the common practice of building burial vaults under the street. In 1823 the city forbade any burials in the built-up portion of the city. In the early nineteenth century, well-to-do New Yorkers drank barreled spring water brought into the city from then-rural Midtown and Upper Manhattan or rainwater, which was drained from the roof into a large brick cistern in the backyard.

In 1834, New Yorkers voted to approve a public water system, following a devastating cholera outbreak two years before, though it would not be completed in time to prevent the disastrous December 1835 fire that completely depleted the Thirteenth Street reservoir in firefighting efforts and destroyed large sections of Lower Manhattan. At a cost of $12,000,000, the city dammed the Croton River in upper Westchester County and built a solid masonry water conduit 45 miles long to the city's 150,000,000-gallon receiving reservoir at Eighty-Sixth Street, later a part of Central Park. Amid great fanfare, water was introduced into the Croton Distributing Reservoir at Fifth Avenue and Forty-Second Street on July 4, 1842. "Nothing is talked of or thought of in New York but Croton water," wrote Philip Hone several months thereafter. "Fountains, aqueducts, hydrants, and hose attract our attention and impede our progress through the streets. . . . Water! water! is the universal note which is sounded through every part of the city, and infuses joy and exultation into the masses."

After a plentiful water supply was assured in the mid-1840s, newly built row houses included one or two bathrooms, and in 1841 George Templeton Strong declared: "Tried our new bath room last night for the first time, and propose to repeat the experiment this evening. It's a great luxury—worth the cost of the whole building." The city tax for introducing Croton water to a row house was $10 a year in a basement-and-two-story-tall dwelling, and $12 a year in a basement-and-three-story-tall house. Often the second-floor hall bedrooms in the back of the house became the family toilet and bathroom, and handsome marble washbasins soon appeared in the old pantries between the front and back bedrooms or in a niche in the wall in the bedroom itself.

The city's finest dwellings, old and new alike, soon included elaborate bath and toilet facilities. In an extreme example, Robert Griffith Hatfield's plan of 1848 for the lavish Henry Parish mansion, included seven toilets and eleven tubs and washbasins. However, the high cost of pipes, valves, and fixtures, not yet mass-produced, limited nearly all row houses of the 1840s and 1850s to far more modest bath and toilet arrangements. Even the magnificent basement-and-four-story-tall brownstone fronts of the 1850s originally had only one or two large bathrooms for the entire family; the servants still used the earlier chamber pots and bathed in a tub in the kitchen. Hot water often had to be carried upstairs from the kitchen, where it had first been heated in a "log boiler" by the hot air and smoke passing up the chimney at the rear of the kitchen stove.

During the 1860s, dramatic improvements in toilet and bathing facilities appeared in New York row houses. Large houses had bathrooms on the several bedroom floors. When the "circulating boiler" or hot-water system replaced the old log-boiler arrangement, hot water was available directly from the tap in the bathroom and bedroom washbasins throughout the house. The circulating boiler was a 30-to-40-gallon copper tank next to an always-lit stove that kept the water nearly at the boiling point. When hot water was drawn from the pipe coil, cold water entered, thus making for an automatic hot-water system.

As plumbing arrangements in the city's dwelling houses improved and expanded, attitudes toward the bathroom also changed. "What was known a few years ago, even as a luxury, is now a necessity," remarked Samuel Sloan in 1869. House buyers now wanted lavish bathroom appointments to complement the splendor of the rest of the house. "Now the polished metal tub and tubular shower, with silver, marble, and walnut setting, are esteemed necessary for comfort, in very moderate houses," wrote Sloan.

Previous pages: Front parlor, West Twelfth Street, Greenwich Village. Many modest houses of the 1840s and 1850s show elements of both the Greek Revival and Italianate styles.

Right: Mantel, West Twelfth Street, Greenwich Village. A typical and handsome white-marble rounded Italianate mantel, with center scrolled bracket and foliate carvings. These mantels were mass-produced in large numbers to satisfy the demand for newly fashionable architectural styles. The mirror is a later Eastlake item, though an overmantel mirror in the Italianate style, since lost, would originally have been installed above the mantel.

Rear parlor, West Twelfth Street, Greenwich Village.

Above: Parlor doors and stairway, West Twelfth Street, Greenwich Village.

Opposite: Hall and stairway, West Twelfth Street, Greenwich Village.

LOS
NO COVER

Previous pages:
Top-floor front and rear rooms, West Twelfth Street, Greenwich Village.

Left: Brownstone-front house on Park Place, Prospect Heights, Brooklyn (ca. 1874–75). Prospect Heights Historic District.

Opposite: Park Place, Prospect Heights, Brooklyn. Impressive double doors open into a vestibule, then into an entry hallway.

HEATING

Improved heating arrangements were the other major advance in comfort for the New York row house in the 1840s. During the eighteenth and early nineteenth centuries, wood-burning fireplaces heated the city's dwellings. During the 1820s, well-to-do families began to burn coal in grates, because it gave a more constant heat with less tending than wood fires. "Coal is here only burned by the opulent," observed one Englishman in New York in the 1830s, "and although fashion has declared in favor of its use, yet wood is the chief, and indeed, almost the only fuel consumed here; it is certainly much healthier and cleaner, than its sable substitute but the matter of dollars and cents has its share of influence."

By the 1830s and 1840s, coal was available to New Yorkers at a reasonable cost because of the opening of the Erie Canal in 1825 to the Great Lakes coalfields, the completion of the Delaware and Hudson Canal in 1828 to the Pennsylvania coalfields, and the growth of the railroad network in the 1830s. Philip Hone believed that coal offered a nearly unlimited source of cheap fuel for heating dwellings. The reduced size of the fireplace opening and the appearance of ornamental cast-iron fireplace grates at that time indicated the triumph of coal over wood for heating the city's row houses.

By the 1840s, forced hot-air heating systems appeared in some New York dwellings. "In many houses, the open stoves, and their unblazing anthracite coal, are now banished, and plain marble slabs, perforated for the passage of hot air substituted in their rooms," wrote Englishman Joseph J. Gurney in 1841. In this period, a coal-burning furnace sat in the cellar in a brick vault about 6 feet by 9 feet. Wide wood troughs brought outside air into the brick vault, where it was heated

Opposite: Front parlor, Park Place, Prospect Heights, Brooklyn.

Right: Front-parlor doors, Park Place, Prospect Heights, Brooklyn. Swinging doors into the front parlor

Following pages: Rear parlor, Park Place, Prospect Heights, Brooklyn. This grand house, constructed in the early 1870s, has particularly generous dimensions. The fine parquet flooring was a new innovation in post–Civil War houses, as the wall-to-wall carpets of the previous decades fell from favor.

MURDER IN AMSTERDAM
Deliciously Dutch

Above: Rear-parlor plaster ceiling cornice molding, Park Place, Prospect Heights, Brooklyn.

Opposite: Mantel detail, rear parlor, Park Place, Prospect Heights, Brooklyn. The grandest Italianate mantels featured carved female figures in white marble.

Above: Rear extension, first floor, in modern use as a kitchen, Park Place, Prospect Heights, Brooklyn.

Opposite: Rear extension, Park Place, Prospect Heights, Brooklyn. This wooden extension, built at the same time as the house, was originally called a conservatory.

Tuesday
Friday
9am - 10:30am
208A

by contact with the hot surface of the furnace and then forced through tin pipes to the upper floors. Often, a small jet of water in the furnace vault restored some humidity to the air after its heating. These tin air ducts, which varied in diameter depending on the room size, led to an elaborate cast-iron or brass floor or wall register. In the 1840s and 1850s, the hot-air system usually heated only the basement and first floors, while the upstairs bedroom floors still relied on coal grates in the fireplaces. By the Civil War, improved furnaces in fine brownstone fronts often heated the entire house.

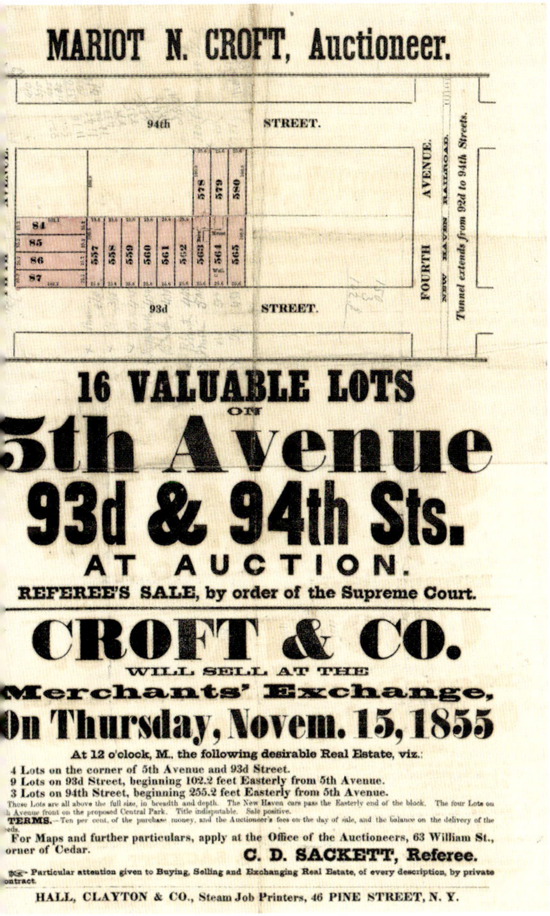

Above: Building-lot auction. North of the building line of major urban development in Manhattan, there was a fervent speculative market trading building lots. Here, an 1855 auction for building lots, which took place when the built-up portion of Manhattan had not yet crossed Forty-Second Street.

Opposite: 208 and 210 East Seventy-Eighth Street (1861–65). Located east of Third Avenue, this row of six brick-fronted Italianate houses represents the earliest stage of development on the Upper East Side, when middle-class houses were constructed shortly after the opening of the Third Avenue Railroad in 1852, making it possible to commute to built-up districts farther south. New York City Landmarks.

THE MARCH UPTOWN

In the mid-nineteenth century, row house construction swept northward up Manhattan Island, slowing only for economic depressions and the uncertainty of the Civil War years. Lower Manhattan neighborhoods that had been the most fashionable a decade or two before were abandoned for commerce. "Broadway has not much to boast of in its houses, and the dearness of land, and the noise and bustle of the great thoroughfare having driven all the wealth and fashion which centered there, into Fifth and Second Avenues, and the neighboring cross streets," observed the *United States Magazine and Democratic Review* in 1846. New fashionable districts appeared to blossom almost overnight. In the March 1854 *Putnam's,* writer George William Curtis observed that "Union Square, Madison Square, Gramercy Park, Stuyvesant Square, and Tompkins Square all contain private residences of palatial pretensions, which have been erected within these few years past."

These neighborhoods, nevertheless, were the result of keen calculations by property owners to favor their uptown properties as prosperous New Yorkers decamped from Lower Manhattan neighborhoods in decline. The largest profits were to be had in constructing grand houses for established families and for the newly wealthy, the latter having few qualms about displaying their newfound material success. In boom years, the demand for the most expensive new brownstones was so strong that development on the fashionable Fifth Avenue corridor often raced up Manhattan at a far quicker pace than the city as a whole.

There was also a healthy market in land speculation far north of the reaches of house development. In 1859, an advertisement ran for 25 lots for "$500 each" that were "located in the most Central and beautiful part of Harlem"—nearly 75 blocks north of the built-up area of the city. The ad boasted that these lots were a "good opportunity for investment, as they must double in value in the next 12 months." Indeed, the speculative market was furious enough that in 1853 building lots were advertised for sale in land that would become Central Park: "A Great Bargain—If purchased immediately, 13 full size building lots on 84th-st., between 5th and 6th—Ave. The lots are free from rock, and level with the grade of the street. Neighborhood free from nuisances. Prices low, terms easy." The ad ran on July 8, 1853, long after plans for the future boundaries of the park were well known, and just two weeks before the New York State legislature passed the Central Park Act formalizing its creation.

Land speculators knew that New York's burgeoning population would force residential development farther and farther uptown as stores, warehouses, and tenements encroached northward again into the newly fashionable residential districts then under development. Wealthy merchants and businessmen building splendid new brownstone fronts in Murray Hill in the 1850s were only outfitting the boardinghouses of the next generation.

FIFTH AVENUE

"Many accidents help to make a particular quarter fashionable," wrote Charles Astor Bristed in his 1852 collection of magazine articles, *The Upper Ten Thousand: Sketches of American Society*. He explained Fifth Avenue's rise as "*the* fashionable avenue" to canny speculation by early landowners "who were influential enough to draw other friends round them, and give a name and reputation to the avenue." Bristed archly observed that "similar attempts are continually made, and frequently without success. Three streets to the east [of Fifth Avenue] there is one fully as broad and convenient [Second Avenue], and two streets to the west another [Seventh Avenue] but that on the east is decidedly second-rate in point of fashion, and that on the west literally nowhere, there not being a house belonging to 'any of us' in it."

Charles Dickens's *American Notes*, which described his tour of the United States in 1842, did not mention Fifth Avenue once. At that point, only a few fine row houses and mansions had been built on Fifth Avenue on the several blocks north of Washington Square. Indeed, as development crossed the latitude of Fourteenth Street—the first 100-foot-wide crosstown street in the 1811 gridiron platte, and the point north of which the entire width of the island was subject to the plan—there was brief uncertainty on the preferred longitude of fine residential development.

By the 1850s, as Bristed described, Fifth Avenue had emerged as the clear north–south axis of New York's finest residential area, a rectangular district bounded by Lexington Avenue on the east and Sixth Avenue on the west. Indeed, the narrow width of this strip, wrote one newspaper, forced status-conscious New Yorkers "to go further and further along it in order to secure fashionable homes." On these favored streets, wrote Englishman William Chambers in 1854, "the edifices are entirely of brown sandstone, and of a richly decorated style of street architecture; all the windows are of plate-glass; and the door-handles, plates, and bellpulls silvered, so as to impart a chaste and light effect. The furnishings and interior ornaments of these dwellings . . . are of a superb kind; no expense being apparently spared as regards either comfort or elegance." In New York, the "avenues are springing up, lined, not with houses, but with palaces," reported one English magazine in 1859. "Neither London nor Paris, with all the accumulations of a thousand years, can show such a street as the Fifth Avenue."

A Fifth Avenue brownstone front was the goal of many an ambitious businessman and his wife, and both residents and houses were the subject of much scorn from more tasteful quarters. The rich,

Fifth Avenue, looking south and including Twenty-Second Street, showing the west side of the avenue (ca. 1870). At the center of the photograph is the Italian palazzo–style Union Club. On either side, brownstone-front Italianate row houses line Fifth Avenue in an unending vista, punctuated by churches. *Putnam's* magazine declared in 1853 that the "prevailing tint" of New York was "fixed" in brownstone.

especially the newly rich, residents of Fifth Avenue and nearby streets were lampooned as "The Avenoodles." "They are fighting hard for the grand, ugly house in the Fifth Avenue, for the gold and damask sofas and curtains that are ever shrouded in dingy coverings, save on the one night of every third year when they are unveiled to adorn the social martyrdom of five hundred perspiring friends," wrote George Templeton Strong in 1857. "I know of no great man, no celebrated statesman, no philanthropist of note who has lived in Fifth Avenue," wrote Anthony Trollope in the early 1860s: "That gentleman on the right made a million of dollars by inventing a shirt-collar; this one on the left electrified the world by a lotion; as to the gentleman at the corner there—there are rumors about him and the Cuban slave trade but my informant by no means knows that they are true. Such are the aristocracy of Fifth Avenue. I can only say that if I could make a million dollars by a lotion, I should certainly be right to live in such a house as one of these."

In its 3-mile-long course from Washington Square to the shanty- and rock-filled fields at the foot of Central Park, Fifth Avenue consisted of several patrician sections—Fourteenth Street, Madison Square, and Murray Hill. The changing architectural styles of the brownstone fronts along Fifth Avenue pointed to their development at different times. "Houses which were considered to be 'just the thing' ten years ago, are out of date today," wrote the 1871 *Traveler's Guide to the City of New York*. "Observe the style of the houses about 14th Street, for instance; then 25th to 30th streets; and, again, those which are now being erected ten or twenty streets farther up."

Only the Salmagundi Club, at 47 Fifth Avenue, remains to give some idea of the original character and scale of lower Fifth Avenue above Washington Square. The house was built in 1852–53 for Irad Hawley, president of the Pennsylvania Coal Company, which had its coal yards about a mile to the west near the Hudson River. With its rusticated basement, high balustraded stoop, and lavish door hood supported on consoles, the Salmagundi Club is a wide, mansion-sized version of the era's fine Italianate-style brownstone-front row house. The parlor floor epitomizes the splendor of the Italianate style in the elaborate white-marble statuary mantels, plaster ceiling ornament, rosewood doors, and two pairs of Corinthian columns between the identical front and back parlors. The dining room, overlooking the backyard, originally was in the Gothic Revival style and is now the club's art gallery. Although the opulence and grand scale of the Salmagundi Club amaze the visitor today, 47 Fifth Avenue apparently was not that extraordinary a dwelling for Fifth Avenue in the 1850s and 1860s—newspapers and guidebooks often described other mansions built on lower Fifth Avenue but never mentioned this fine building.

With Fifth Avenue built up with mansions, merely grand basement-and-four-story-tall 22- , 25- , and 30-foot-wide brick- and brownstone-front row houses lined the quiet side streets from Sixth Avenue on the west to Second Avenue on the east. Particularly favored by fashion was Fourteenth Street itself, described by *Putnam's* in 1854 as "a hundred feet in width, and containing residences of great beauty and truly splendid proportions." The same article pointed out West Twenty-

220 and 222 Fifth Avenue, between West Twenty-Sixth and West Twenty-Seventh Streets, (1851–52), photographed in 1881. These two florid Anglo-Italianate dwelling houses—one altered into a shop on the first floor—epitomize the extravagance of Fifth Avenue in the 1850s and 1860s and the elegant city residences of the famed "Upper Ten Thousand." Such richly ornamented brownstone fronts led visitors to proclaim Fifth Avenue a "street of palaces." Demolished.

VONHAUS
W. VONHAUS
220
TAILOR
AMIDONS HAT ESTABLISHMENT

Above: Fifth Avenue at Thirty-First Street. In 1869, Junius Henri Browne's *The Great Metropolis* guidebook referred to the street as an "unbroken line of brown-stone palaces" as far north as Fifty-Ninth Street. Demolished.

Left: William B. Astor and A. T. Stewart Mansions, Fifth Avenue and Thirty-Fourth Street. Both demolished. The A. T. Stewart Mansion at right was built in 1869 and hailed by *Putnam's* magazine as the "most costly and luxurious private residence on the continent," though it was panned by other New Yorkers for its vulgar pretensions. The Astor Mansion at the center is more typical of the grandest mansions on Fifth Avenue of the era, which resembled larger-scale versions of typical brownstone-front Italianate houses.

First Street between Fifth and Sixth Avenues as a typical block of this splendid area, where "the quiet tone of color of these buildings, the inviting elegance of doorways and flights of steps, the absence of noise, the verdure of the shade trees against the brilliant sky, and some spire or tower picturesquely terminating the vista—all combine to produce an agreeable frame of mind in the passer-by."

The Fifth Avenue district's residential fashion near Fourteenth Street lasted only through the Civil War—a scant fifteen or twenty years after the area's first development. "At one time a location is pleasant and even fashionable, and in a few years, presto! change—it has become degraded and almost uninhabitable by certain classes," wrote the *Real Estate Record and Builder's Guide* in 1868. The first store on Fifth Avenue opened in a house on the southeast corner of Seventeenth Street, and in the years after the Civil War the area became known for its "pianoforte" showrooms. The Parish and Benkard mansions became elegant clubhouses, and the Haight residence was enlarged and converted into one of the city's first apartment buildings. One by one, the handsome row houses of the pleasant side streets near Fifth Avenue became boardinghouses, and by 1875 one magazine observed that "in Fourteenth Street, today, the entire block between Fifth and Sixth Avenues, with the exception of the Van Buren mansion, is occupied by boarding-housekeepers."

Farther uptown during the prosperous late 1840s and early 1850s, row house construction swept into the East Twenties and Madison Square, the center of fashionable New York by 1860. "This part of the city is rapidly filling up with private dwellings, in many places entire blocks are going up, and in a few years this will be one of the most thickly settled parts of the city," wrote the *New-York Evening Post* in 1847. Madison Square, originally a potter's field, was opened as a park that year and soon attracted the dwellings of the wealthy and fashionable. And in the 1860s, row house construction crossed Thirty-Fourth Street into Murray Hill, an area that took its name from the old country house of Robert Murray, at the present-day intersection of East Thirty-Seventh Street and Park Avenue. During the 1860s, mansions and elegant brownstone fronts were built along Fifth, Madison, and Park Avenues and Thirty-Fourth Street, and fine row houses filled Lexington Avenue and the side streets from Sixth to Third Avenues.

This stretch of Fifth Avenue epitomized the wealth and social whirl of 1860s New York. "Fifth Avenue has consistently represented the rage for lavish expenditure which characterizes the newly-rich, while with this class still remains mingled a considerable leaven of those who give the uppermost stratum of 'society' its laws," observed *Appleton's* in 1869. After the Civil War, one magazine estimated that none of the 340 houses on Fifth Avenue cost less than a then-handsome $20,000, and one newspaper reported that $100,000 and $200,000 mansions with $30,000 to $50,000 in furniture "are rapidly making their appearance" on Fifth Avenue. In 1865, house rents ranged from $4,000 a year—"never less"—to a "gentle and genial" $12,000, according to *Leslie's*. Fifth Avenue's residents, reported the *Traveler's Guide* in 1871, largely were "retired and active merchants and business men" who "live in a most princely style. They seem to float in an ocean of wealth, and their number is legion."

Following pages: Anglo-Italianate houses on Stuyvesant Street, part of the Triangle formed by Stuyvesant and St. Mark's Place, attributed to James Renwick Jr. (1861). Fine examples of the Anglo-Italianate style, they have nearly the same appearance today as when they were originally constructed. The contrast in color and texture between the red Philadelphia pressed brick and dark brownstone window trim and rusticated first floor is particularly striking. St. Mark's Place Historic District.

The grandest Fifth Avenue house in post–Civil War New York was the A. T. Stewart Mansion at the northwest corner of Fifth Avenue and Thirty-Fourth Street. With its marble facade, mansard roof, and lavish drawing rooms and galleries, the A. T. Stewart Mansion epitomized the wealth and occasional vulgarity of the post–Civil War city. "This will unquestionably be, when completed, the most costly and luxurious private residence on the continent," wrote *Putnam's* in 1869. On the other hand, the A. T. Stewart Mansion did not impress aging architect Alexander Jackson Davis, whose designs had fallen from the favor they had enjoyed in the decades before. Davis described the Stewart house as "the most vulgar house in ostentatious vain show, and unmeaning ornament."

The fashion of Fifth Avenue and its haughty residents was also not as solid as appearances indicated. Only several blocks east or west of its "unbroken line of brown-stone palaces," in one 1869 description, one found overcrowded tenements, factories, stables, and littered and noisy streets. One British visitor reported the "incongruous sight" on Fifth Avenue of a "huge filthy hog devouring a putrid cabbage on a marble door-step." Indeed, the proud brownstone fronts on the streets near Fifth Avenue were not always simply the residences of wealthy merchants or businessmen. In an era of soaring house rents and prices punctuated by occasional depressions, hard-pressed families on fashionable streets often took in boarders to make ends meet. "Many of the handsomest mansions in the upper part of the city were establishments of this nature," wrote one Englishman in the 1860s, "and I was not a little amused by the interviews I had with the pompous dames who received me in elegantly furnished drawing rooms, before showing me the dear and shabby apartments upstairs."

STUYVESANT STREET AND LOWER SECOND AVENUE

In an ever-changing New York, the "Triangle," a group of Anglo-Italianate row houses on Stuyvesant Street completed in 1861, has retained much of its original dignity and setting. The houses are markers of a district that once was among the most fashionable in the city but fell by the wayside into relative obscurity as new fortunes favored brownstone districts farther uptown.

Attributed to James Renwick Jr., the houses of The Triangle stretch from 23–35 Stuyvesant Street around the point of the Triangle to include 112–128 East Tenth Street. The ensemble is a stunning architectural solution to the strangely shaped intersection of East Tenth and Stuyvesant Streets, midway between Second and Third Avenues. The houses of the Triangle form an impressive single composition rather than two rows of narrow houses on an awkwardly shaped lot. Inside, the houses have different interior plans, varying in width from 16 to 32 feet and in depth from 16 to 48 feet, and the house at the point of the Triangle is cut off flat at the end rather than following the lot lines to a sharp point.

The unusual street pattern near the Triangle came from the Stuyvesant family's holdings here, which stretched back to the seventeenth century and Peter Stuyvesant, the last Dutch governor of New Amsterdam. Peter Stuyvesant's mansion stood near what became the intersection of Second Avenue and East Tenth Street, and today's Stuyvesant Street was a road from the house to the Bouwerie Road. Several generations later, Petrus Stuyvesant, the Dutch governor's great-grandson, inherited the family farm and, as early as 1789, mapped out the land into building lots on a grid street plan running exactly north to south and east to west. Because the old road to the Peter Stuyvesant mansion ran exactly east and west, it was incorporated within that street plan as Stuyvesant Street. As the city laid out streets according to its 1811 gridiron plan, all streets at variance with the grid were normally closed, the buildings torn down or moved, and the owners compensated for losses in houses or land. However, Stuyvesant Street became a part of the regular street plan, in the words of the Common Council in 1830, "both for Public convenience and for the accommodation of a large and respectable Congregation attending St. Mark's Church as well as the owners and occupants of several large and commodious dwelling houses . . . all of which would be destroyed, or rendered of little value, if that street were closed." In 1812 the city opened Third Avenue in this area, in 1816 Second Avenue, and in 1826 Eighth, Ninth, Tenth, Eleventh, and Twelfth Streets.

In the following decades, the streets near lower Second Avenue were built up, forming one of the city's finest neighborhoods in the 1830s, 1840s, and 1850s. "The two great avenues for elegant residences are to be the Second and the Fifth," reported the *New-York Evening Post* in 1846. "Like the Fifth, the Second has its character established as a good neighborhood, by the number of elegant dwellings erected." The presence of notable families such as

the Stuyvesants and their concern that the area be developed in an elegant manner contributed to its fashion, and Second Avenue was also just east of the elegant Bond Street area and Lafayette Place.

From the late 1820s to the late 1850s, elegant row houses and mansions were built along St. Mark's Place, the three blocks of Eighth Street east of Third Avenue. Although St. Mark's Place has the standard 60-foot width of a New York side street, the row houses were built a uniform 10 feet behind the front property line and gave the block an extraordinary spaciousness and dignity. The real estate advertisement for "A DESIRABLE RESIDENCE IN ST. MARK'S PLACE" in 1845 points out the street's one time fashion and describes a New York mansion before the appearance of the Fifth Avenue palace about 1850:

> The subscriber offers for sale the three story brick house No. 101 St. Mark's Place, his present residence, being 37 feet 6 inches front by 54 feet deep, the property extending through to Ninth street, and embracing three lots of land.
>
> The under cellar is divided into pantries, wine vault, wood room and coal bin.
>
> The basement contains a kitchen, laundry, breakfast room, store room and pantries.
>
> The first floor is divided into two spacious drawing rooms, dining room, study and pantries.
>
> The three upper floors contain each four large rooms, besides water closet, bath room, pantries, &c. and the Croton water is introduced as high as the third story.
>
> The House is finished throughout in the most approved manner, without regard to cost and in perfect order.
>
> The stable is 37 feet 6 inches by 30, including coach house, harness room and stalls for four horses, with court yard, well, cistern, &c.
>
> Apply to JAS B. MURRAY, 101 St. Mark's Pl. or 12 Old Slip.

At its peak during the 1840s and 1850s, lower Second Avenue was one of the most fashionable thoroughfares in New York. Below Eighteenth Street, it was lined with palatial Greek Revival and brownstone-front Italianate dwellings, some of them among the first in both styles in the city. However, by the eve of the Civil War, lower Second Avenue had lost favor to uptown Madison Square and Thirty-Fourth Street. In the 1880s, one Englishman remarked that "early in the century it was what Fifth Avenue has become to-day, the fashionable residence avenue; and even yet some of the old Knickerbocker families cling to it, living in their roomy, old-fashioned houses, and maintaining an exclusive society, while they look down with disdain upon the parvenues of Fifth avenue. Stuyvesant Square . . . is one of the quarters of the ancient regime."

THE HEIGHTS AND SOUTH BROOKLYN

In the mid-nineteenth century, Brooklyn, a separate city, enjoyed rapid population growth and a frenzied building boom. Its population increased from 139,000 in 1850 to 279,000 in 1860 and reached 420,000 in 1870. Although a large number of rich families lived in Brooklyn in palatial row houses or countrified mansions, the city was renowned for street after street of substantial middle-class dwellings. "Our architectural greatness," wrote Brooklyn resident Walt Whitman in the early 1860s, "consists in the hundreds and thousands of superb private dwellings, for the comfort and luxury of the great body of middle class people—a kind of architecture unknown until comparatively late times, and no where known to such an extent as in Brooklyn."

Despite its thriving economic and social life, Brooklyn was of course tied, practically and emotionally, to New York across the East River. Brooklyn residents, rich and middle class alike, usually worked in downtown Manhattan, and the city's omnibus lines and horse-drawn street railroads converged at the several ferries to Manhattan. Well-to-do women preferred to shop on glamorous Broadway rather than in downtown Brooklyn, and after the morning rush hour, ladies' carriages jammed the ferries. Real estate advertisements in Brooklyn always stressed a property's proximity to Manhattan and the East River ferry stations.

Throughout the nineteenth century, Brooklyn's most fashionable residential district remained Brooklyn Heights. Men of "solid respectability and well-lined simplicity," often bankers and merchants who worked in

Above: 2–3 Pierrepont Place, Brooklyn Heights (1856–57). Designed by architect Frederick A. Peterson for Alexander M. White and Abiel Abbot Low, they were among the most elaborate Italianate mansions built in Brooklyn.

Opposite: 210–216 Columbia Heights, Brooklyn (1850s and 1860s). Brooklyn Heights Historic District.

Following pages:
131 St. James Place, Clinton Hill, Brooklyn (ca. 1871). A typical high-stoop Italianate brownstone-front house, with a later Queen Anne addition. Clinton Hill Historic District.

Pages 210–211: 185–189 St. James Place, Brooklyn (ca. 1865–67). A handsome trio of brick-front Italianate houses. Clinton Hill Historic District.

downtown Manhattan, favored the area's quiet tree-lined streets. In the 1850s, brownstone-front Italianate-style row houses—constructed with a basement, four stories tall, and 22 to 25 feet wide—introduced the splendor and monumental scale of the brownstone era to the Heights.

The finest Italianate and Second Empire brownstones were built along Columbia Heights, Montague Street, Montague Terrace, and Remsen Street. Arguably the greatest houses constructed in the era were the trio of brownstone-front mansions at One, Two, and Three Pierrepont Place, designed by architect Frederick A. Peterson and completed in 1857. Nos. Two and Three, respectively the Alexander M. White and the Abiel Abbot Low Houses, are still standing and feature handsome doorways with twinned rectangular Corinthian columns on either side of the entrance supporting the heavy entablature. Many other Italianate houses along envied Columbia Heights have remained in largely original condition and continue to enjoy the spectacular view of New York Bay and the ever-changing Lower Manhattan skyline across the East River. "The situation on the Heights overlooking the bay can hardly be matched in any great city of Christendom," remarked George Templeton Strong, a resident of the fashionable Gramercy Park area in Manhattan, in 1865. "How often have I wished I could exchange this house for one of them, and that I could see from my library windows that noble prospect and that wide expanse of sky, and the going down of the sun every evening!"

By the 1840s, row house construction extended beyond Atlantic Avenue into what was then known as South Brooklyn. (It was renamed Cobble Hill in the mid-twentieth century.) The area's earliest growth had begun two decades before, when Henry Street was opened south of Atlantic Avenue in 1828, which with the long-existing Red Hook Lane, linked Cobble Hill with Brooklyn Heights, and thus to the Fulton Ferry to Manhattan. By 1834, the grid pattern was imposed from Atlantic Avenue south to Butler Street. To the south of Butler Street, a partial grid coexisted for some years with the old country lanes.

Small groups of row houses were built that stood in surreal splendor in the still-open fields. The Reverend Sewall S. Cutting, pastor of the Strong Place Baptist Church, recalled the scene of the 1840s:

> On this side of Atlantic Street I recall no instance, in the streets running either way, unless near the river, where any street was built from one corner to another. In all the district from Atlantic Street to Carroll, the buildings were dwellings in detached clusters. Whole blocks were without a building on them, or with no more than two or three or four. Everywhere were footpaths across the blocks to make shorter routes to the South Ferry. My own family had been in 1845 the first to occupy a house in the row of houses on Harrison [now Kane], fronting Strong Place.

In the 1850s large-scale construction finally connected these isolated houses into complete, architecturally diverse rows. In Cobble Hill, large brownstone-front row houses were built on Clinton and Henry Streets, which run north to south, and modest row houses on east-to-west streets such as Warren, Baltic, and Kane, as well as on the unusual one-block-long north to south streets such as Cheever, Strong, and Tompkins Places. In Cobble Hill, as throughout the city, builders constructed houses narrower than the standard 25-foot-wide lots to fit more dwellings onto expensive land. A common Cobble Hill construction pattern was three 16-foot-8-inch-wide row houses, sometimes in the Anglo-Italianate configuration, on two 25-foot-wide lots.

A handsome instance of good site planning with narrow houses remains at the blockfront 206–224 Kane Street and around the corner at 10–12 Tompkins Place and 301–313 Clinton Street. Built in 1849–54 by Gerard W. Morris, a New York lawyer, these eighteen row houses are 14 and 15 feet wide but, having been designed as a cohesive group, appear larger than their narrow widths. Adjoining doorways appear paired in projecting sections, which add an unusual spaciousness and rhythm.

Immediately to the south, in the neighborhood today known as Carroll Gardens, fine brownstone fronts were constructed near Carroll Park and at the high ground of Bergen Hill near the intersection of Clinton Street and First Place. The June 1872 listings from the *Wyckoff and James Real Estate Bulletin* for Brooklyn show that row houses in the district varied greatly in size and cost, with a seven-fold difference in price between the most modest and the grandest:

> SACKETT ST., betw. Hoyt and Bond; 2 story brick, 20 x 34, 9 rooms, all modern improvements. Lot 100. $5,000.
>
> SACKETT ST., bet. Henry and Hicks, 3 story marble, 19.3 x 43, extension 10 ft., lot 100. $7,500.
>
> SACKETT ST., between Clinton and Court, 3 story brownstone 16 x 50, lot 100, $8,500.

189

CARROLL ST., bet. Court and Clinton, 3 story brick 23 x 40, lot 100, $12,000.

UNION ST., betw. Smith and Hoyt; 3 story brown stone 20 x 45, 12 rooms, all modern improvements. Lot 115. $14,500.

THIRD PL., corner Court, 3 story marble front, 20.10 x 45. Lot 133, $16,000.

PRESIDENT ST. bet. Court and Smith, 3 story brown stone, 20 x 50, lot 100, $17,000.

CLINTON ST., bet. Sackett and Union, 4 story brown stone, 25 x 50, finished in hard wood throughout, billiard room, dome in fourth story, and all modern improvements, lot 90, $35,000.

THE HILL: FORT GREENE AND CLINTON HILL

By the 1840s, row house construction had spread eastward from Brooklyn Heights to an elevated area known as the Hill, which comprises today's Fort Greene, Clinton Hill, and a small part of Bedford-Stuyvesant. The Hill's position was not unlike that of the Heights, but its elegant residences were fewer in number and their owners slightly further removed from the traditions of genteel respectability. It abounded in churches and middle-class houses, the majority of whose owners worked in New York but took pride in living in Brooklyn.

Clinton Avenue, the highest point of the area, was the Hill's most fashionable street, and by the 1830s and 1840s was lined by large-frame country houses and occasional mansions on spacious grounds. During the 1850s and 1860s, substantial middle-class brick- and brownstone-front row houses in the Italianate style began to fill in the numerous vacant lots in the area and replace country villas. And in the 1860s Frederick Law Olmsted and Calvert Vaux, the landscape architects of Manhattan's Central Park and Brooklyn's Prospect Park, converted the site of old Fort Greene into the elegant 30-acre Washington Park, later renamed Fort Greene Park.

An unusually detailed advertisement in 1871 for three fine brownstone-front row houses with mansard roofs on Clinton Avenue recalls the splendor of these dwellings then rising on Clinton and Washington Avenues:

FOR SALE IN BROOKLYN, On the northwest corner of Clinton and Lafayette avs., some of those elegant blocks of four-story high-stoop brown-stone front French-roof houses, 21, 22, and 23 x 48; lots 90 to 110 feet. . . . These houses have been built by day's work in the most thorough and substantial manner, under the supervision of the owner; all modern improvements replete; black-walnut front and vestibule doors; stairs and stair-casings of the most elegant design; black-walnut sash and polished plate glass; dining-room and hall wainscotted in black-walnut; independent laundry, two bath-rooms, three water-closets, eight wash-basins, butler's pantry, &c.; about eighteen rooms, twelve pantries, and any amount of drawers for table linen, &c. hot-air furnaces; 15 to 20 minutes by Green-av. cars from Fulton Ferry; five to seven blocks from Prospect Park grand entrance. Price $25,000, $30,000, and $35,000, about one-half cash. Must be seen to be appreciated. Immediate possession. Apply on the premises, to THOMAS FAGAN, Owner.

After the Civil War and the completion of Washington Park, fashion favored the blocks at the park's southern and eastern edges. In the frantic building boom of the late 1860s and early 1870s, palatial brownstone-front row houses and occasional mansions—selling for $25,000, $30,000, and even $40,000—rose along South Portland Avenue, South Oxford Street, and Washington Park, the two-block-long stretch of Cumberland Street facing the park. Fine Italianate and Second Empire dwellings were built on nearby blocks in the area. New houses sometimes did not destroy the modest wood houses they replaced; the wood houses were instead simply sold to be relocated just outside the frontier of development. An ad from 1871 stated that the wood-frame house "220 Cumberland St, near DeKalb ave" was "to be removed in thirty days" and was a "bargain to any one owning a lot within a mile."

By the 1870s, row house construction in Fort Greene had virtually ceased, and the area settled into several generations of genteel stability—something basically unknown in the wealthy neighborhoods in Manhattan constructed at the same time. On warm evenings and weekends, area residents strolled in Washington Park, which in 1870 Henry Reed Stiles in his *History of the City of Brooklyn* described as "one of the most central, delightful and healthful places for recreation of which any city can boast."

306–308 Clinton Avenue, Clinton Hill, Brooklyn (1877–78). Italianate brownstone-front houses continued to be built even after the Panic of 1873 in Brooklyn, where the demand for up-to-date architectural styles lagged behind more fashionable Manhattan. Clinton Hill Historic District.

306

HOUSE

BROWNSTONE MONOTONY DECRIED

The brownstone front was so popular for dwellings in New York for so many years that the material was transposed to become the name for the house itself—that is, a row house became known as a brownstone. Today, any row house in New York, from any era and faced in any material, not just brownstone, is still popularly termed a brownstone.

Indeed, the universality of the brownstone-front house sparked a severe backlash among critics following the Civil War. "When he has seen one house he has seen them all," complained the *Architects' and Builders' Guide* in 1868, "the same everlasting high stoops and gloomy brown-stone fronts . . . the same huge cornices bristling with overpowering consoles and projections." The Italianate brownstone-front row house's excess ornament only served to mask an underlying uniformity: "[W]hat we lack in invention, we can cover over by 'ornamentation,' and hence we have miles of reiterated and unmeaning rope mouldings, filigreed jambs, and window-heads twisted into all sorts of conceivable contortions."

Indeed, what appeared so elegant in the late 1840s was merely commonplace or even vulgar to New Yorkers several decades later. "The architecture" of Fifth Avenue "is not only impressive, it is oppressive," wrote journalist Joseph H. Howard Jr. in 1885. "Its great defect is in its monotony, which soon grows tiresome. A variation, a contrast—something much less ornate or elaborate—would be a relief."

Brownstone itself had also fallen into disrepute as a building material, though it would continue to be used as a primary facade material on many houses through the end of the nineteenth century. Its rich brown hues turned nearly black when covered by the soot of New York's pollution, which, combined with the death of many of the street trees that had lined pleasant row house blocks a quarter century before, created block after block of uniformly somber streetscapes. In her 1920 novel *The Age of Innocence*, which was set in the 1870s, Edith Wharton archly noted the disdain with which Gilded Age architects held the previously fashionable building material—brownstone was the "uniform hue" that "coated New York like a cold chocolate sauce."

462 West Twenty-Third Street, Chelsea (ca. 1860), photographed in the 1910s. Built as a fine one-family residence on once-fashionable West Twenty-Third Street, this brownstone front—though still well maintained—had become a boardinghouse by World War I. These houses still stand, though many are heavily modified.

893
895

IV

1873–1893
THE ECLECTIC DECADES

The financial collapse of the Panic of 1873 led to the worst economic depression in the United States to that date, and with it came a lull in building activity in New York that lasted nearly the rest of the decade. In 1874 the *Brooklyn Daily Eagle* wrote that the real estate industry was "so greatly depressed by the extreme dullness in other branches of business, the lack of public and private confidence, and the uncertainty of the future that it was brought almost to a stand still," with the "demand for unimproved property or building lots" having "ceased entirely." Four years later, in 1878, after a modest upswing in demand, the *New-York Times* still cautioned against talk of revival after years in which real estate had been "flat and expressionless as pancake."

Finally, an economic upswing beginning in 1878 and taking full force in 1879 coincided with a sharp rise in population in Manhattan, as well as in the still-independent city of Brooklyn. New York grew from 942,000 people in 1870 to 1,440,000 in 1890, while Brooklyn's population doubled from 420,000 to 839,000 in the same two-decade span. In both cities, transit improvements made large new swaths of land more accessible for speculative construction. The scope of building, and the rate of survival of buildings from this period compared to earlier ones—especially in Brooklyn—means that this era of row houses is the most widely represented in New York City's contemporary streetscape.

Amid this rapid growth, multifarious forms and styles proliferated—as did house sizes and price points—meaning that there is hardly a house "typical" of the period. At the same time, the sheer volume of speculative building still gave opportunities for the architectural press to issue its long-levied complaint of uniformity. "The conventional brown stone, three or four story and basement house, plain, but eminently respectable, is to be found everywhere in Brooklyn," wrote the *Eagle* in 1885—the "eye wearies of the monotony." The *Eagle* lauded architects who planned "more rows of buildings with bay windows and deeply recessed doors," which would relieve the otherwise flat plane of the all-too-typical block front. It was an "improvement"—but the *Eagle* still complained that "even in bay windows there can be too much uniformity."

895 Union Street, Park Slope, Brooklyn (1889). In a severe break from the brownstone era, New York row houses built from the 1870s through the Panic of 1893 show remarkable eclectic variation. Though certain styles—including Neo-Grec, Romanesque Revival, and, here, the Queen Anne—flourished, none predominated, both from house to house and often on the same house. Park Slope Historic District.

The *Eagle*'s critique summarized a slew of sometimes contradictory trends. The emergence in full of the modern professional architect brought a new emphasis on individual, "artistic" residential creations for wealthy clients, each potentially setting a particular fashion to be imitated. But the large-scale development of new neighborhoods continued to lend itself to the mass production of rows. Industrialization and standardization of building materials allowed for easy duplication and thus monotony but also, through modularity of components, made certain forms of variety easier and more inexpensive to attain.

A variety of styles appeared in the two decades following the Panic of 1873, including Neo-Grec, Queen Anne, and Romanesque Revival. None gained absolute dominance in the era's speculative construction; they coexisted as much as competed, often in the same facade, as fashions trickled down and the market for residences expanded to new populations and new frontiers of urbanization across the city. The stylistic terms themselves were used loosely by real estate promoters and reporters, for whom, in fact, the most common catchword for any style was the evergreen *modern*.

In 1882, the *Real Estate Record and Builder's Guide* surveyed the city's residential building scene, with a long view of the city's history across the "architectural gulf" between the present and "any previous period of building activity." The author suggested that the Greek Revival had signified the city's striving to metropolitan maturation following the completion of the Erie Canal and was followed by a period of decline symbolized by the application of thin brownstone veneers to brick-built houses, solely for the appearance of expense.

But now, the author observed, "What we see about us are gropings after a new type." In place of the "academic Gothic" and "Renaissance"—and the "vernacular brown stone" of the pre-1873 era—"We can now count 'Colonial,' Queen Anne, Florentine Renaissance, English Renaissance, Dutch Renaissance, Hispano-Moorish, Neo-Grec and 'Old New York,' not to mention Japanese and even Celtic motives in decoration and detail." The multiplicity of styles in the late nineteenth century drew on the information about trends within architecture and about the art-historical heritage of the world made more widely available through national and international architectural publications and the spread of photography. This, together with the consolidation of the architectural profession, facilitated the provision of houses that could be advertised, at least, as "built by an individual for an individual." Once, when a "20-foot three-story" house was advertised, the *Record and Guide* wrote that "we knew exactly what to expect"—houses "built on the assumption that men were all alike, income only excepted." But now, "it cannot be said that there is a type of New York house."

ECLECTICISM AS A STYLE

Since the 1830s, American architects had evoked historical architectural styles for their stirring Picturesque forms and associative power. The sheer number of faraway times and places that an architect could evoke had proliferated—in the 1860s, for example, the celebrated

Redbrick Chateauesque corner house and neighbors, 11–13 Mount Morris Park West, Harlem, architect James E. Ware (1887–89). Mount Morris Park Historic District.

FILLMORE
BROOKLYN
FOR SALE
718-486-5200

architect Alexander Jackson Davis offered to execute designs for country houses in the following long, almost comical catalog of fanciful styles: "American Log Cabin, Farm Villa, English Cottage, Collegiate Gothic, Manor House, French Suburban, Swiss Chalet, Swiss Mansion, Lombard Italian, Tuscan from Pliny's Villa at Ostia, Ancient Etruscan, Suburban Greek, Oriental, Moorish, Round and Castellated."

In the eclecticism of the last decades of the nineteenth century, however, the employment of numerous past architectural influences transcended fidelity to discrete historical styles. Writing in the mid-1880s in *Artistic Country Seats*, George William Sheldon wrote that "[s]o far as style is concerned," many of the buildings in the volume simply could "not be classified." The architect, Sheldon wrote, no longer had to "assume that non-compliance with any set style necessarily deprives a dwelling of features on which the artistic imagination may be worthily exerted, and in which new ideas may be brought into place. The value of the results depends upon the freedom of the architect within the range of the vitalizing ideas of his art."

Sheldon wrote that the "disciples of the eclectic school" were those architects who had "become conversant with the best that has been thought and done in architecture," exercising the "untrammeled freedom of the artist of the nineteenth century." Other strict revivalists ("Classicists, Gothic, Italian and French Renaissance") were, in this view, "mere copyists" bound by a rigid interpretation of the past. Eclecticism was, unlike these revivals, itself a style, and a modern one.

In contrast to the revivalist's Romantic desire for association with a distant time, the panoply of styles employed in late nineteenth-century eclecticism was a palette available to the modern and sophisticated architect-as-artist. The rise of specialized architectural journals and magazines, as well as of photography and mass pictorial media more generally, provided architects and their customers with unprecedented access to depictions of exotic styles, archaeological discoveries that enriched the consciousness of the long-emulated ancient world, not to mention European and national trends in design. The *American Architect and Building News* began publication in 1876 and was joined in the early 1890s by others including the *Architectural Record* (created by the publisher of New York's *Real Estate Record and Builders' Guide*) and *The Brickbuilder* (later *Architectural Forum*).

This broader consciousness of architectural options encompassed the discarded past of American architecture as a historical style in itself. The 1876 Centennial Exhibition in Philadelphia helped stoke a renewed appreciation of early American architecture, which became one strand in the synthesis of varied influences and elements that would make up what was known as Queen Anne architecture.

THE STREETSCAPE: ECLECTICISM AS URBANISM

Artistic eclecticism was embraced not only as a means for individualistic expression by architects (and home buyers) but as an urbanistic goal. The midcentury stately ideal of the unified

Above: Convent Avenue, Hamilton Heights, photographed 1889. This trio, part of a block of fifteen houses, shows the variation possible in a single house row in the eclectic 1880s. In place of a uniform monumental streetscape of the brownstone era, architects and builders now differentiated houses, on these three with Queen Anne, pyramidal, and Dutch gables, and with an even wider variety across the entire row.

Opposite: Picturesque, asymmetrically massed roofline and variations in facades in a trio of houses developed together on Montgomery Place, Park Slope, Brooklyn, by developer Harvey Murdock and designed by architect C. P. H. Gilbert.

Following pages:
305–307 West Seventy-Ninth Street (1885–86). Flemish Renaissance Revival. Riverside–West End Historic District.

Moorish, Romanesque, and Renaissance elements melded in brownstone, 130–132 West Seventy-Eighth Street, architect Rafael Guastavino (1886). Upper West Side/Central Park West Historic District.

130
132

monumental blockfront was instead now viewed as providing only dullness and uniformity, and gave way to calls to create streetscapes with pleasing variation to endow any given block with true uniqueness. In 1885, the *Brooklyn Daily Eagle* complained not only of uniform rows of houses, but also that "builders erect in different streets rows of buildings which are exact duplicates." "In the erection of city houses," the author of *Palliser's New Cottage Homes and Details* wrote in 1888, "it has always been a mystery to us why those building them should persist in making the fronts all alike; in many cases they are so for whole streets, and look like a lot of bakers' loaves set on end." The *Eagle* pleaded for an "architect" serving as a "public benefactor" who "will give Brooklyn a row of houses that, while embracing one central idea and forming a united whole, will be so varied in points of detail that every man can recognize his own doorway."

By the mid-1880s, such differentiation was commonplace on many new row house blocks. In 1886, summarizing the extensive development in recent years on the Upper West Side, the *New-York Times* noted:

> Nearly all of the dwellings built by money furnished by Mr. [William E. Dodge] Stokes are architectural novelties. Where six or a dozen are constructed in one block, care is taken to have the front of each house distinctive in appearance. While one house may have an entire front of gray sandstone, the house next to it will display a front of half red brick and half rock-face granite. The designs for the front doors and windows are different in each building. This idea in appearances has been carried out by many other builders in that locality, and the result is that some of the newly erected blocks present a very unique appearance.

Where critics of uniformity had complained that builders placed identical rows of houses across numerous sites in the city, Stokes employed multiple architects for the various blocks he built, including William J. Merritt and Berg & Clark, and sold more lots for development to the architects Lamb & Rich.

Unrestrained eclecticism and strivings for startling originality did give rise to criticism that they resulted in an "incongruous, inharmonious jumble of houses," as the *Record and Guide* complained in 1887. But even those scandalized by mediocre architects, "each man designing as though he were a law in himself," granted that a row of houses should have a "unity of effect" that was achieved by variations, albeit carefully composed ones.

The *Record and Guide* claimed to identify the sole remedy for the "'nightmarish' results" of completely ungoverned variety: "someone with large capital to purchase both sides of the street, and employ one good architect to design all the houses," so that "a great variety of architecture is embraced, yet the whole is strictly harmonious." Similarly, in 1889, the same publication praised a row of houses on East Forty-Seventh Street for having a "general effect" with "individual variations":

> Here we have six dwellings all in the style of the modern Renaissance, with effective and graceful arches, some of which have a leaning toward the Moorish type, all grouped under one coping; and yet each home differs from its neighbor—some being built with Amherst stone with Berea stone trimmings, and others of Connecticut brown stone, while some have bay windows in the second and third stories, and others only in the second, and others again differ somewhat in the treatment of their entrances and windows, while all are enticed with carving of unique and artistic design.

THE RISE OF THE PROFESSIONAL ARCHITECT

The post–Civil War era saw the rise of American architecture as an academically trained profession, with New York naturally one of its centers. Formal architectural education in the United States, as opposed to apprenticeship, had its origins in this period as well, and the American Institute of Architects (AIA) was founded in New York in 1857 and grew to include chapters across the nation in the subsequent decades. Emblematic of the new American architect were Richard Morris Hunt and Henry Hobson Richardson, the first two United States–born students to enroll at the École des Beaux-Arts in Paris and perhaps the two most influential figures in New York City residential architecture in the late nineteenth century.

Even beyond the realm of such elite figures, though, the practice of everyday house design and construction—previously thought of as "building"—became "architecture." The *Real Estate Record and Builder's Guide* observed in 1882, "The young architects have ransacked all times and all countries" for stylistic sources, "with more or less success, according to their place in the long scale of professional skill and competency." Newspaper columns that previously reported mere "Building News" were supplemented by such features as, in the *Brooklyn Daily Eagle*, "An Architect's Views of the Practice of His Art in Brooklyn," "Architectural Art," and "Architectural Fads," to help keep up with the "diversified styles" of desirable homes. The prospective tenants of a New York house became consumers of an architectural art that aspired to an expression of individuality through a proliferating number of variables, interior and exterior.

The *Times* noted in 1880 that "originality in architectural designs is very much in demand," including "artistically carved door and window trimmings, mullioned windows, gabled roof, massive stone steps, and interiors finished in carved woods." The author shrewdly added: "As a result of this demand clever architects can command good compensation, despite an unusual degree of competition."

THE SPECULATIVE BUILDER AND THE RULES OF HOUSE DEVELOPMENT

The *Real Estate Record and Builders' Guide* published its first issue in March 1868. It was the first New York publication devoted exclusively to the building trade. The editorial of the opening issue noted that the "Real Estate and Building interests of the metropolis are enormous and widely ramified, and demand vastly more attention than they have heretofore had from the press." Though speculative building had of course flourished before the Civil War, it was now increasingly recognized as a business concern on par with New York's financial and dry-goods trade—that is, among the key sources of the city's wealth and power, not just their reflection.

Just as the professional architect emerged as a separate profession from the architect-builders of the pre–Civil War era, the division of the real estate speculator and developer as distinct professions from the building trades was now identifiable. The *Record* distinguished between the class of "real estate dealers and owner" on one hand and the "architect, builder, mason, carpenter, lumber merchant, brick and marble dealer, cement and lime trader, seller of paint and putty" on the other. Together, these two sides constituted all who dealt "in any thing which enters in the composition of a house."

A decade later, in 1878, just as New York's building trades were reviving from the long depression with renewed demand, the *Record* ran an extended series devoted to the "Economics of Building," one of the most detailed exegeses of the operations of the city's real estate market, where the construction and sale of first-class "private dwellings" was viewed as the "chief activity of the buying demand" and thus the "most conspicuous and noticeable branch" of real estate development, and "apt to be taken as a true index to the condition of building interests."

The *Record* classified the city's master builders into three classes: "legitimate builders," "speculative builders," and "architect builders."

Following pages: Queen Anne row with gable-fronted faux mansards and Venetian Gothic variations, 145–153 West 118th Street, Harlem (1887). Note the A-shaped gable fronts and slate tile in the intervening spaces, which give the appearance of pitched roofs, even though part of the house elevations. Mount Morris Park Historic District.

147

The first class were effectively general contractors, working for fixed fees on architect-designed works; they did not participate in the project's financial upside (or downside). Architect-builders were, according to the *Record*, not traditional row house architect-builders, but the enterprising trained professional architects who saw the only way to enforce the completion of "superior dwellings" was to develop and construct them themselves—a new development in the 1870s.

Nevertheless, it was the second class of builders, the speculative builders, who were responsible for the bulk of the city's housing construction: "The physical progress of New York city in the past, as is certain to be the case in the future, has been due mainly to the efforts and, we may say, sacrifices of speculative builders," the *Record* wrote. "They scan the surface of the island, state its capacities for improvement, and determine the need of additional building accommodation." This was not unalloyed praise, however; while New York derived "the questionable benefit of a rapid extension of its building area," the "inferior quality of many of these projections detracts serious[ly] from the value of the quality thus afforded." Speculative builders were apt to produce a more generic private dwelling than afforded by the one where architects played a greater role—in the latter case, design would be held in esteem equal to profit.

In the *Record*'s taxonomy of the New York real estate market, buyers for private houses in the city were classified as "High-Priced," "Medium-Priced," and "Low-Priced"—not necessarily an indication of the buyer's income, but rather of the sale price of the houses they sought. Even after the downturn in house prices in the economic slough of the 1870s, there were effectively no purchase options for the low-priced category, which was sought by potential buyers of "moderate means." In the high-priced-house category, New York was distinguished from other major American cities as the only one where the "erection of high-priced city mansions, upon speculation" could be met with the "confident expectation, which has never been disappointed, of finding a purchaser at the completion of work." However, though at the peak of the market in the early 1870s such high-priced houses could be sold for almost $80,000—and $125,000 to $190,000 for the rarer, larger mansions on Fifth Avenue—their sale price was subject to major market corrections and thus carried a greater risk in undertaking, though also the potential for greatest profits.

The "most reliable and acceptable staple" of demand was to be found in medium-priced homes, ranging from $25,000 to $40,000, though the same range had been as high as $40,000 to $65,000 before the Panic of 1873. The buyers of these homes were the "easiest and readiest seen of patrons" representing the "thrift, wealth and culture of the city"—that is, the city's aspiring and often newly moneyed upper middle class. The "most comfortable and lucrative service which the speculative builder" could engage in was "satisfying the tastes and necessities of medium-class buyers," a demand that was considered insatiable.

Indeed, the pitfall of speculative construction of houses, according to the *Record*, was not a want of buyers, but rather location and timing of construction. Though the uptown movement of fashionable neighborhoods was inexorable—the "peculiar formation of the island [of Manhattan] compels all improvements to take one course—northward" wrote the *Record*—speculative builders could not risk moving too far from already built areas. Though a builder might try to leapfrog north over "some intermediate vacant space" to as-yet-developed environs, such "pioneering" was "hazardous and unprofitable" and better left to land speculators rather than developers. Instead, market forces forced the speculative builder to "follow the sluggish growth of the city, keep close the line of improvements, and exercise his finest abilities as surveyor and prospector in determining good and wholesome locations."

Madison Avenue, southeast corner of East Seventy-Eighth Street, photographed in 1914. A row of Neo-Grec brownstone houses, with angular-bracketed cornice and flattened, incised window and door surrounds. Demolished.

THE NEO-GREC STYLE

In the mid-1870s, the Neo-Grec style supplanted the Italianate style in New York row houses, though the two differed less in overall building form than in the details in which their elements were executed. The Neo-Grec style first appeared in the 1840s at the École des Beaux-Arts in Paris, and French architect Henri Labrouste was the style's foremost advocate. Although American architect Richard Morris Hunt returned to New York from France in 1855 with a familiarity in the Neo-Grec style, he did not employ it in the United States until after the Civil War—on 480 Broadway, the old Lenox Library on Fifth Avenue, and for the base of the Statue of Liberty. The Neo-Grec influence appeared on fine brownstone fronts in the Fifth Avenue district in about 1870 and, with resumption of construction in the late 1870s after the hiatus of the Panic of 1873, came to dominate row house architecture in New York for the remainder of the decade. "The tendency is now towards a purer and simpler style than has of late prevailed," observed one magazine on the shift from the Italianate to Neo-Grec in brownstone fronts.

In the eyes of contemporary observers, the Neo-Grec style emerged against the background of a continuing theoretical debate between the virtues and appropriateness of classically inspired architecture on one hand and Gothic forms on the other. The *Real Estate Record and Guide* in 1875 noted that the highly elaborate ornament of the Gothic was not generally appropriate to residential architecture from a cost perspective and favorably cited a new house at Fifth Avenue and Fifty-Seventh Street constructed instead in a kind of "modern Gothic" that combined "classical repose with Gothic light and shade, while avoiding both the heavy cornices of the one and the interminable details of the other." The critic praised the synthesis of Gothic and Neoclassical virtues as "susceptible of all variations, responsive to all thought . . . alone possessed of that natural elasticity which is an absolute necessity of modern street architecture." The *Record* referred to the style as "Neo-grec" but with some reservations—as "why it is so named would be hard to say, since it is neither new nor Greek."

1009

ONE WAY

In practice, the Neo-Grec row house, at first glance, appeared to be nearly identical to row houses in the preceding Italianate style, and, indeed, it did retain the smooth brownstone front, protruding cornice, and heavy doorway and window enframements of earlier years. But in a reaction against the round forms and foliate ornament of the long-standing Italianate style, the forms and details of the Neo-Grec row house took on a rectangularity and precision. "It is an established principle in the theory of design that decorative art is degraded when it passes into a direct imitation of natural objects," wrote English architect Charles L. Eastlake in his influential 1868 *Hints on Household Taste*. "Nature may be typified or symbolized, but not actually imitated."

Opposite: Corner bookend to block-long Neo-Grec row, 241 Lenox Avenue, Harlem (1883–85). Mount Morris Park Historic District.

Above: Continuous sill courses unify a Neo-Grec row, 227–229 West 112th Street, Harlem. In general, the Neo-Grec style carried on the forms of the Italianate brownstone front, but with heavier, more angular features

Comparing Neo-Grec row houses to their Italianate neighbors, analogous elements were evoked in more stylized and restrained gestures but exhibited a similar overall organization and effect. On the Neo-Grec row house, the projecting cornice rested on angular brackets rather than on the earlier rounded consoles faced with acanthus

leaves. The massive door hood and full window enframements were rectangular in form and had squared-off edges. The stoop had immense newel posts and balustrade railings, but with squared-off edges and ornamental knobs and strapwork.

An important feature of the style was incised ornamental detail cut into the smooth brownstone. The two most popular details were a stylized single-line flower or vine design known as the "Eastlake motif" and long, parallel, narrow channels. These usually appeared on door hoods and pilasters, windowsills and lintels, stoop railings and fences, and brackets at the cornice. The squared-off forms and incised detail of the Neo-Grec style were more economical than the round forms and naturalistic ornament of the Italianate style. With the mechanical planers and groove-cutting routers of the period, incised detail was cheaper to cut than consoles and acanthus leaves and, in the contemporary view, lent a feeling of modernity and individuality to a row house.

Unlike the luxuriant brownstone front of the Italianate style, the mixture of delicate single-line incised detail with the heavy, squared-off doorway, windows, and cornice on the Neo-Grec row house front sometimes presented a disturbing inconsistency in the scale and character. Indeed, the *Record*'s 1875 paean to Neo-Grec's highest forms warned that, as it gained a hold on "public taste" in New York, it had "become burdened with a solidity and harshness at variance with its real character."

Above left: Two-story Neo-Grec brownstone, 357 Macon Street, Bedford-Stuyvesant, Brooklyn (1884). Note the incised ornament on the lintel, a typical feature of Neo-Grec houses. Lower land costs on the farther reaches of Brooklyn trolley lines meant that it was still possible to construct such modest houses in large numbers through the turn of the twentieth century.

Above right: Neo-Grec cornice details and carved window enframements, 32–34 Mount Morris Park West, Harlem (1880–81). Mount Morris Park Historic District.

Opposite: Pioneering "Coignet stone" (concrete) Neo-Grec fronts, 536–540 Clinton Avenue, Brooklyn (1870s). These houses are among the earliest uses of concrete in residential architecture in the United States, using concrete produced at the New York and Long Island Coignet Stone Company in Gowanus, Brooklyn. Three of the original four survive.

538
536

THE QUEEN ANNE

During the 1880s, the architectural fashion that each row house have a measure of individuality—and the streetscape a visually exciting appearance—reached its culmination in a style that was known loosely as Queen Anne.

The term *Queen Anne* even in its heyday was often a malleable catchphrase whose precise meaning was the subject of debate. An 1878 article on the "Queen Anne, so-called, of to-day" in furnishings described an array of tendencies variously congruent with both the Neo-Grec and what we now refer to as Queen Anne: "severely square and straight . . . a great deal of carving in the face, that is, in sunk relief, of the conventional forms of fruit, flowers, foliage, birds, and animals, and their idealized suggestions." In 1882, still early in the life of Queen Anne in New York, the *Real Estate Record* reported hearing that "the so-called Queen Anne style is said to be laid upon the shelf" in favor of "catholicity"—that is, the term *Queen Anne* was itself becoming a victim of the flight from established labels that it was a very part of. "'Queen Anne' is a comprehensive name," wrote architectural critic Montgomery Schuyler in 1883, "which has been made to cover a multitude of incongruities, including, indeed, the bulk of recent work which otherwise defies classification." More definitively, *Harper's* in 1886 wrote that the "epoch of Queen Anne is a delightful insurrection against the monotonous era of rectangular building."

In the United States, the Queen Anne style typically referred to the combination of the "Free Classic" work of the esteemed British architect Richard Norman Shaw and American colonial ornament made newly popular by the Centennial Exhibition in 1876 in Philadelphia. Shaw's inspiration for the Free Classic mode was the early Georgian-style brick city house of the eighteenth century. Besides the warm textured-brick facade, Shaw's country houses in the Free Classic mode included an irregular plan and silhouette, a pitched-gable roofline with large chimneys, large windows, and simple white trim. The Queen Anne style emerged in the United States in the mid-1870s when architects added such colonial ornament as delicate pilasters, wreaths, and garlands to Shaw's robust and fairly simple Free Classic buildings.

By the late 1870s, Queen Anne forms appeared in New York on residential and commercial buildings. Many dwellings featured redbrick fronts with light- and dark-colored stone and wood trim. On row houses, architects freely mixed brick and stone of different colors and textures or employed brick laid or cut in a decorative pattern, or terracotta or encaustic tiles. After decades of dominance of the brownstone front, and attendant complaints of the resulting monotony, the Queen Anne style allowed individuality and "artistic" expression in houses through a broader palette of materials and stylistic references. And the long-lived streetscape of flat row house fronts and uniform cornice line finally lost sway in favor of a large A-form gable and small dormer windows, with tile or slate roofs and massive chimneys enhancing often asymmetrical rooflines. For an even more Picturesque appearance, the stoops of some New York row houses, beginning in the 1880s, abandoned straight flight of stairs for an entry stairway with at least one landing and change in direction.

Above: Shared Queen Anne parapet of 1087 and 1089 Dean Street, Crown Heights, Brooklyn.

Opposite: Queen Anne house, 295–297 Jefferson Avenue, Brooklyn. Unlike the horizontal and uniform cornice lines of the previous era, Queen Anne houses often had dramatic gabled fronts, providing variety and the appearance of individuality even within a multiple-house row constructed by one builder. Bedford Historic District.

20
DOCTOR'S OFFICE

Left: Queen Anne and Neo-Grec styles abut at 10–18 Arlington Place, Bedford-Stuyvesant, Brooklyn (both rows completed 1886). The Queen Anne houses on the left were designed by Amzi Hill, a prolific architect of hundreds of Brooklyn houses built by various developers. Bedford Historic District.

Following pages:
240 and 242 Hancock Street, part of a five-house row from 236 to 244 Hancock Street, Bedford-Stuyvesant, Brooklyn, architect Montrose Morris (1886). Morris was perhaps the greatest architect of preconsolidation Brooklyn, and his houses along the south side of Hancock Street east of Marcy Avenue are among the most spectacular ever constructed. Morris was the developer of the five lots as well as their architect. Bedford Historic District.

"The staircase is no longer a railed ladder but has risen into a chief ornament of the house," observed *Harper's* in 1886.

These new-style row houses often had recessed porches, set several feet into the house behind a half-circle arch, to break the flat row house front dramatically with a dark volume. Normally, the porch appeared on the top floor of the house or as a sheltered entryway for the front doorway, but some city houses employed a stone half-circle arch on the flat front, known as a "blind arch," to recall the recessed porch. A three-sided bay window at the first floor or running from the basement to the roof was another popular way to break the flat row house front, particularly those with brownstone facing. Some new dwellings, especially those on a corner, had oriels, a small one-story-tall bay window that sprang from the second- or third-floor wall on a bracket.

The windows often varied in size and shape and imaginatively employed different-size glass panes for striking visual effect. Although New York row houses had employed plate-glass windows for several decades by the 1880s, some windows on a Queen Anne–style dwelling often included small panes, about 4 inches by 4 inches, which reflected the style's eighteenth-century early Georgian-style antecedents. The diminutive wood panels on the front door recalled these small, quaint panes of glass. Decorative stained glass also appeared in first-floor windows or the sidelights of the front doors.

Nevertheless, few Queen Anne–style row houses in New York adopted such variations in material and massing all at once. Indeed, many modest New York row houses still employed the respectable brownstone front and, in the tradition of the earlier revival styles, relied upon such applied ornament as garlands, sunbursts, and foliate forms on the street front for their Queen Anne notes.

As the Queen Anne was a more dramatic departure from past fashion than Neo-Grec, some owners took pains to alter existing row houses of earlier eras in the newest ornamental style. In 1886, the *Eagle* praised Queen Anne details found on Willow Street in Brooklyn Heights—already notable for its Federal and Greek Revival homes:

> Here one finds structures of brick ornamented with terra cotta, in which are combined Byzantine and Queen Anne style and the most delicious applications of terra cotta. . . . The signs are there that there is going to be here a revival of Byzantine modified by Queen Anne Tudor and by terra cotta decoration, and that out of those modifications will come an American dwelling house, truly original. It will be of brick; it will be decorated with terra cotta, and possibly with encaustic tiles; it will be rather small, exceedingly comfortable, with a highly decorated façade and a Queen Anne gable roof.

The popularity of the Queen Anne style was brief in New York row house construction. It lacked any strong champions in the United States and, rather than becoming a relatively defined style, remained to its critics a loose collection of Picturesque forms and ornament. By the late 1880s, one New Yorker wrote that "the extravagances of 'Queen Anne' have disappeared . . . that strange mode of building has spent its force."

Queen Anne row, 889–903 Union Street, Park Slope, Brooklyn (1889).
This row, located on the north side of Union Street between Seventh and
Eighth Avenues, is one of the most sophisticated Queen Anne blocks
in the city. Park Slope Historic District.

Left: Multilight transom in a sheet-metal Queen Anne bay, 300 Clinton Avenue, Clinton Hill, Brooklyn (1889). Clinton Hill Historic District.

Center and opposite: Details, 244 and 242 Hancock Street, Bedford-Stuyvesant, Brooklyn (1886). Bedford Historic District.

Romanesque Revival–tinged Queen Anne row, 1257–1265 Dean Street, Brooklyn (1892). The blocks located east of Grant Square in Brooklyn, one of the centers of preconsolidation Brooklyn's wealth, feature spectacular row houses and even some freestanding mansions along St. Marks Avenue. The scale of such houses, whether individually or in rows, makes these streets some of the most urbane in all New York. Crown Heights North Historic District.

THE ROMANESQUE REVIVAL

Intertwined with the practice of Queen Anne architecture on New York's row houses was the application of the Romanesque Revival, a major contemporaneous trend in American architecture, whose historical inspiration was the eleventh-century Romanesque buildings of southern France and Spain. However, the Romanesque mode of the 1880s and 1890s was not simply a revival style relying on historical forms and details for its elements. As with the concurrent Queen Anne, a Romanesque Revival building employed asymmetrical massing, building materials of varying colors and textures, and vigorously applied ornament for visual and architectural excitement.

The *Brooklyn Daily Eagle*, praising the Herman Behr Mansion at Henry and Pierrepont Streets in Brooklyn Heights in 1890, heralded the Romanesque as emblematic of the "emergence of architecture out of existing commonplace into art," after the Queen Anne had led the way in "practical protest against the house of bandbox smugness and of packing box outline." To the ornamental strategies introduced by the Queen Anne, the Behr House's Romanesque added a fully rough-hewn first floor and robust turrets: "The effect is to combine something of feudal strength with the elegance of the Renaissance and the comfort of the American home."

In large part owing to the influence of its leading exponents, Henry Hobson Richardson and John Wellborn Root, the Romanesque Revival style fulfilled the taste of the era, and for nearly a decade was the foremost architectural mode in the United States. With its easily adapted forms, ornament, and plan, the Romanesque Revival style was suited for buildings as varied as city row houses and mansions, high-rise office buildings, warehouses, prisons, and railroad stations. Besides the heavy stonework and massive arches, the Romanesque building evoked a comforting sense of solidity and pastness.

The style's massive scale and austere ornament, which favored squat, monumental buildings, was difficult to design with grace within the confines of the tall and narrow row house facade. Its most successful application as a pure style was in rows of four or five houses designed as an ensemble. Together, such small rows could give the appearance of the weighty mass of a single building rather than separate houses. More typically, the Romanesque was combined in Picturesque fashion with the Queen Anne or other eclectic details on the same facade. "One may find Romanesque features in countless houses that cannot be described as examples of Romanesque," wrote Montgomery Schuyler. "[T]here are comparatively few houses which an archaeologist would allow to have been designed in the Provençal Romanesque."

The chief form of the Romanesque Revival style was the round arch at doorways and windows. Though best suited to large openings, the round arch often appeared in a modified form in handsome round-top windows on the second or third floor of a row house. To set off the doorway or window from the row house front, the arch itself was often a different color or material from the rest of the facade.

On most Romanesque Revival row houses, combinations of limestone, brownstone, granite, and red, yellow, or brown brick replaced the brownstone front. In many row houses, large rough-hewn blocks of stone appeared at the basement wall, as trim in round-arch openings and for window lintels. Another common feature was a vigorous applied detail of spiky, intertwined leafwork known as Byzantine leafwork. The rough-hewn stone and Byzantine leafwork, in theory, enhanced the structural elements of a building and were not applied ornamental detail in the tradition of earlier styles. A properly designed building's "decorative system," wrote English historian and architect Edward Augustus Freeman in his treatise "Romanesque Architecture," which appeared in 1872, "should be such as in no way conceals or masks the construction, but makes the construction features themselves ornamental." Or, as the *Eagle* quipped in 1886: "Ornament your construction, instead of constructing your ornament."

In the 1880s and early 1890s, some architect-designed mansions and row houses in New York lacked such specifically Romanesque forms and details as large round arches and Byzantine leafwork but nonetheless were in the Romanesque style because of their materials, massive scale, and overall severity. The severe Romanesque design of 848 Fifth Avenue, wrote Montgomery Schuyler, "testifies to the architect's conviction, which is also that of a good many other people, that at present distinction in our domestic architecture can be attained in no other wise so surely as by extreme plainness." Although "the simple massing, the large unbroken wall spaces of rough granite, the severity of the treatment of the openings

Above: 880–888 Carroll Street, Park Slope, Brooklyn (1894). Park Slope Historic District.

Right: Carroll Street, about 1893, north side, between Eighth Avenue and Prospect Park West, Park Slope, Brooklyn. Romanesque Revival house on an eclectic block in development. The round arch, here seen at the entrance, was one of the most common features of the Romanesque Revival style. Many houses on Carroll Street were commissioned by owners, designed by architects, and built singly. The typical rows of speculative construction are seen in the background on President Street.

237-9

Above: Romanesque Revival cornice, Dean Street, Crown Heights, Brooklyn. Squat columns, here appearing to be compressed by the sheer weight of the building, are a common Romanesque Revival decorative element, even when rendered in the lightweight pressed tin used for most row house cornices. Crown Heights North Historic District.

Right: Romanesque Revival Byzantine carved leafwork in limestone, 1249 Dean Street, Crown Heights, Brooklyn (1892). Crown Heights North Historic District.

Opposite: Triple-width mansion in Romanesque Revival fantasia, 237 Hancock Street, Bedford-Stuyvesant, Brooklyn (1890). At a distance, this giant house appears to be three row houses and blends seamlessly into the rest of the block. Bedford Historic District.

Romanesque Revival and Renaissance Revival ornament on facades of varying stone, 297–303 Park Place, Prospect Heights, Brooklyn (1890s). These blocks feature charming variations in size of the same basic row house form. Prospect Heights Historic District.

and the very sparing use of ornament give the house individuality and character," Schuyler wondered "whether this character is domestic."

With the death of Richardson in 1886 and Root in 1891, the Romanesque Revival style lost its two most sophisticated proponents, and the halt of building with the Panic of 1893 and the ensuing very deep depression largely condemned the style to its demise for New York row houses, though Romanesque details still appeared on some Brooklyn house rows through the 1890s.

ROW HOUSE INTERIORS AND TECHNOLOGY IN THE 1870s AND 1880s

Despite the convulsions in style, the floor plan and mechanical equipment of a New York row house in the 1870s and 1880s remained largely unchanged from previous decades. The first floor had a long, narrow front parlor and a back parlor across the full width of the house, which was typically used as a dining room. Deeper houses had an additional interior room between the front parlor and the rear dining room, often referred to on plans as a music room or a stair hall, a variation on the triple-parlor configuration pioneered in Italianate houses in the 1850s. At the rear of the house there was often a handsomely appointed butler's pantry with a dumbwaiter located near the stairway to the basement. In the basement, the front room was an informal dining room and the back room, overlooking the garden, a kitchen and laundry, though the front room also served as billiard room in the grandest houses. Family bedrooms, servants' rooms, and several bathrooms filled the two or three upper floors of the house.

The interior design of houses shifted toward decorative ideals of relative simplicity and coherency in forms and materials, though still within a very wide range of potential eclectic styles. The fashionable black walnut and dark red mahogany of the Civil War era gave way to lighter woods. More than one critic welcomed the demise of "the dark age of house decoration"—echoed when Charles Wyllys Elliott asked in his 1876 *Book of American Interiors* "whether the goodness and cheapness of black walnut has not led us into making our rooms too sombre and heavy for cheerful life." The newly fashionable woods of the 1870s and 1880s were mahogany, quartered oak, bird's-eye and plain maple, cherry, tulip, sycamore, hazel, ash, birch, and poplar. These woods, polished to show a natural finish, dominated the front parlor and back dining room—in mantels, doorways, pier-mirror frames, built-in sideboards and china closets, and wainscoting or paneling. Another handsome decorative innovation of the 1870s was parquet flooring, which when partly covered with rugs complemented the fine woodwork and the relative simplicity of parlors and dining rooms.

Unlike earlier eras, where the record of the original configuration, mechanical equipment, and decoration of houses must be gleaned from newspaper advertisements, contemporaneous accounts, and the physical (often altered) records of the houses themselves, numerous prospectuses for houses from the 1870s and 1880s survive describing houses and their interiors in elaborate detail. Indeed, in contrast to the comparatively

293 and 295 Park Place, Prospect Heights, Brooklyn (1890s). A pleasant contrast in which two similar house rows of varying sizes meet. Prospect Heights Historic District.

293

primitive speculation and marketing of the first half of the nineteenth century, these brochures show a sophisticated real estate industry.

One prospectus from 1879, "How to Build Good Houses," by architect-builders Duggin & Crossman, touted itself as a template for the construction of the "first-class home." These builders—whom the *Real Estate Record and Guide* elsewhere had esteemed the greatest architect-builders in the city—boasted of having constructed 140 houses in Manhattan, most of them between Fifth and Park Avenues from Thirty-Fourth to Fiftieth Street. They described the baseline decoration and conveniences of their houses in a list:

> All of the Houses have the Bath Rooms fitted up with hard wood.
>
> Hinges and Fittings to those portions trimmed with hard wood, are of Bronze Metal ...
>
> Houses are heated by Patent Moist Warm-air Wrought Iron Furnaces
>
> All of the Fireplaces on the First Floor are arranged to burn either wood or coal, and are fitted up with Fancy Tiled Hearths, Ornamented Iron Backs, Brass Frame and Fender, and Basket Grates.
>
> All of the Houses have every possible convenience, such as:
>
> Bedroom Doors have night bolts as well as locks.
>
> Hot-air Registers up to the Fourth floor.
>
> Speaking tubes on each floor, leading to the Kitchen; also a speaking tube from Basement entrance to the Kitchen.
>
> Linen Closet and Housemaid's Sink and Closet in each house.
>
> Coal Bins fitted up in Cellars.
>
> Water Closet seats hinged, and leaded underneath.

The brochure described a seven-house development located at the southeast corner of Thirty-Ninth Street and Park Avenue, with the houses ranging in price from $26,000 to $34,000, all of them four-story, high-stoop brownstone fronts, save for the corner house, which was of "Philadelphia Brick, with Brownstone trimmings," boasting "Octagon fronts on the street and avenue." Inside,

> All of the Houses have Basement, First and Second floors finished in hard woods, many of them polished, other finished with a dead gloss.
>
> Hardwood Mantels on First and Second floors. Marble Mantels on the Third floor.
>
> These houses have large and elegant Consol Mirrors in Parlors and Mirrors and Frames over the Mantel in the Dining-rooms. Also Plate-glass Mirrors on the Second Story.

The exact same list of finishes and conveniences were published in another prospectus for eight far more expensive houses by the same builders at the more fashionable location of Madison Avenue at Forty-Seventh and Forty-Eighth Streets, indicating the underlying uniformity in speculative construction across price points, even as builders attempted to distinguish house exteriors as more individualistic than those of the decades before.

Another prospectus from 1880 published by the builder William Noble described "Nine Elegant Residences" under construction with a "Front on Central Park, West" between Eighty-Fourth and Eighty-Fifth Streets. This extensive guide is a wordy record, accompanied by line drawings, of the interior details of the highest-end speculative construction in the city on the West Side. The copy next to the lavish illustration suggested that little additional interior decoration would be needed with such a grand finished state delivered to a buyer: "It requires no great elasticity of the imagination to picture the magnificence this suite will have when decorated and fitted with rich hangings at the openings, with a long line of sparkling chandeliers, whose brilliancy is doubly enhanced by the mantel mirrors in every room. The loftiness of the ceilings give dignity and roominess to the whole." Notably, the description of sumptuous appointments was not limited to the parlors, but to all the rooms of the house, including the bathrooms, which received special emphasis. Each bedroom chamber in the house had "its own toilet-room," in which there were "wardrobes, dressing-cases, closets and set basin. . . . The plumbing is all exposed to view, the floor under the basin being of marble, and the walls at back and ends faced up with English tile. . . . Over the basin in connection with the dressing-case is a large beveled-edge French plate mirror."

Though these prospectuses were for high-class houses in Manhattan, the same principles of interior decoration and the collection of modern conveniences were common in less lavish homes

in Brooklyn. The *Eagle* regularly featured descriptions of newly decorated interiors—both in new houses in new neighborhoods, and redecorations of existing homes in the latest styles. In 1888, the paper visited a three-story brownstone at 85 Hancock Street in the Stuyvesant district, with a "drawing room" in "Louis XVI style" and an adjoining room "Moorish in conception." Upstairs rooms included one "in the Japanese style with wood trimmings of maple" and a third-story space altered to serve as a "smoking room" with Gothic arches "supported by antique columns." Throughout were wall coverings of paper, silk, and tapestry variously treated in blue, "electric green and silver," and details of "peach blossoms."

In 1889, the *Eagle* featured remodeled interiors of older houses in Brooklyn Heights "modernized by artistic decorators," many with wallpapers or paint in colors ranging from light cream, buff, or robin's-egg blue to "terra cotta" or "a dark Pompeiian red." Plasterwork details were accented by gold leaf, "bronze effects," or otherwise "metallized." Woods were often ash, tulipwood, or cherry, though a library "in the Tudor style" might have features in "black oak" distinct from lighter woodwork in other rooms.

Romanesque Revival stone details, 264 Prospect Place, Brooklyn (1892). Prospect Heights Historic District.

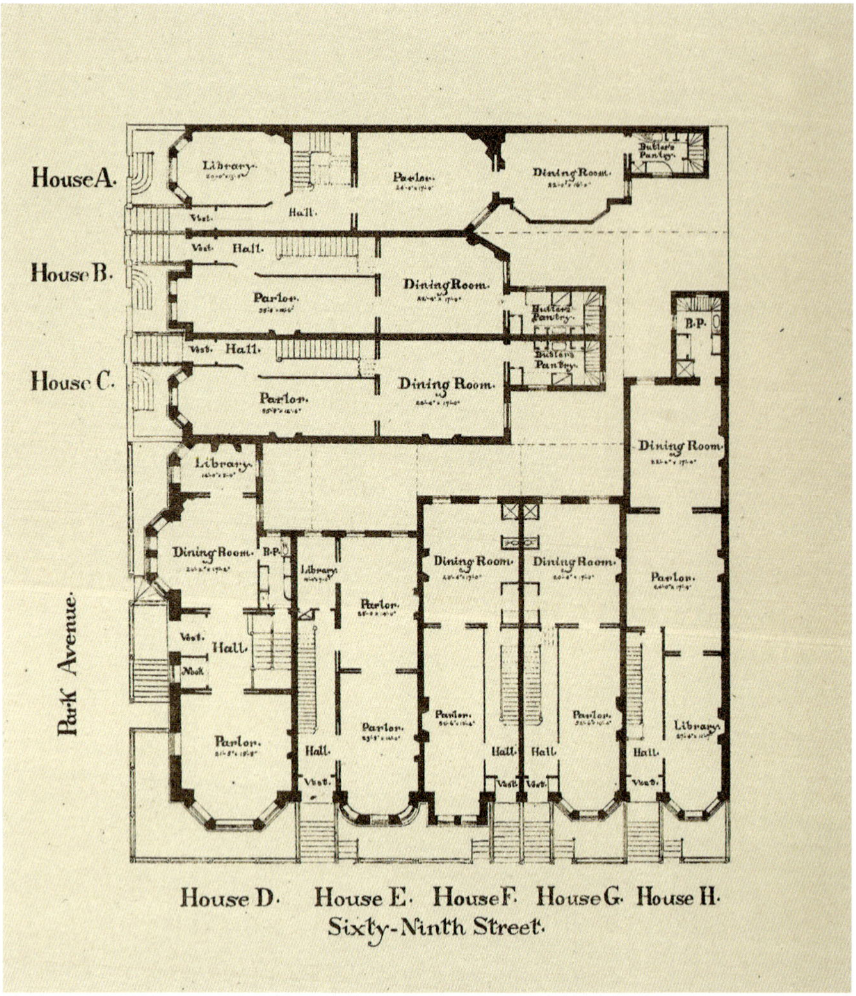

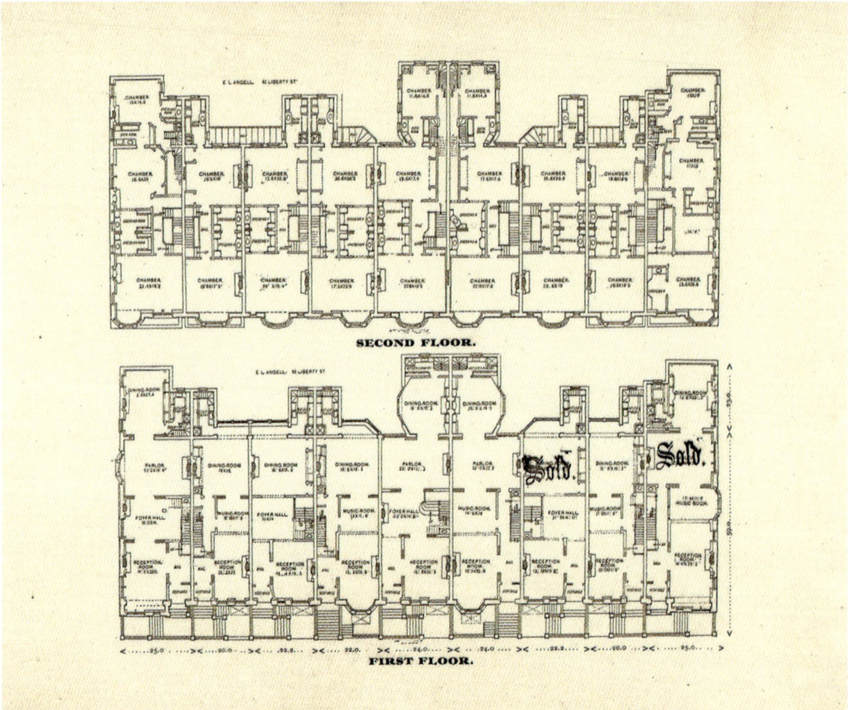

Above left: Floor plans, Park Avenue and East Sixty-Ninth Street, architects Lamb & Wheeler (1878–82). The eight houses grouped together show the overwhelming lot coverage possible in a corner location.

Left: First- and second-floor plans from the marketing brochure, "Description with illustrations of nine elegant residences fronting on Central Park, West, bet. 84th and 85th Sts., New York City," architect E. L. Angell, builder William Noble (1888). The grandest houses at the center and the flanks of the row are four rooms deep, covering nearly the entire building lot. Note the variation in configuration of the stoops and internal stairs.

Opposite: Foyer looking into parlor, rendering from "Description with illustrations of nine elegant residences fronting on Central Park, West, bet. 84th and 85th Sts., New York City" (1888).

FOYER HALL LOOKING INTO PARLOR IN HOUSE No. 1.

Above left: Second-floor interior renderings from "Description with illustrations of nine elegant residences fronting on Central Park, West, bet. 84th and 85th Sts., New York City" (1888). The brochure boasted that each bedroom chamber had "its own toilet-room," in which there were "wardrobes, dressing-cases, closets and set basin," shown here in elegant detail for prospective buyers.

Opposite: Hall in a house on Montgomery Place, Brooklyn, photographed about 1893.

Above: Dining room in a house on Montgomery Place, Brooklyn, photographed about 1893.

Left: Stairway from parlor, Decatur Street, Bedford-Stuyvesant, Brooklyn.

Opposite, top: Looking toward front parlor from rear parlor, Decatur Street, Bedford-Stuyvesant, Brooklyn. Decorative screens separating parlors were common features in late nineteenth-century row houses.

Opposite, bottom: Rear parlor and mantel, Decatur Street, Bedford-Stuyvesant, Brooklyn.

Following pages: Parlors, Decatur Street, Bedford-Stuyvesant, Brooklyn.

ELEMENTS
OF

Opposite: Mantel and overmantel mirror, 1190 Dean Street, Crown Heights, Brooklyn.

Right: Door details, 1190 Dean Street, Crown Heights, Brooklyn.

Following pages:
Rear extension from rear parlor, Decatur Street, Bedford-Stuyvesant, Brooklyn.

Closet passageway, second floor, Decatur Street, Bedford-Stuyvesant, Brooklyn.

Above: Kitchen, Decatur Street, Bedford-Stuyvesant, Brooklyn.

Opposite: Kitchen dining nook, Decatur Street, Bedford-Stuyvesant, Brooklyn.

Following pages:
Top: Neo-Grec houses, 241–251 East Seventy-Second Street, photographed about 1920. The East Side streets between Madison and Third Avenues were heavily built up with row houses by the early 1880s. These houses were originally home to prosperous middle-class families. Several houses in the row survive, now flanked by tall apartment buildings.

Bottom left: 19 East Ninety-Second Street (1890s), photographed in 1920. While architect-designed mansions for the very richest New Yorkers lined Fifth Avenue across from Central Park, speculatively built row houses were constructed on side streets just east of the park for the merely wealthy.

Bottom right: West 121st Street, photographed about 1891, south side between Lenox and Seventh Avenues. Houses combining Romanesque Revival and Neoclassical elements.

THE EAST SIDE AND HARLEM

During the 1850s and 1860s, the East Side of Manhattan was a far different setting from today's district of elegant apartment buildings and town houses. In 1867 George Templeton Strong described Madison Avenue in the Forties and Fifties as "a rough and ragged track . . . hardly a thoroughfare" but "rich in mudholes, goats, pigs, geese." Huge outcroppings of rocks, bare hills, occasional frame dwellings and villas, piles of trash, and decrepit shanties of the poor marked much of the East Side at the time of the Civil War.

Fifth and Madison Avenues and the adjacent side streets north of Forty-Second Street did feature speculatively built houses and mansions similar to those in Murray Hill, but on Park Avenue, factories, saloons, and seedy tenements overlooked the railroad tracks leading into Grand Central Station. Fashionable New Yorkers raced their fine horses up and down the gentle hills of muddy Third Avenue, which was then "the exercise and trial ground of all the fast trotters and pacers in the city," and frequented the taverns and blacksmiths' shops along the way, according to *Fraser's* magazine in 1850. The foot of Forty-Second Street, at the East River, was Dutch Hill, "a droll-looking hamlet" of shanties teeming with garbage, dirty and poorly clothed children, dogs, and pigs. Farther north, in the East Sixties, summer houses, vanishing patches of onetime forest, and beer gardens lined the East River.

During the post–Civil War building boom, city growth crossed Forty-Second Street, and fine brownstone fronts and modest brick-front row houses began to fill lots in the East Forties, Fifties, and Sixties. Palatial brownstone-front row houses and mansions soon lined Fifth Avenue from Forty-Second Street to the foot of Central Park. Above Fifty-Ninth Street, wrote *Appleton's* magazine in 1869, "the Avenue is so far very little built up; but the lots are held at extravagantly high prices, and it cannot be doubted that ere long all this portion of the street, overlooking Central Park, will be built up with a succession of elegant villas and mansions." Prosperous middle-class families soon settled in row houses along the side streets as far east as Third Avenue. The *Times* in 1878 reported that "the greatest activity in the building line is found to prevail in a line lying between Fourth and Fifth Avenues, above Forty-second and below Fifty-ninth Street, although there are several important enterprises under way along this same line still further north."

Few one-family dwelling houses were built east of Third Avenue, and these streets were soon lined with tenements, factories, shops, and carriage houses. Some respectable row houses were built on the quiet side streets off the East River from the Forties to the Eighties. "Beekman Place, on the East River," wrote Strong in 1871, "is unlike any other part of the city and dimly suggests Brooklyn Heights. Its brownstone houses look very reputable but are separated from civilization by a vast tract of tenement rookeries and whiskey mills, and streets that absolutely crawl with poor little slatternly pretty children."

The New York and Harlem Railroad had provided a connection between the East Side and the built-up areas of Lower Manhattan since the 1830s, but it was the opening of the Second Avenue elevated train in 1878 and the Third Avenue line in 1879 from downtown to Harlem that encouraged a surge in building activity there. In 1881, the *New-York Times* observed, "So far, the growth of the City above Fifty-ninth-street has been entirely on the East Side, where it follows the route of the horse and elevated railroads. Madison-avenue is already lined with costly dwellings as far as Seventy-ninth-street." In the 1880s and 1890s, builders filled up the side streets with dwellings in the Seventies, Eighties, and Nineties, generally adhering to the social patterns to the south in the Forties and Fifties during the 1860s. Between Madison and Third Avenues, speculative builders erected rows of dwellings for prosperous middle-class families. In contrast, by the 1880s the blocks from Third Avenue to the East River were "an almost unbroken series of tenements . . . for the full five miles above Fourteenth Street."

On Fifth Avenue and adjacent side streets in the Forties and Fifties, "[O]ur millionaires are vieing [*sic*] with each other in the erection of private dwellings," wrote *The Builder and the Woodworker* in 1881. "These new palaces surpass in comfort and elegance anything we have yet seen in this city. Their massive and fortress-like foundations give token of buildings which will be not only ornaments to the finest part of the city but landmarks for the future." Nevertheless, just as the city's most affluent neighborhoods had gradually moved up Fifth Avenue from the Washington Square area, ahead of encroaching commercial development, the *New-York Times* warned in 1881, "Business has already made its way far up Fifth-avenue, and we

FOR SALE

Left: Row houses in the fields, about 1877. View of 53, 51, 49, vacant lots, and 31, 29, 27, and 25 West 133rd Street, between Fifth and Lenox Avenues, Harlem. A view of a nineteenth-century New York street only partly built up with row houses. Though such photographs are rare, this was, in fact, a common condition, since it sometimes took several years—or longer, when an economic panic intervened—for small sets of houses to coalesce into a uniform row.

Below: Sylvan Terrace, Manhattan (1882). Ten wood row houses line each side of Sylvan Terrace in a spectacular vista, terminating at the Morris-Jumel Mansion. Jumel Terrace Historic District.

have intelligent friends who think it a great mistake to spend much money upon dwellings anywhere below the Central Park."

Farther uptown, development began in earnest in Harlem in the 1880s. Long a target of land speculators, building lots finally began to be developed with house rows once transit improvements reached the streets directly north of Central Park. Building activity was clustered around Mount Morris Park, which had been laid out as Mount Morris Square long before, in 1839. The row houses built on the blocks immediately west of the park, especially the grand houses facing wide Lenox Avenue, are some of the handsomest constructed in Manhattan in the era, and were originally sold to prosperous upper-middle-class families seeking comparable houses at a lesser expense than those located farther downtown. Row house development crossed into the Bronx in 1886, when the Suburban Rapid Transit Company constructed a bridge over the Harlem River. Houses were built in Mott Haven through the turn of the twentieth century, though never in large numbers, including the charming Bertine Block on East 136th Street between Willis Avenue and Brown Place.

Farther west, in Harlem, on the Hamilton Heights, houses were also constructed beginning in the late 1880s when the Ninth Avenue elevated train was opened on the West Side. One of the most spectacular house rows of the eclectic period are the fifteen houses at 311–339 Convent Avenue completed in 1887–90 by builder Jacob D. Butler and architect Adolph Moak. Sitting on Convent Avenue's east side between 141st and 144th Streets, the Picturesque ensemble, with redbrick and brownstone clothes in various Flemish, Tudor, and Romanesque forms, has a varied roofline of stepped Dutch gables, slate pyramids, and turrets. The thirteen middle houses of the fifteen are configured in symmetry around the center house in an A-B-C-D-E-F-G-F-E-D-C-B-A pattern, but the diversity of styles in the ensemble belies the fact that there is any repetition at all. This charming district of houses became known as Sugar Hill when it became home to Harlem's prominent African American families in the 1930s.

THE WEST SIDE

The growth of the West Forties and Fifties below Central Park generally began in the 1850s and 1860s. "The work of clearing the rocks from the Sixth avenue, above 44th street, is rapidly progressing," *Leslie's* magazine observed in 1856. "A large number of buildings are going up in the vicinity of 47th, 48th, 49th, 51st, and other streets. The selection of the site for the Central Park has given an impetus to the work." Fine row houses were built along most blocks in the West Forties and Fifties, with the blocks generally growing more fashionable closer to Fifth Avenue. Unlike the East Side, however, row house construction on the West Side in the 1860s and 1870s did not go beyond Fifty-Ninth Street and into the blocks opposite Central Park. According to a later account, "On the West Side in 1868 there were not more than half a dozen modern houses."

When building activity in New York resumed in the late 1870s after the Panic of 1873 and the following depression, today's Upper West

Following pages
Top: West Seventy-Second Street, photographed about 1893, south side between Broadway and West End Avenue. Deliberate variation in a row designed by C. P. H. Gilbert.

Bottom: Eclectic stone fronts, 41–49 West Seventy-Fourth Street (1880s). On the Upper West Side, row houses constructed in the last decades of the nineteenth century took on heights over three times their width, a sign of high land costs, which forced speculative builders to cater to the wealthy upper middle class, some of whom were beginning to live in nearby apartment houses rather than row houses. Upper West Side/Central Park West Historic District.

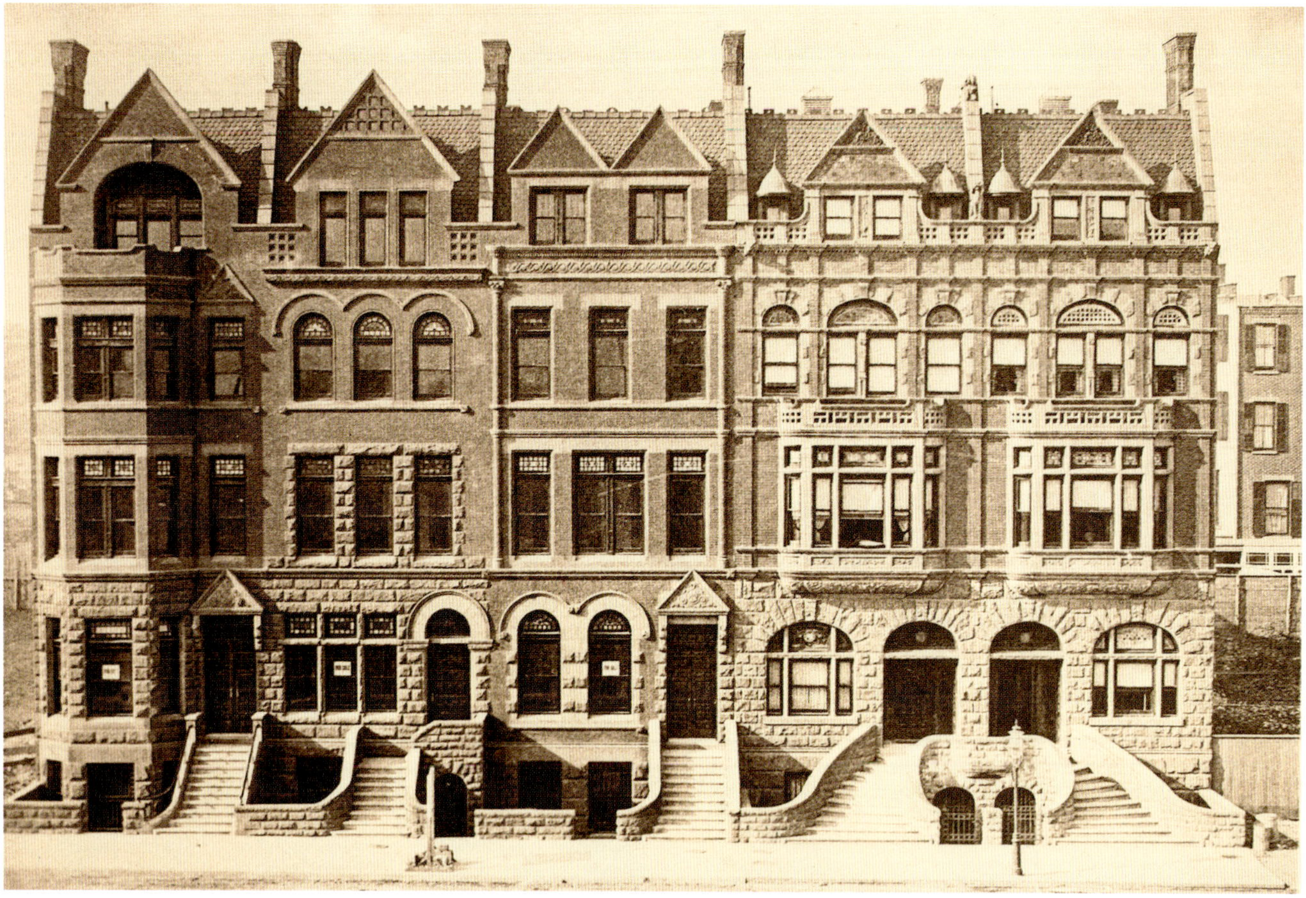

Side remained a barren, open land marked with occasional shanties, vegetable gardens, menacing rock outgrowths, lowly taverns, and decrepit country mansions. Indeed, the West Side's development was effectively nearly two decades behind that of comparable latitudes on the East Side, as it was far removed from the thrust of the city's northward growth along Fifth Avenue.

The foremost hindrance to the growth of the West Side, however, was the virtual absence of transportation to downtown Manhattan. Before 1870, the Eighth Avenue omnibus line only ran a single car from Fifty-Ninth Street to Eighty-Fourth Street at long intervals, which turned around and then returned south on the same track. With the completion of the elevated railway line along Ninth Avenue in 1880, now Columbus Avenue, building on the West Side finally began in earnest. The first developments of the early 1880s sprang up along Ninth Avenue at the elevated railway stops at Seventy-Second, Eighty-First, Ninety-Third, and 104th Streets and then along all of Ninth and Tenth Avenues and Seventy-Second Street.

Nevertheless, row house construction on the West Side was still slow in the early 1880s. Streets were either in terrible condition or had not yet been graded and opened, and the city's large speculative builders were busy erecting rows of houses on the East Side and in Harlem. New Yorkers also were uncertain of the West Side's future social composition. Would it become an area of tenements or working-class and middle-class row houses or the dwellings of well-to-do and rich New Yorkers?

The only assured patterns of development seemed to be tenements just north of Fifty-Ninth Street and fine mansions along Central Park West and newly laid-out Riverside Drive. The West Side, thought Montgomery Schuyler, echoing the sentiments of many other New Yorkers, had "offered an opportunity for a quarter of small houses"—none of which had been built in Manhattan for a half century—because "so much land was at once thrown open to settlement by the completion of the elevated railroad that its price was low enough to encourage speculative builders to provide for the wants of people of moderate means."

Others predicted the opposite. "There can be no question that this section must become in time the most exclusive part of the city," wrote one magazine in the 1880s. The wide avenues of the area and nearby Central and Riverside Parks contributed to the fashion and sanguine forecasts for the West Side. "The conclusion is inevitable" that the West Side "has been held in reserve until the time when the progress of wealth and refinement shall have attained that period of development when our citizens can appreciate and are ready to take advantage of the situation," Egbert Ludovicus Viele wrote in 1879. Viele, the famous civil engineer instrumental in the creation of Central Park and Prospect Park, boasted: "This entire region combines in its general aspect all that is magnificent in the leading capitals of Europe. In our Central Park we have the fine Prater of Vienna, in our grand boulevard [Broadway] the rival of the finest avenues of the gay capital of France, in our Riverside Avenue the equivalent of the Chiaia of Naples and the Corso of Rome, while the beautiful 'Unter den Linden,' of Berlin, and the finest portions of the West End of London are reproduced again and again." It was Viele's prediction that proved victorious. In the mid-1880s, New York's row house builders left the heavily built-up East Side for the more open and lower-priced West Side, and the West Side entered a decade of frantic building. "The west side of the city presents just now a scene of building activity such as was never before witnessed in that section, and which gives promise of the speedy disappearance of all the shanties in the neighborhood and the rapid population of this long neglected part of New York," reported the *Times* in 1886. "Streets are being graded, and thousands of carpenters and masons are engaged in rearing substantial dwellings where a year ago nothing was to be seen but market gardens or barren rocky fields."

By the turn of the twentieth century, the West Side, apart from some tenement districts, had largely become a well-to-do area of handsome town houses and mansions, as well as early apartment houses and apartment hotels. Mansions on spacious grounds and palatial row houses rose along Central Park West and Riverside Drive, which was completed in the 1890s. Riverside Drive, wrote one New Yorker at the turn of the century, "is universally acknowledged to be the most beautiful and picturesque [street] in the world. This dreamlike region [is] but little removed from the distracting noises of a busy section of the city."

West End Avenue, north of Seventy-Second Street, also became a fashionable residential avenue with "some of the most charming houses in New York." Broadway, which had been named the Boulevard

Above: Part of the eclectic Renaissance Revival row at 343–357 West End Avenue, Upper West Side, architects Lamb & Rich (1891). Though created by the hand of a single architecture firm for one developer, these houses were designed to appear as an accretion of individually built houses. This row is a rare survivor on West End Avenue, since rebuilt into the familiar tall elevator apartment houses of today. West End–Collegiate Historic District.

or the Western Boulevard until 1899, had a handsome grass and shrubbery-planted mall in the center and soon was lined with fine shops and apartment buildings. In keeping with the fashionable tone of the West Side, humble Ninth Avenue, north of Fifty-Ninth Street, was renamed Columbus Avenue in 1890, and Tenth Avenue, for similar reasons, was renamed Amsterdam Avenue.

"The houses that now characterize the West Side are without doubt the most interesting examples of domestic architecture that New York has to show," wrote Montgomery Schuyler in 1899. When the West Side's growth began in the early 1880s, the fashion for eclecticism on a single house and on a row of houses was at its peak, and this taste was represented more thoroughly on the West Side's houses than in any other area of Manhattan. Examples include the coherent row of twenty-seven Queen Anne houses on the north side of West Seventy-Third Street, between Central Park West and Columbus Avenue, built in 1883 and designed by Henry J. Hardenbergh of the Dakota Apartments and Plaza Hotel fame, and in the few surviving row houses remaining on West End Avenue. But the fashion for architectural individuality often led to excesses, and Montgomery Schuyler singled out several blocks on the West Side for "a clamoring restlessness all their own" which made the passerby "sea-sick."

Right: 145 West Eighty-First Street (1886). Upper West Side/Central Park West Historic District.

Slope, the renewed growth generally marched up the slope from Sixth Avenue toward Prospect Park, and from Flatbush Avenue and its omnibus line into the blocks to the south. The pleasant row houses of a prosperous middle class lined the side streets leading to the park, and palatial row houses and mansions rose along Eighth Avenue and Ninth Avenue, which overlooks the park and is now Prospect Park West. Park Slope, observed one New Yorker in the 1880s, is "a location unexcelled for beauty of situation, orderliness and cleanliness." An 1881 advertisement in the *Eagle* from the Wyckoff Brothers real estate firm touted "A Bird's Eye View of All the Prospect Park Lots For Sale" as available for view in the firm's office, allowing them "to give full information regarding present and prospective value of every lot of the park slope"—presumably the entire district was desirable.

Today, some of the finest late nineteenth-century row house architecture in New York survives in the area. Although the elevator apartment buildings replaced many of the mansions and their grounds along Prospect Park West and Eighth Avenue in the 1920s and 1930s, generally unaltered row houses in the Italianate, Neo-Grec, Queen Anne, Romanesque Revival, and Renaissance Revival styles stand along Park Slope's tree-lined streets. Sixth Avenue, for the seven or eight blocks off Flatbush Avenue, is one of the few streets in New York that retains a semblance of the scale and character of the city's handsome mid-nineteenth-century avenues. Here, the basement- and three-or-four-story-tall brownstone fronts in the Italianate or a faintly Neo-Grec style enjoy the proper scale of a wide avenue not found on the usual side street. Farther up the slope, Montgomery Place between Prospect Park West and Eighth Avenue displays all the architectural styles of New York row houses of the 1880s and 1890s on a single block. Despite its diversity, the street is the work of one hand, architect C. P. H. Gilbert, who completed the development scheme of builder Harvey Murdock.

Beginning in the 1870s and increasingly in the 1880s and 1890s, the other newly built well-to-do Brooklyn neighborhood was the expansive area today known as Bedford-Stuyvesant and Crown Heights. Costly row houses and occasional mansions rose on the streets north of Fulton Park and west of Brower Park. In 1873, the *Eagle* noted that the area—until recently one of farms—was being "marvelously developed" in two distinct classes: freestanding "villa residences" and more modest rows, mostly of brownstone, boasting "shower baths" and systems of speaking tubes and bells. In the 1890s, one magazine praised the "beautiful part of town" near Brower Park, in today's Crown Heights, "where New York, Brooklyn, and St. Mark's avenues pursue their ways between noble houses, decorating ample grounds. This is more modern, more beautiful, and is, perhaps, supported by greater wealth than the older beauty-spot of the town," Brooklyn Heights and the Hill.

The large amount of development in this vast area of eastern Brooklyn included significant numbers of houses more modest in scale, some "plain brownstone fronts," others aspiring to partake in the more current, eclectic fashions. In an 1885 survey of new construction, the *Eagle* described the house "most in favor in Brooklyn" as "the two story and high basement brown stone front cottage," occasionally with a mansard providing a third story. Two years later, describing the

Above: 1146–1150 Dean Street, Crown Heights, Brooklyn, architect George P. Chappell (1891). By the early 1890s, many of the more exuberant variations of the previous decade had started to fade for a more academic yet still freeform classicism. Crown Heights North Historic District.

Opposite: Renaissance Revival brownstones with triple windows, 275–279 Jefferson Avenue, Bedford-Stuyvesant, Brooklyn, architect George P. Chappell (1887). Renaissance forms began appearing up on brownstone-front houses in the eclectic 1880s before reaching a full flowering in the following decade. Bedford Historic District.

Above: Cornices, Park Place, Prospect Heights, Brooklyn. Prospect Heights Historic District.

Right: Stoop railings, 325 and 327 Park Place, Prospect Heights Historic District.

Opposite: Stoop railings, 264 Prospect Place, Prospect Heights, Brooklyn (1892). Prospect Heights Historic District.

Above: 246 Hancock Street, gable detail, Bedford-Stuyvesant, Brooklyn (1889). Bedford Historic District.

Right: 246–252 Hancock Street, Bedford-Stuyvesant, Brooklyn, architect Montrose Morris (1889). The masterful Morris composed a unified Queen Anne front out of four houses. The effect is almost of a Shingle-style mansion rendered in the more solid masonry of New York row houses. This is one of the most stunning house rows of the eclectic era. Bedford Historic District.

1369

emergence of an "elegant and opulent section" in Stuyvesant Heights, the *Eagle* found hope that mass taste was being "emancipated from the thralldom of the brown stone idea," with the use of pressed brick and iron-framed window bays. Even just novel facade designs, such as a ganged triple window with panes of ornamented glass instead of two punched openings on an upper floor, the *Eagle* opined, could lend more interest to a brownstone front.

By 1891, however, the *Eagle*'s observers were leery of undisciplined eclecticism in mass construction, suggesting that Brooklyn would soon have as many "turrets, towers, campaniles and cupolas . . . as a Moslem village has of minarets."

FROM PANIC TO PANIC

Another long, severe economic depression, initiated by the Panic of 1893, halted New York's building activity and with it the hothouse diversification of the city's residential architecture. As the nation's financial center, the effects of the collapse of credit across the country were greatly magnified locally, slumping New York real estate financing and building operations. In December 1893, a representative advertisement in the *Eagle* offered "Panic Prices" for a ten-room house to rent at $20 per month. In July 1894, the *Eagle* stated, "We have a number of people in Brooklyn who have invested in real estate in anticipation of considerable profit. The financial depression through [which] the country has just passed has to a very great extent defeated their desires."

Taken as a whole, the span between the Panic of 1873 and the Panic of 1893 saw the most diversity in style in row house architecture built at the greatest volume—indeed, perhaps no two decades had a wider impact on the single-family residential architecture of New York City as it is handed down to this day. In those twenty years, vast areas of the city were developed at the hands of a new class of builders and professional architects, deploying an unprecedented array of materials, industrial products, and stylistic options to create homes for a broad range of home-buying classes. The eventual revival of building following the 1893 downturn would see a turn to a more restrained style—and the end of the row house as the foremost engine of real estate development in New York.

1369 Dean Street, Crown Heights, Brooklyn, architect George P. Chappell (1892). Crown Heights North Historic District.

V

1893–1917

CLASSICISM AND THE DECLINE OF THE ROW HOUSE

In May 1893, the World's Columbian Exposition in Chicago opened, marking the four hundredth (plus one year) anniversary of the landing of Christopher Columbus in the New World. The centerpiece of the Exposition was the Court of Honor, the fabled "White City" of pavilions arrayed around waterways on the fairgrounds off Lake Michigan. Each of the fourteen buildings was designed by a celebrated American architect, among them New Yorkers Richard Morris Hunt, George B. Post, and the firm of McKim, Mead & White. With the sole exception of Louis Sullivan's polychrome Transportation Building, all were designed in a gleaming white Neoclassical style.

The White City was a stark contrast to the sooty chaos of the typical American city, and the uniform Beaux-Arts design an antithesis to the eclecticism of the past two decades of American architecture. The ensemble was seen by the millions of visitors to the exposition, and was reproduced endlessly in countless newspapers, magazines, and postcards. Though the buildings were made of plaster, not stone, and were only designed to survive the duration of the exposition, they had an impact far more measurable than any permanent building of the era. "The influence of the Exposition on architecture," stated architect Daniel Burnham, the fair's director of works, "will be to inspire a reversion to the pure ideal of the ancients."

The U.S. Congress had selected Chicago for the exposition over New York and other competing American cities. The choice rankled civic and business leaders in Manhattan, who worried that their city, long the premier metropolis of the United States, would be overtaken in population and standing by the Second City. "The world is impressed by bigness," wrote the *Real Estate Record and Guide* in 1894. "New York would undoubtedly lose a great deal in prestige the world over—and in actual dollars and cents, too—should Chicago or any other city on the continent count a larger population."

12–18 Jumel Terrace, Manhattan (1896). The World's Columbian Exposition in Chicago in 1893 popularized Beaux-Arts and Renaissance Revival architectural forms nationwide. These classical forms would predominate in New York row house styles for nearly three decades. Here, the traditional high-stoop row house is clothed with tasteful Renaissance ornament and, apart from the stoop, is rendered in limestone rather than the darker shades of brownstone or brick. Jumel Terrace Historic District.

Financial and real estate interests in Manhattan and Brooklyn pushed for the consolidation of the two cities and nearby counties into a greater metropolis. With Brooklyn drawing against the limits of its own water supply and thus needing access to Manhattan's water system for continued expansion, the effort gained traction, and in May 1896, New York's governor signed legislation consolidating Manhattan, Brooklyn, Queens, the Bronx, and Staten Island under a single metropolitan government. On January 1, 1898, Greater New York—dubbed the "Imperial City" by its longtime proponent, reformer Andrew Haswell Green—came into being, with a population of well over three million, second in the world only to London.

The consolidation of Greater New York was a self-evident milestone in the city's history. To mark the occasion, the editors of the *Real Estate Record and Builder's Guide* published a sweeping history of the city's real estate development from 1609 to the present, titled simply *A History of Real Estate, Building and Architecture in New York City*. The volume concentrated on the period "From the Close of The Civil War to Consolidation," underlining the primitive quasi wilderness of ungraded land and shanties that had existed only three decades earlier in what were now built-up portions of the city: "At the close of the Civil War the city's northern limit of building improvement was in the neighborhood of 42d street. Beyond that, streets were for the most part ungraded and unpaved. . . . Below 86th street the city contained, in 1865, 25,261 vacant lots. It was a city with a low sky-line. Square miles of territory were covered with houses of three and four stories." In the subsequent three decades, according to the volume, "the productive power of real estate" had been revolutionized by the technological advances of the "passenger elevator, rapid transit, and steel construction," all of which together increased the "earning capacity" in central locations by favoring vertical construction. For real estate interests, it was now clear that the primary force of development in Manhattan would be the redevelopment of existing, already built sites. Already, "comparatively little of the city" of 1865 "as it then was" remained—"except in the form of obsolete survival."

Throughout the nineteenth century, newspapers and the real estate press had referred to the "building line," a moving frontier of northward development on Manhattan Island. The first properties developed on the building line as it moved north from the Battery were always houses. That northern latitude was now of almost irrelevant interest to real estate speculation in Manhattan, as the true development frontier was now skyward. The long primacy of the row house in New York was waning.

POST-ECLECTIC CLASSICISM

Though row houses were increasingly a minor part of the speculative real estate industry in Manhattan by the 1890s, they remained bellwethers of architectural style. The slump in building that occurred in the years following the Panic of 1893 underlined the stylistic break with the preceding decades, with a backlash against eclecticism in full force. In 1897, *Architectural Record*, reflecting the prevailing sentiment, attacked

Opposite: Bow-fronted Renaissance Revival brownstone, 109 West 118th Street, Harlem (1890s). The bow front was a common measure to break the uniformity of the street wall in a row of otherwise similar houses. Mount Morris Park Historic District.

Following pages: Brownstone Renaissance Revival at 2–9 Mount Morris Park West, Harlem (1890s). Architects and builders in the 1890s sometimes used brownstone with surprising verve and imagination, after the material had fallen into disrepute in the previous two decades. Mount Morris Park Historic District.

109

5

552
550

548–552 First Street, Park Slope, Brooklyn (1909). Fine Renaissance Revival houses, among the final house rows to be constructed on the blocks near Prospect Park. Park Slope Historic District.

the eclectic era as little different from the preceding brownstone era in end result: the "speculative builder" had been "credibly informed that the buyers and even the tenants of dwelling houses demanded 'variety' in the fronts" but had satisfied the "new demand by instructing the same incompetent draughtsman whom he had before instructed to make the fronts all alike, to make them all different." Both had resulted in the same "awful" results, as evident to the author, in the majority of houses built on the West Side since the Civil War.

The pendulum of taste now swung back toward relative uniformity in residential building and favored the use of academically correct classical forms as ornament. The *Real Estate Record and Guide* in 1894 wrote that "we are on the threshold of an era of better construction, the improvement being in the line of gratifying the aesthetic demands of a more refined and cultivated sensibility."

The World's Columbian Exposition raised the Beaux-Arts style to national prominence and offered a logical escape from the confusion of post–Civil War styles. Indeed, so great was the attraction of the exposition's architecture that, for the next few decades, public and commercial buildings throughout the United States adopted the white-marble or limestone facade, classical columns and domes, and elaborate ornament of the Beaux-Arts style. In less complicated forms and often more plebeian materials, the same style could be found on much of the commercial and residential architecture in New York constructed over the next three decades.

The widespread adoption of the Renaissance Revival mode opened a schism in form and scale between the highest-end row houses in Manhattan—whether architect-designed or speculatively built—and the generic upper-middle-class and middle-class houses, which were now for the large part only financially feasible to construct in Brooklyn or far northern Manhattan. Since the very earliest days of residential construction in New York, there had typically been a continuum in appearance between modest row houses and the grandest houses of the same style, typically only a matter of scale. For example, the widest brownstone-front mansion on Madison Avenue in Murray Hill was little different on the exterior than a smaller, narrower house several blocks away on a side street. Montgomery Schuyler observed that through much of the nineteenth century in New York, "the mansion" had been "merely a more expensive expansion and elaboration of the small house."

Beginning in the 1890s however, the grandest houses often took on appearances wholly different from modest speculatively built typical houses, even if clothed in nominally similar classically inspired Renaissance forms. In part, this was due to the fact that houses for the very rich in Manhattan were now often designed as individual town houses rather than as rows. In 1901 *Architectural Record* described the "Architecture in the Billionaire District of New York City" and the Beaux-Arts ornament now popular on the mansions of the East Side, drawing a parallel with the brownstone era:

Opposite: 332–344 West Eighty-Eighth Street, photographed 1895. A resolutely continuous cornice line unites a symmetrical Renaissance Revival row.

Following pages: A Renaissance Revival palazzo formed by five houses, adjacent to a pair of Neo-Gothic houses, all designed by architect Clarence True, on Riverside Drive between West Seventy-First Street and Seventy-Second Street, 1893. Demolished.

[W]hen the centre of fashion was at Madison Square or below, a millionaire, or more likely a mere five hundred thousandaire, who had his house front profusely decorated with the carving of the period, was admonished that, if he would hang a statement of his bank-balance on the front of his house, it would serve the same purpose and he would keep the money. It is not intrinsically different now, when the cartouche and the palm and the festoon and the rope of bulbs have succeeded the "ornaments" of those old days, to become, two generations hence, equally ridiculous.

Such ostentatious exuberance, however in fact did not extend to the much more modest Renaissance Revival houses of the era, the majority of them constructed in Brooklyn. The row house construction boom there from the 1890s to World War I created huge numbers of nearly interchangeable, relatively generic Renaissance Revival houses, none of which had any ready analogue in the few high-end houses built in the same period in Manhattan. Indeed, with the extreme variations of the eclectic era now out of fashion, most builders of middle-class speculative row houses could hew to a stock house formula that had really changed little since the 1850s. Much as Neo-Grec and Queen Anne ornament had appeared on brownstone-front houses in the post–Civil War era without altering the basic house form established in the Italianate era, Renaissance classical forms now appeared as applied ornament on the otherwise largely similar row house fronts, whether in brownstone or the newly popular limestone.

In contrast to the brownstone era, the repetition on display in such modest house rows was celebrated by the real estate industry rather than decried for its monotony. In an 1896 column on so-called "Limited" architecture, the *Real Estate and Record and Guide* was candid on the need for such effectively ready-made architecture and style for most New York buildings, commercial or residential. "Architecture is consequently more than ever a process of duplication and the architect has to deal only with a well-defined repertoire," the *Record* opined. With the house buyer or renter—again, save for the richest clients—accepting that there was little truly distinguishing one building from another, the simple classical language of Renaissance forms allowed for a baseline decoration that perhaps was not even truly a style as had been previously understood. The *Record* wrote: "Originality of any kind is superfluous. A limited number of stereotyped forms is all that the public expectation requires."

THE RENAISSANCE REVIVAL

Though the 1893 World's Columbian Exposition later served as a convenient historical marker for mature classical revival styles, the Renaissance Revival had, in fact, first appeared during the chaotic architectural scene of the 1880s. Classically inspired motifs such as wreaths, garlands, and pilasters decorated otherwise nominally Romanesque Revival and Queen Anne row houses. "A change is rapidly taking place in the style of building and decorating," wrote *The Builder and the Woodworker* in 1884. The "Eastlake and the so-called Queen Anne have each had their day, and we are now turning to the Renaissance for fresh inspiration."

The first New York dwellings in a coherent Renaissance style were the Villard Houses (1883–86) on Madison Avenue between Fiftieth and Fifty-First Streets, designed by McKim, Mead & White. The Villard Houses carried out the Renaissance style with a symmetrical plan, low roof, smooth-cut stone set off by quoins at the corners, and classical window treatment. The McKim, Mead & White design originally called for a light-colored stone, but Henry Villard specified traditional brownstone for the facade. "The external treatment is an Italian Renaissance fashion," wrote architectural critic Mariana Griswold Van Rensselaer in 1886 about the Villard Houses. "The effect is very quiet, a little cold, perhaps a little tame; but it is extremely refined."

Other critics pointed to Renaissance architectural language as appropriate for the buoyant economic and technological achievement of the era. The sixteenth-century "Renaissance was essentially optimistic, cheerful, gay in all its conceptions, and contrasted markedly with the ages preceding that were mystic and sombre, and full of weirdness and dim religious obscurities," wrote the *American Architect and Building News* in 1890. "Is not after all the Renaissance much more in keeping with our civilization of today which is sanguine and self-satisfied to an extraordinary degree, convinced of its own advance beyond achievement of any preceding age?"

By the mid-1890s, New York row houses fully embraced the Renaissance Revival style, which ranged from academically correct to wilder creations recalling the architectural fantasies of the eclectic era if with a more consistent vocabulary. Though grouped under the general label of the Renaissance Revival style, these houses took inspiration and much form and ornament from many sources—Roman, the Beaux-Arts, Italian Renaissance, French Renaissance, French Classic, and German Renaissance, among others. The Renaissance Revival–style dwelling relied upon applied detail for its stylistic impact, with the most popular motifs being wreaths, baskets of fruit, garlands of flowers and leaves tied with ribbons at the ends, and numerous foliate forms. The fluted pilaster was another common applied motif and often appeared in the front doorway enframement.

Many houses returned to the familiar brownstone, which remained the "most suitable material for domestic architecture," as the *Real Estate Record and Guide* wrote in 1894, praising a group of bow-front brownstone dwellings at 3 to 11 West Seventy-Fifth Street. The houses were "of that more refined class of modern renaissance which imitates the French and Italian art more closely." They were "very gratifying specimens of the modern brownstone house; not the old-fashioned brownstone front made up of thin slabs cut to get the most out of the block, but the brownstone front of to-day—made up massively, relieved by carving and set scientifically." Indeed, the newspaper wrote, that like "a black silk, Connecticut brownstone never goes out of style."

181–189 Maple Street, Prospect Lefferts Gardens, Brooklyn (1908–9). Limestone- and brownstone-front Renaissance Revival houses with either curved or octagon-front bay windows. Prospect Lefferts Gardens Historic District.

However, the Renaissance Revival–style row house often used limestone or limestone and yellow brick together, a sharp break with the darker materials previously popular in residential design. A full limestone front was also often used next to a full brownstone front within the same house row, providing a variation between otherwise identical house designs.

Opposite: Renaissance Revival detail, 209 Midwood Street, Prospect Lefferts Gardens, Brooklyn (1910). Prospect Lefferts Gardens Historic District.

Right: 255 Fenimore Street, Prospect Lefferts Gardens, Brooklyn (1907). Prospect Lefferts Gardens Historic District.

Perhaps the greatest houses in the Renaissance Revival mode are the King Model Houses in Harlem, which incorporated 158 row houses on four blockfronts on West 138th and 139th Streets between Seventh and Eighth Avenues, completed in 1891. Developer D. H. King Jr. employed three architectural firms—James Brown Lord; Bruce Price & Clarence S. Luce; and McKim, Mead & White—to design three different uniform blockfronts, with Price's design repeated on the north side of 138th and south side of 139th Street. The McKim, Mead & White row, on the north side of 139th Street, adapted the Renaissance palazzo form to the entire row house blockfront in spectacular form. In 1919, following the rest of Harlem, the houses were opened to black residents and became known as Striver's Row and as the most desirable blocks for the city's African American elite.

The wide vocabulary of potential Renaissance-inspired classical architectural references carried over to house interiors. Herbert Croly, writing on "The Contemporary New York Residence" in *Architectural Record*, in 1902 stated that "few general statements" could be made about the interior decoration of the era's upper-class houses, architect-designed or speculatively built. Interior decoration was in a "much more transitional state even than that of exterior design: and it is to be hoped in the end some specific forms, adapted to local conditions, will be evolved out of the present chaos of borrowing and imitation." Among the rich, the "current taste" was "at present running strongly in the direction of the use of definite French and Italian styles, and the use wherever possible, of old furniture and tapestries."

Indeed, where exterior design relied on careful academic re-creation of elements of French and Italian design, interior design for the wealthy relied on the original artifacts themselves, purchased from Europe, not only "old fabrics and wood work" but also major building elements like "columns, mantel pieces, floors, ceilings." Croly quipped that American designers would shortly need to step up, as "Europe will have parted with all its relics of domestic life" from American plunder. There was even less coherency in the interiors of speculative construction. Croly observed, "Even the speculative builders make allowance for individuality of taste in such matters by having the drawing-room, dining-room and library undecorated, until a purchaser is found and his wife consulted."

The most remarkable aspect of the Renaissance Revival was its longevity. Architectural critic Montgomery Schuyler was skeptical of the potential of its long-term appeal, writing in 1898 that an "observer who has lived through two or three architectural phases finds it difficult to believe that the present phase is destined to more permanency than its predecessors," but his prediction would be proven wrong. In New York, the Renaissance Revival was the de facto standard style, remaining popular for three decades stretching from the 1890s to the 1910s. The *Record and Guide* in 1896 correctly predicted that the "public taste, after much restlessness and long circulation among the 'styles,' has apparently settled down to a permanent acceptance of Renaissance forms."

Typical Neoclassical interior details of the parlor floor of the houses at 35–57 West Eighty-Eighth Street, photographed 1895. The exteriors of the row were Renaissance Revival in style but varied with Gothic and Romanesque details.

THE COLONIAL REVIVAL

In the 1890s, architects in New York looked to the Georgian and Federal styles of the eighteenth and early nineteenth centuries for the design of houses. The style came to be known as the Colonial Revival, a misleading name, since many of the buildings whose inspiration was taken for the style dated from after American independence. The most optimistic observers hoped that the adoption of early American forms would blossom into a new, wholly American national style.

Domestic observers had not always admired the simple and small buildings of early American architecture. In the 1840s, Louisa Caroline Tuthill scorned New England's eighteenth-century farmhouses in her *History of Architecture*. "Happily they were all of such perishable materials that they will not much longer remain to annoy travelers in search of the picturesque through the villages of New England." By the end of the nineteenth century, tastes had changed, especially against the backdrop of successive revival styles based on European rather than American antecedents. "All our 'styles' have failed of real currency because they have been remote from our vernacular building language," wrote Montgomery Schuyler in 1898, attacking the wholesale importation of foreign styles, which had ignored American traditions.

The Colonial Revival style first appeared on a popular level during the Centennial Exhibition of 1876 at Philadelphia, which focused national attention on all aspects of the nation's eighteenth-century past. After looking to distant times and places for architectural inspiration throughout the nineteenth century, American architects began to admire the restrained and thoroughly American city and country dwellings of the late eighteenth and early nineteenth centuries. Architect H. Hudson Holly in 1877 asked, "Would it not be well for us to consider if there is nothing in our country which might contain the germ of an American style of architecture, and if so, should it not be found and brought to light?" In this vein, Edith Wharton's novella *Summer* depicts an architect of the era gathering sketches of "Colonial houses" in New England for a publication. Holly wrote the study of "primitive buildings" of the American past would ensure that "the second century of the Republic would not result in the "feeble copy of foreign styles of questionable fitness and in little sympathy with our institutions, but something distinctly American."

One of the first vaguely Colonial Revival houses in New York was the Hugh J. Jewett residence (ca. 1879–80) at 289 Madison Avenue, designed by architect G. E. Harney. The Jewett House included such distinctly colonial features as a redbrick front, a bow window such as those on New York's West Sixteenth Street and Boston's Beacon Street, and a heavily molded late Federal doorway that had once been so prominent on Bond Street and St. Mark's Place. Despite these Federal details, the Jewett house revealed its late nineteenth-century origin in its plate-glass windows and such rich details as inset Adamesque panels beneath the windows, heavy stringcourses, and marble rather than brownstone trim. The *American Architect and Building News* described the Jewett House as "an exact reproduction" of the Federal-style dwelling with a "most characteristic doorway of old New York." However, another architect in the eclectic 1880s believed that "the

Colonial Revival/Neo-Federal house, 109 Willow Street, architect John Petit (1905), Brooklyn Heights. At the turn of the twentieth century, many architect-designed houses looked backward to the houses of the early nineteenth century for design inspiration. Brooklyn Heights Historic District.

effect of the copy . . . is at best simply void of offense" and advised Harney to return to the creative designs fashionable at the time.

The foremost features of the Colonial Revival row house were a redbrick front and marble or limestone doorway and window trim. The front doorway, whether in the high stoop or American basement (see below) arrangement, had sidelight windows with an elaborate leaded pattern similar to those found on fine Federal dwellings of the early nineteenth century. Colonial Revival dwellings also employed the elaborate Federal fanlight doorway of the 1820s and generally ignored simpler rectangular toplight doorways. In general, the street-front forms and ornament in these row houses often were more elaborate or more intricate in composition than any early nineteenth-century Federal dwelling.

As row house construction slowed to a halt in Manhattan in the early twentieth century, it was ironic that New York's rich and prominent families still willing to occupy houses rather than apartments looked to Federal "second-rate, genteel houses" of the 1820s for the inspiration and design of their sumptuous town houses. Indeed, architects were often unable to transplant the charm and character of the simple and small-scale, century-old dwellings to large, costly town houses. Montgomery Schuyler wrote that the "modern instance mainly fails to carry out the spirit of the older work," pejoratively naming the style "Old New York" when used on new mansions on the East Side.

THE AMERICAN AND ENGLISH BASEMENT CONFIGURATIONS

In the 1890s, the long reign of the high-stoop house and its traditional plan came to an end for upper-class houses in Manhattan. Under the new configuration, known as the American front or American basement plan, the entrance doorway appeared in the center of the building, one or two steps above the sidewalk. This entrance opened into a large reception room, which occupied nearly the full width of the house. A large stairway, with several dramatic landings and turns in direction, occupied the center of the house in place of the traditional long stairway at the side. With the stair at the center, the parlors and bedrooms on the upper floors could occupy the house's full width, allowing more generous (and generously lit) interior spaces even with relatively narrow building lots. A similar plan, the English basement, featured an entrance at the side of the house rather than at the center, echoing the Anglo-Italianate configuration of the mid-nineteenth century.

"The high stoop house," wrote architect Russell Sturgis in 1893, "is the survival of early and simpler habits, and should have been abandoned long ago for all city dwellings." If "thronged receptions and dancing-parties are to be made as agreeable as their nature allows," wrote Sturgis, "the houses must really be planned with some regard to their requirements." The reception room, sweeping stairway, and large parlors of American basement houses lent themselves to the extravagant lifestyle of rich New York families at the turn of the twentieth century.

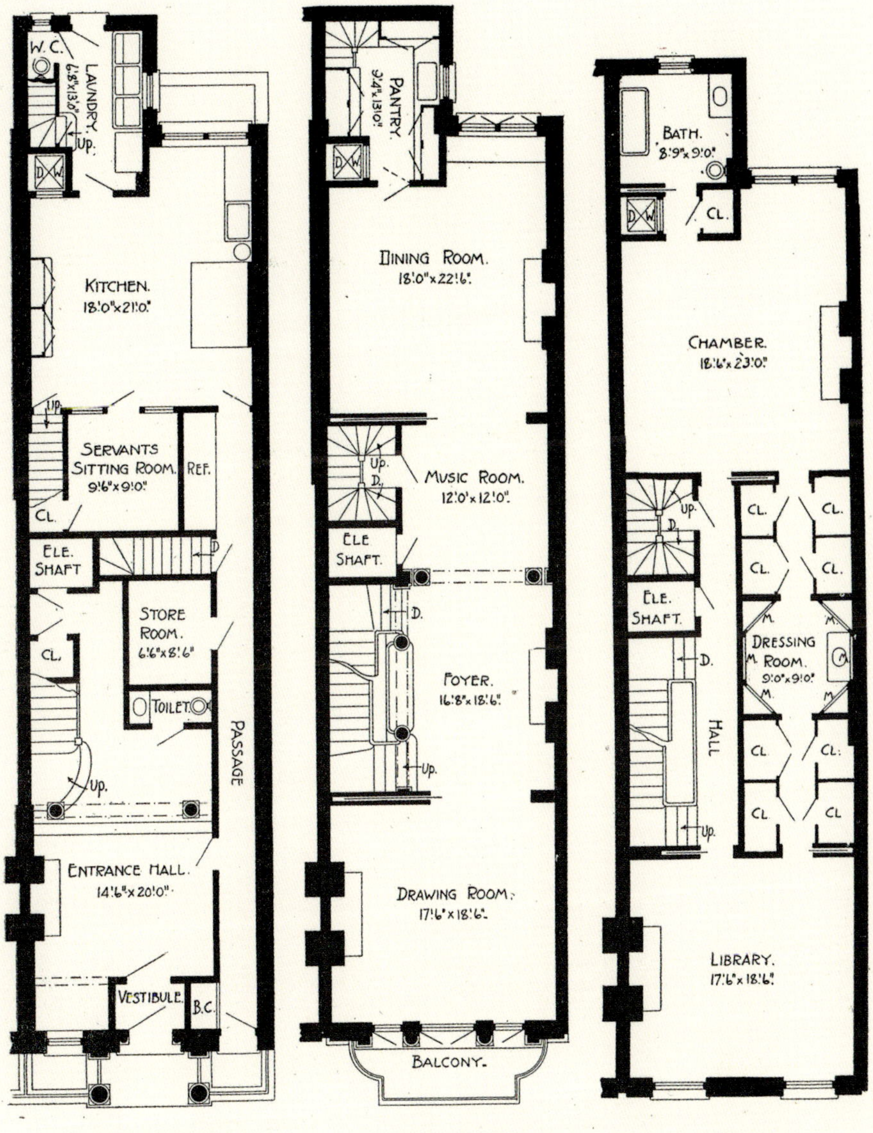

Entrance — 2*d* Floor — 3*d* Floor

Floor plans of American basement houses at 40–44 East Fifty-First Street (1903). The entrance to the house is at the center of the ground floor, which from the vestibule opens into an entry hall. An impressive stairway at the center leads to the parlors on the second floors. This configuration allowed the upper-floor front rooms facing the street to stretch the entire width of the house.

These configurations all but displaced the traditional high-stoop house in new Manhattan construction and resulted in the "destooping" of many earlier dwellings. Indeed, in 1912, the *Real Estate Record and Guide* provided a taxonomy of the "three principal types of attached houses" in New York City, classifying them as the "High Stoop, American Basement and English Basement" with the first considered as a nearly extinct subspecies against the other two more contemporary configurations.

However, though celebrated in the architectural press, neither the American or English basement configurations took hold in any great numbers in the many modest houses constructed in Brooklyn in the same period. There, the traditional high-stoop configuration continued to dominate. Indeed, the high stoop allowed houses to be purpose-built as two-family residences. From the outside, they retained the traditional New York row house form, but they were split into an owner's apartment and renter's apartments, with the latter accessible from the doorway under the stoop.

32
30
32

Left: 30–34 West Seventy-Fourth Street. American basement Georgian Revival and Beaux-Arts houses (1902–4). Upper West Side/ Central Park West Historic District.

Following pages:
"Types of New York Entrances," *Real Estate Record and Guide* (1899), featuring new styles of street-level and side-access stoop entries.

413–417 West 144th Street, Hamilton Heights (1898). English basement houses with side entrances and low stoops. Hamilton Heights Historic District.

Types of New York Entrances.

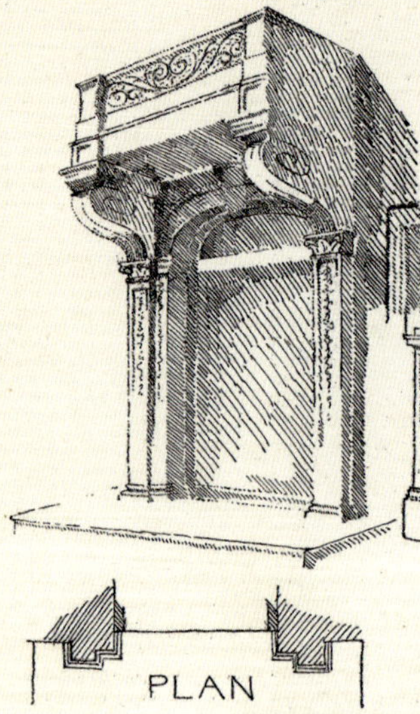

A MODERN FRENCH ENTRANCE.

DESIGN EMBRACING THE WINDOWS ON BOTH SIDES OF DOORWAY.

ENTRANCE TO AMERICAN BASEMENT HOUSE.

ENTRANCE APPROACHED FROM THE SIDE.

ENTRANCE APPROACHED FROM THE SIDE.

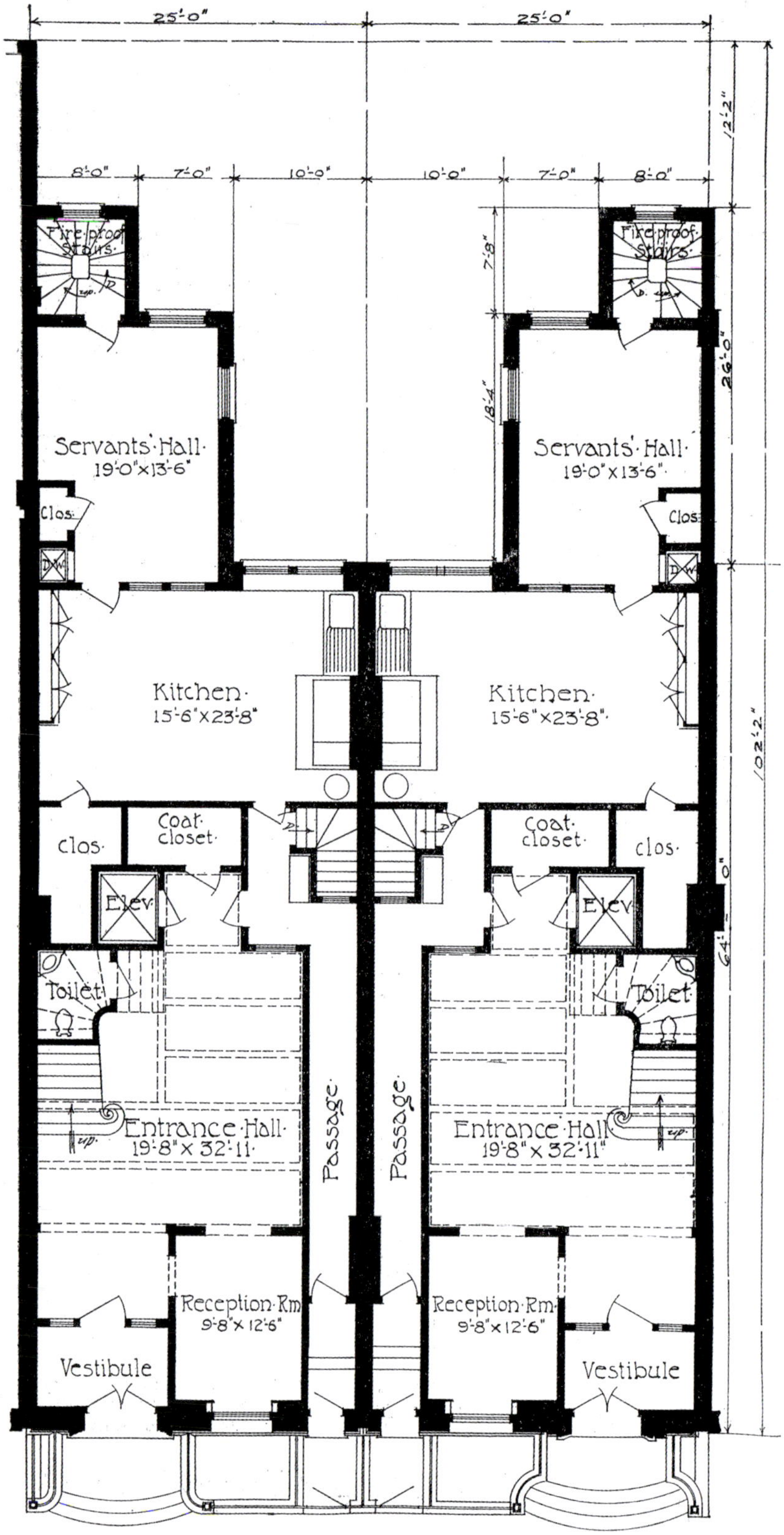

First Floor Plan

No. 20 No. 22

[14]

First- and second-floor plans from prospectus for English basement houses at 20–28 West Eighty-Sixth Street (ca. 1900–1910). In the English basement plan, the main entrance to the house was at the side, only several steps up from street level. In this particularly well-thought out design, the entry hall contains a small reception room and coat closet, as well as an elevator. The relatively compact central staircase, as opposed to the straight-run stairs of the traditional row house plan, allowed for a generous front parlor even on a narrow building lot.

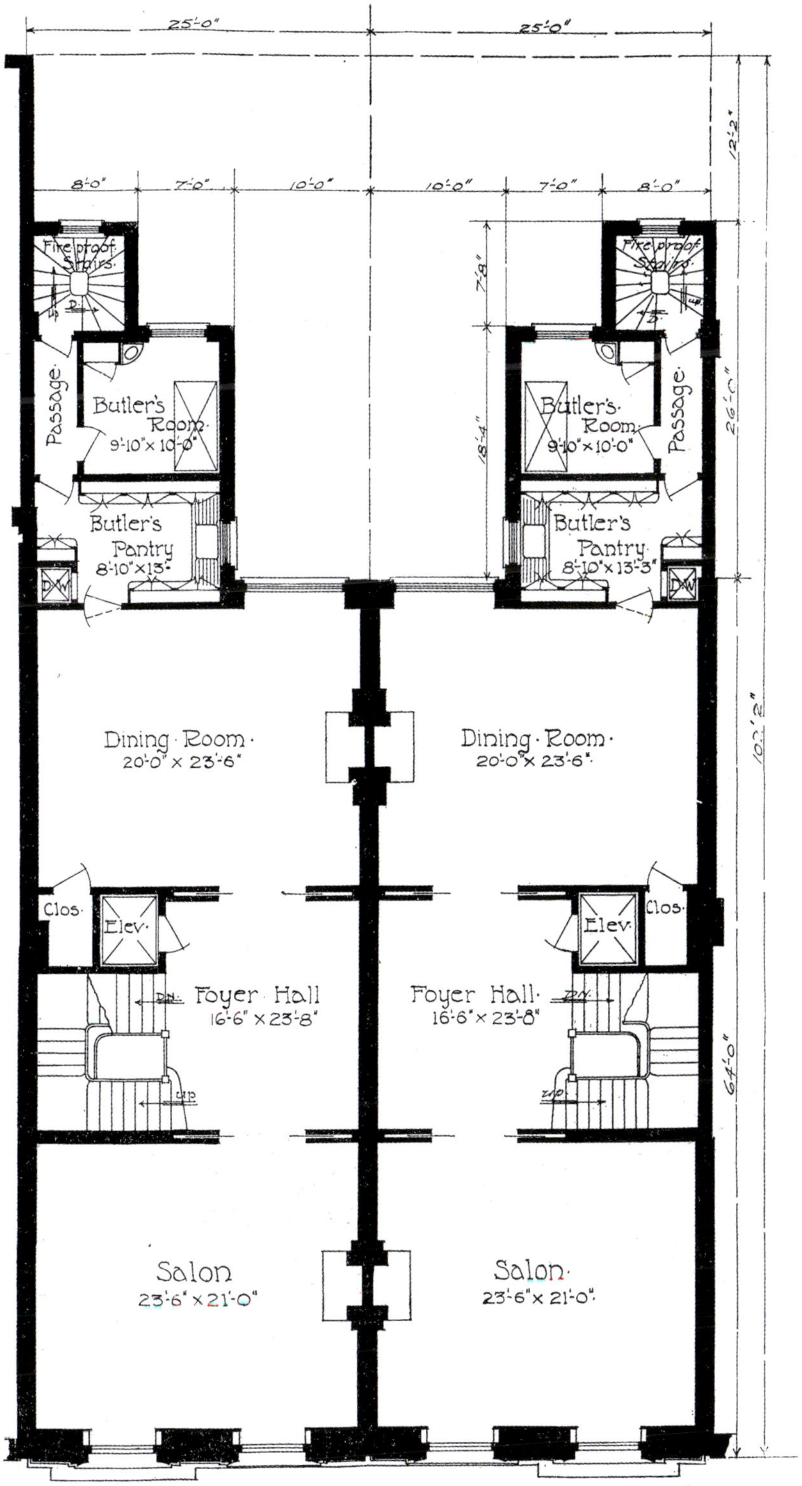

SECOND FLOOR PLAN

No. 20 No. 22

English basement Renaissance Revival houses in pairs, 309–331 West Seventy-Eighth Street, Manhattan, photographed 1895. Demolished.

THE EAST SIDE: ROW HOUSES INTO TOWN HOUSES

In 1873, *Harper's Bazar* [*sic*] published lithographs of vistas of Fifth Avenue south from Forty-Third Street and Lexington Avenue north from Thirty-Sixth Street, which, according to the magazine, were the corners of what was "at present the fashionable quarter of New York." However, the magazine cautioned that "the bounds of this quarter are as shifting as quicksands," predicting that "rapidly advancing business" will probably drive it back ere long to the region about the Central Park, where it will establish itself permanently."

In 1878, with development on the East Side underway, the *Real Estate Record and Guide* expressed hope that restrictive covenants would prevent new neighborhoods under development from succumbing to the nuisances and creeping commerce that had invaded neighborhoods downtown: "In the house building quarters of the future, where business is not likely to invade until a very remote period, if ever, it is hoped that lot owners will combine together, and impose whole restrictions and building covenants upon land, such as will create desirable neighborhoods, and relieve the building business of a constant menace and serious source of loss." As society moved uptown through the nineteenth century, such predictions assumed that a permanent fashionable district would establish itself as a relatively uniform quarter of new construction somewhere above the current building line.

However, it was at the already built-up East Side where the uptown march of fashion halted in the late 1890s. Herbert Croly wrote in his 1902 survey "The Contemporary Metropolitan Residence" that the "very rich from all over the country" were "flocking to New York, and seeking dwellings regardless of cost." Where before they might have chosen the West Side, it had now become "definitely settled that there was only one section of the city, in which people who were both rich and fashionable could live." That "one fashionable district" was the "region east of the Central Park" and also "south thereof between Madison and Sixth Avenues, to about Thirty-fourth Street."

These East Side streets had already been developed with brownstone-front houses constructed in the decades after the Civil War. In the absence of available land, these older houses were now completely reconstructed as Colonial Revival or Georgian Revival town houses, often designed by noted architects. In a survey of such construction in 1906, Montgomery Schuyler deemed such residences "The New New York House." Indeed, as true individual town houses, these houses arguably represented a break from the long New York row house tradition.

That break was underscored by the fact that these town houses very consciously obliterated the brownstone-front houses that had stood on the same lot. The buyer of "modern residences," wrote Croly, insisted upon an "individual design," thus "the use of brick or some more attractive stone, and among the moderately well-to-do people of good taste, this demand has frequently resulted in the erection of a totally new facade in place of the old brownstone front." Typically, the new facade was built much closer to the sidewalk lot line, eliminating the front areaway on the traditional high-stoop dwelling. On some blocks,

Opposite: In an illustration from Montgomery Schuyler's 1906 article "The New New York House," flanking Colonial and Renaissance Revival houses eclipse a surviving brownstone-front house, with their basement fronts pushed into the former stoop areaway, creating a new street wall. Today's town houses on the side streets of the Upper East Side are often rebuilt brownstone-front houses originally constructed in the 1860s and 1870s that were completely transformed in the first decades of the twentieth century.

Following pages: Striver's Row/King Model Houses, 203–217 West 139th Street, Harlem, architects McKim, Mead & White (1891). Perhaps the most impressive Italian Renaissance–inspired house row in the city. Developer D. H. King Jr. commissioned three major architectural firms to design entire blockfronts. St. Nicholas Historic District.

Striver's Row/King Model Houses, 253–273 West 138th Street, Harlem, architects Bruce Price & Clarence S. Luce (1891). St. Nicholas Historic District.

Opposite: Renaissance Revival mantel and mirror, West 121st Street, Harlem.

Above: Renaissance Revival reception room and entry hallway woodwork, West 121st Street, Harlem.

Renaissance Revival stair hall,
West 121st Street, Harlem.

Opposite: Renaissance Revival front reception room, West 121st Street, Harlem. This house is part of a row of identical high-stoop houses on narrow building lots, with a single window bay lighting the front of the house next to the entry door and hallway.

Above: Second-floor bedroom, West 121st Street, Harlem. This front room facing the street spans the entire width of the house.

Right: First-floor rear parlor, West 121st Street, Harlem.

Basement kitchen,
West 121st Street, Harlem.

unrenovated brownstone-front houses were marooned, with their facades submerged 10 or more feet behind the adjoining fronts of the new houses. Most cheered the destruction of the brownstone fronts, by now viewed as hopelessly old-fashioned. Croly looked forward to the time "when the brownstone dwellings, if not entirely demolished, will at least cease to dominate that part of the city in which it once prevailed."

BROOKLYN: "THE BOROUGH OF HOMES"

"New York is growing Brooklynward at a marvelous pace," the *New York Sun* wrote in 1899. The newspaper's judgment, "as Viewed From the Other Side of the East River," was that Brooklyn was foremost "the borough of homes," the greatest agglomeration of urban houses in Greater New York, if not the country as a whole.

The *Sun* attributed Brooklyn's boom to the fact that nearly the entire borough, from the "old city" of Brooklyn Heights to the outskirts, was no more than thirty-five minutes from the Manhattan end of the Brooklyn Bridge. The trolley lines fanning out across Brooklyn from the base of the bridge made development in many directions possible, unlike in Manhattan, where it could only travel north. There were thus "hundreds of acres of land now practically vacant" that were "fast going into the hands of the real estate syndicates that are taking a large part in the development of the new city."

"Towns seemed spring up in a night, as they say in mining camp towns in the West," wrote the *Sun*'s reporter. At the time, there were "more than four thousand residences in course of construction in the new part" of Brooklyn. Traveling the various trolley lines, the reporter saw "pretentious houses and unpretentious houses, the very expensive and the moderate cheap"—however, there were "no very cheap ones," as land speculators had created restrictive covenants preventing such construction to buoy values. The *Sun* wrote that in Brooklyn for $500 it was possible to buy a $4,000 house, with the balance payable as rent to the owner, and sometimes with no down payment at all.

This report came one year after the consolidation of Brooklyn into Greater New York. The union, somewhat ironically, in many ways only served to amplify the borough's separate identity as distinct from Manhattan, even if it was no longer an independent city. Brooklyn's self-image was one of sober restraint and domesticity against the material excesses across the East River, where middle-class life had been all but impossible for decades. By contrast, Brooklyn houses, though never inexpensive, remained affordable to a much broader range of the middle class, not just the wealthy upper middle class. Even though apartment houses were built in Brooklyn neighborhoods beginning in the 1890s, the single-family row house—along with the two-family house—remained the preferred form of residence well into the twentieth century, and it was still economically viable for builders to construct.

There was less need to be fashionable in Brooklyn row houses, and styles often lasted far longer in popularity. An 1897 advertisement in the *Eagle* for homes in "The Finest Residential Section" of Brooklyn, on Bergen

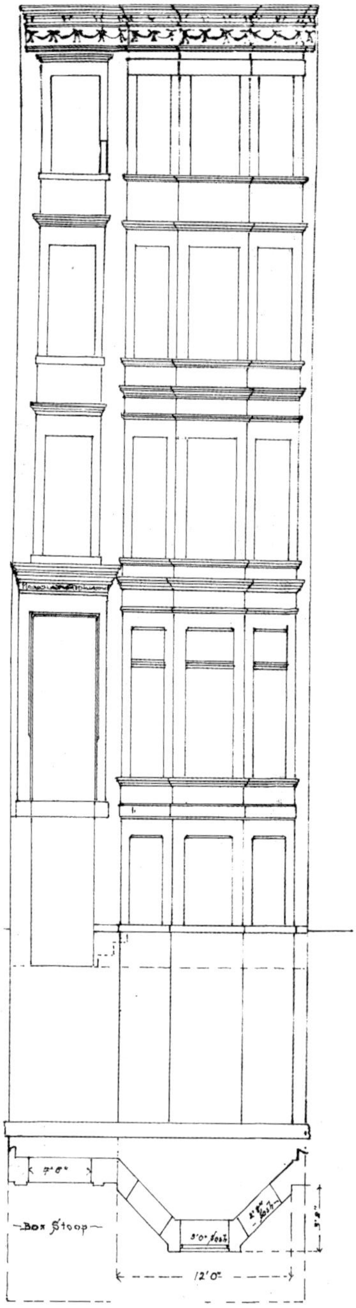

Above: Elevation of a house on the north side of Carroll Street between Eighth Avenue and Prospect Park West, filed as part of a building permit application in 1894 by builder-developer William Flanagan. Over a span of more than three decades, Flanagan constructed nearly one-quarter of the houses in Park Slope. They hewed to a similar basic design, and such permit filing drawings often did not depict the final planned exterior decoration of what were otherwise identical houses.

Opposite: 841–843 Carroll Street, Park Slope, Brooklyn. Completed in 1896 by developer William Flanagan, these houses show how builders trimmed out houses with fashionable exterior decoration on an otherwise effectively standard-model template, as shown in the filing plan for the same building. Park Slope Historic District.

Street in the St. Mark's district in today's Crown Heights, was typical. Though touting "Romanesque, Gothic, and Colonial style of architecture"—the first two long succeeded in fashion—the houses were, per the accompanying illustration, effectively uniform and bearing few of those features, with the only variation among the otherwise identical octagon-front, high-stoop houses the finish of either limestone or Roman brick. Inside, each house featured the typical "interior trimming" of "oak, ash and mahogany."

Another 1897 advertisement in the *Eagle* proffered "Styles for 1898" for a row on Bainbridge Street between Stuyvesant and Lewis Avenues, but did not specify any style beyond "richly carved stone fronts." Indeed, as had been the case even in the eclectic era, the most important description of the houses was simply "modern"—here, "High Class Modern Dwellings, all known improvements." The major selling point for most Brooklyn houses remained their relative economy. Offered at $14,500 and up, the houses were touted as "Equal to a $30,000 New York house" across the river in Manhattan.

Many builders whose careers had started in the 1870s boom continued to work through the first decade of the twentieth century and profited by replicating the same house formula over and over in only slightly varying styles. William Flanagan was one such example, a builder-developer whose career spanned from the 1870s to the 1900s, when he served as vice president of the Speculative Builders' Association of Brooklyn. The *Brooklyn Eagle* in 1902 identified Flanagan as the builder of "one-fourth of the modern houses on the Park Slope," a boast borne out by the historical record as true.

That 1902 *Eagle* article described four houses at 791 to 797 Carroll Street, which, as the last to fill the remaining vacant lots on the street, would "finish the block." This block, the north side of Carroll Street between Seventh and Eighth Avenues in Park Slope, is a remarkable record of the steady conservatism of Brooklyn speculative construction. Twenty-five of 26 houses—effectively the entire blockfront—were developed either by Flanagan or the architect-builder John Magilligan starting in 1887. Though clothed in vaguely Neo-Grec ornament, supplanted by Renaissance Revival details on the 1902 row, the houses are all effectively identical save for the configuration of their bay windows as either octagon or rounded fronts and for the use of limestone on two of the last four houses. Indeed, a Department of Buildings filing from Flanagan for another house on Carroll Street between Eighth and Ninth Avenues shows a similar stock row house plan and elevation without any specific ornament whatsoever—presumably the basic plan and elevation could be reused with little modification over and over.

The most distinguished Brooklyn row house neighborhood of the era, Prospect Lefferts Gardens, presented an alternative model of development, with strict covenants to assure quality design. In 1893, James Lefferts, an heir to the vast Lefferts family landholdings in Brooklyn, divided the Lefferts farm in Flatbush into 600 building lots, placing restrictions against development as apartments and tenements and requiring the land to be developed as single-family houses for sale for not less than $5,000. The restrictions required uniform setbacks and massing, leading to a remarkably urbane neighborhood as the lots were developed over the next two decades. Unlike more piecemeal development common elsewhere in the borough, a handful of developers, working with the same architects, built dozens of houses at once, mostly from 1905 and 1910. In particular, the relatively uniform blockfronts on both sides of Maple Street between Bedford and Rogers Avenues represent a coherent urban design unmatched by other Brooklyn row house blocks of the era.

Elsewhere in Brooklyn, Renaissance Revival details and classical motifs served as the standard exterior decoration on countless modest one- or two-family brownstone-front or limestone-front houses, which were constructed in large numbers until 1917, when the U.S. entry into World War I halted building across New York. Afterward, houses would continue to be built across Brooklyn and the outer boroughs through the twentieth century, but in forms generally unrelated to the traditional New York row house.

Opposite: Central, two-story octagon oriel at 250 Decatur Street, one of a twenty-five-house row, Bedford-Stuyvesant, Brooklyn (1894–97). Many houses built in the 1890s in Brooklyn appear largely similar to those constructed the previous decade, a testament to the conservatism of Brooklyn builders and house buyers as well as to the underlying uniformity of speculative row house construction in the four decades following the Civil War, whatever the convulsions of exterior styles. Stuyvesant Heights Historic District.

Following pages: 138–144 Maple Street, Prospect Lefferts Gardens, Brooklyn (1910). Divided from the old Lefferts farm in Flatbush, building lots in the neighborhood were required by covenants to be developed with uniform setbacks and massing. Prospect Lefferts Gardens Historic District.

250

208
206

Opposite: 856 and 858 Prospect Place, Crown Heights, Brooklyn, architect George P. Chappell (1894). Some architects looked to New York's Dutch past for inspiration, as in these two Dutch Renaissance Revival houses, creating fantasies far more elaborate than anything that would have been found in New Amsterdam centuries before. Crown Heights North Historic District.

Above: 174–208 Lincoln Road, Brooklyn (1907). Prospect Lefferts Gardens Historic District.

Following pages: Albemarle Terrace, Flatbush, Brooklyn (1917). These houses were completed the same year that the U.S. entry into World War I halted the building trades in New York. As the most fully realized Neo-Federal houses in the city—especially the smaller, gabled houses with dormers—they represent perfect bookends of New York's row house building history stretching from 1783 to 1917. Albemarle–Kenmore Terraces Historic District.

2107

2109

THE END OF THE ROW HOUSE IN MANHATTAN

The *Real Estate Record and Guide* in June 1904 published a sweeping overview of standard building types in New York. "Each successive generation creates its peculiar type of building," wrote the *Record*, and it was the apartment house, not the row house, that was now deemed the typical high-class New York residential building at the opening of the twentieth century.

The *New York Times* wrote in 1905 that one reason for the "prevailing apartment craze" was "perhaps traceable to the approval given the so-called *maison de convenience* by ultrafashionable folk" who now rented apartments, even though they could afford to own and maintain houses. But the real reason was economic: "New York is shy of homes because, in the aggregate, it is shy on such incomes as the equipment and maintenance of a private residence demand." Only several thousand households out of the two million residents of Manhattan could afford private homes—so economic reality had enforced the revolution in the "pace and style of living the metropolitan life" to live in the "honeycombs" of apartment buildings rather than in private residences.

As early as 1857, the *Times* had praised apartment living, as yet unaccepted in New York, but "universally adopted in Paris, generally in Edinburgh, and recently introduced in London." The newspaper advocated for the wholesale demolition and reconstruction of much of the city below Fourteenth Street. The "remedy for a narrow area is to go into the air," the *Times* recommended, calling for flats buildings to replace aging houses that had been converted into boardinghouses. Building apartments would displace these boardinghouses—a "system so fraught with pernicious consequences to the rising generation, and especially hurtful to female reserve and delicacy"—and allow both rich and poor to be housed downtown and thus "check the absurd increase of rents up town and enable those whose families require the luxury or convenience of a whole house to obtain such accommodation at something like a rational cost."

Still, even two decades later, the apartment house, despite significant early examples, had yet to be accepted. The *Times* in 1876 again introduced the "Parisian System of Living" of French flats, dividing them into two classes: the "flat proper or apartment-house" and the apartment hotel. The latter, considered indigenous only to New York, featured small suites where meals were served from a central dining room. The French flat, or apartment house, by contrast, was like its foreign analogues a substitute for the private house, "where the suites of rooms embrace kitchen, dining-room, and bed-rooms, and accommodations for private housekeeping." The newspaper admitted that with private houses largely out of reach whether for purchase or for rent, many New Yorkers effectively already lived in such conditions in the shared accommodations of boardinghouses, themselves converted from single-family homes. The purpose-built apartment house would ratify what was already widely accepted, in economic if not quite social fact.

Indeed, one of the stumbling blocks to the adoption of apartment buildings in New York was arguably not mores favoring single-family housees, but rather the conventions of real estate speculation, which prized the development of 25-by-100-foot building lots into row houses rather than their assemblage into larger sites for apartment buildings. However, soaring Manhattan land prices in the 1890s made it difficult or even impossible for speculators to make money constructing houses for all but the wealthiest New Yorkers, quickly tilting the preference of developers toward apartment construction. The "steady increase in the value of real estate in Manhattan," the critic Herbert Croly wrote in 1902, had caused "an ever stronger tendency for apartment houses to take the place of private dwellings." When the seven-story flat building was introduced in 1898, it provided a valid model for speculative development of apartment buildings, Croly wrote. "So many of these flats were erected within a year or two that values were forced up beyond the reach of the builders of inexpensive residences, and a sudden diminution of the number of such residences" was effected.

From 1889 to 1892, plans were filed for 700 first-class private dwellings to be constructed in Manhattan, to be sold for about $25,000 apiece. By 1899, only 338 house plans were filed, and by 1900 there were just over 100 house plans filed, with the expected purchase prices for those houses well over $100,000. On the West Side, the number of house plans filed dropped from some 500 annually in 1890 to 68 in 1900, then to only 28 in 1901.

"It is an extraordinary fact that at the present day," Croly wrote in 1902, that "there is practically only one class of private dwelling erected on the island of Manhattan—the dwelling intended for comparatively rich people." It was a "radical transformation." Twenty-five years before, there had been space and economic possibility to create Manhattan districts that were "chiefly a collection of private dwellings, small and great"—but no longer.

"Search the history of the city," the *Times* wrote in 1905, "and there has been but one period when fewer private houses were in process of construction or contemplation, and that was during the Revolutionary war," a century and a quarter before. A long chapter in New York's architectural history was at an end. Row houses were no longer the vanguard of the city's development. Instead, they had become relics of an earlier New York.

EPILOGUE

In 1926, the *New York Times* published a valedictory titled "The Brownstone Era is Coming to a Close." The newspaper reported that the physical remnants of the "age of the brownstone front" were quickly disappearing: "Long blocks of these stolidly respectable houses are yielding to the wrecker. Before long the saunterer who looks for remains of old New York will have to look twice to find a brownstone front. In almost every cross street of Central Manhattan, from river to river, the dignity of brownstone gives way to shining new structures that rise higher. A hundred families come to live where two or three have dwelt as the panorama of New York moves on." The *Times* wrote that "men and the house they inhabit are much alike. And surely there never could have been a stronger resemblance between men and houses than was reflected in the brownstone front." The destruction of these surviving houses meant the spirit of the era, which had survived even after its human actors had long passed on, was also being erased.

A testament that such a link between person and house was deeply felt at the time, not just a historical memory, was the Federal mansion of merchant Stephen Whitney at 7 Bowling Green. The house had been constructed in 1817, and Whitney lived there long after the neighborhood had fallen from fashion. At his death in February 1860, Whitney's obituary stated, "Perhaps no fact exhibits this conservative element of his character more forcibly than his persistent refusal to follow his old acquaintances and neighbors who, years ago, resigned their downtown mansions to look for more quiet and fashionable homes in the upper part of the City." His wife, Harriet, died two months afterward, and two photographs of the front and rear elevations taken shortly after show a sort of death mask for the house as a residence for the Whitneys. The surviving family members are perched in the windows on the upper floor, already half ghosts. The house survived as a steamship passenger line office until it was demolished in the early twentieth century for the new United States Customs House. No trace of it, or of any of the stately residences that once fronted Bowling Green, remains.

But many houses do survive in Manhattan and Brooklyn, modest or great, landmarks or not. "A hundred years hence, or ever so many hundred years hence, others will see them," as Walt Whitman wrote in "Crossing Brooklyn Ferry." These houses are records that outlast people and remind us that even in the most impermanent of cities not all is transitory.

7 Bowling Green, Whitney Residence, constructed 1817, photographed in the 1860s.

ACKNOWLEDGMENTS

Like a work of historic preservation, this edition of *Bricks & Brownstone* represents an adaptation of an already significant work into a new form. My first acknowledgment thus must be to Charles Lockwood, who trusted me to take this book beyond its own original life as well as his own. I am eternally grateful.

Charles wanted to dedicate this book to the brownstoners, in particular, to the late Evelyn and Everett Ortner, with whom Charles lived at their home on Berkeley Place in Park Slope, who were instrumental in his understanding of New York row houses. With the Charles Lockwood estate, I thank his executor, Isaac Malitz, and Maureen Baum, Charles's husband, Carlos Boyd, his brother, John Lockwood, and Lucia Aparicio. Also, thanks to donors Jeffrey Hyland and Christian Kessee, who set this edition moving, along with the Greenwich Village Block Association.

Furthermore, a program of the J. M. Kaplan Fund provided a generous grant, thanks to Joan K. Davidson. I am grateful for the New York Landmarks Conservancy's role as a fiscal conduit and official partner—thank you to Scott Leurquin, Alex Herrera, and Peg Breen. I thank Otis Pratt Pearsall and Nancy Pearsall, Margaret Gardiner of the Merchant's House Museum, Leslie Mason, Paul Kolbusz, Linda Yowell, and all the house owners whose interiors are featured here. The historical depth that informs the book is due to the librarians and staff of the New York Public Library, the Museum of the City of New York, the New-York Historical Society, Columbia University's Avery Library and Drawings & Archives, the Brooklyn Historical Society, the Athenaeum of Philadelphia, and the Winterthur Library.

I owe deep gratitude to the following people: Janet W. Foster, who first connected me with Charles at Columbia in 2006; Fran Leadon, for his opening essay and insightful comments and corrections throughout; Daniel B.F. Fox, for reading the entire manuscript once it finally came together; Flora Esterly, for her sage advice about the publishing world; Matthew B. Harrison, for giving me the goods; Fabian Friedland, for trusting me with the best day job I could want; Aldo Sampieri, the designer, for his magnificent interpretation of the book's visual riches; Douglas Curran, my editor at Rizzoli, for his infinite patience; my parents, Michael and Joanne, for their unflagging support.

And though I have already described their contributions in my introduction, I again must call out my collaborators, Jonathan D. Taylor and Dylan Chandler—this book is a testament to your great efforts.

Finally, I thank my wife, Kristin LaBuz. We met the month after Charles's death in 2012, and *Bricks & Brownstone* has remained up to this point a book in the future tense. It would never have become the book you hold in your hands today without your love—you made this possible.

—Patrick W. Ciccone

I would like to thank my parents, for pushing me toward a life of art and creativity from a young age; and my wife, Anna Ziemski, for her boundless support.

—Dylan Chandler

I would like to thank Patrick Ciccone for involving me in this endeavor and others; mentors in thinking about New York's houses, Andrew S. Dolkart and Chris Neville; my colleagues at Higgins Quasebarth & Partners for an ongoing seminar on researching and interpreting our city; my parents, Gordon and Tatiana; and David Schleifer, with whom I will always share my New York dwelling.

—Jonathan D. Taylor

INDEX

First published in the United States of America in 2019 by
RIZZOLI INTERNATIONAL PUBLICATIONS, INC.
300 Park Avenue South, New York, NY 10010
www.rizzoliusa.com

Front cover: 800–802 Carroll Street, Park Slope, Brooklyn (1889). Park Slope Historic District. Back cover: Interior detail, 37 West 11th Street, Greenwich Village, Manhattan.
Pages 2–3: Washington Square North, Greenwich Village (1831–33). Greenwich Village Historic District.
Page 4: Plaster details, Merchant's House Museum, 29 East Fourth Street, Manhattan (1831–32). National Historic Landmark, New York City Landmark, and New York City Interior Landmark.
Page 10: Writing desk, bedroom, Merchant's House Museum.
Page 12: 11–15 South Oxford Street, Fort Greene, Brooklyn (ca. 1869). Fort Greene Historic District.
Page 16: South Portland Avenue, Fort Greene, Brooklyn. Fort Greene Historic District.

Publisher: Charles Miers
Editor: Douglas Curran
Design: Aldo Sampieri
Production Manager: Rebecca Epperson
Managing Editor: Lynn Scrabis

This publication is sponsored in part by a grant from Furthermore: a program of the J. M. Kaplan Fund, Inc.
Printed in Hong Kong

2021 2022 2023 2024 2025 / 10 9 8 7 6 5 4 3

ISBN-13: 978-0-8478-6589-5
Library of Congress Control Number: 2019942317

Visit us online:
Facebook.com/RizzoliNewYork
Twitter: @Rizzoli_Books
Instagram.com/RizzoliBooks
Pinterest.com/RizzoliBooks
Youtube.com/user/RizzoliNY
Issuu.com/Rizzoli

Principal photography for this book is by Dylan Chandler, except as here noted and gratefully ackowledged by the author and the publisher: **Athenaeum of Philadelphia**, 168; **Avery Library Drawings & Archives**, 154; **Avery Architectural and Fine Arts Library**, 298, 301, 307 (top & bottom), 311, 314, 316, 317, 318, 320; **Brooklyn Historical Society** 221, 247 (bottom), 258 (bottom), 259, 274 (top); **Historic American Buildings Survey, Library of Congress**, 29, 60, 131; **Metropolitan Museum of Art**, 23, 172; **Museum of the City of New York**, 73 (top & bottom), 75 (top & middle), 77, 171 (top & bottom), 197, 202 (bottom), 206, 220, 271 (top & bottom left), 279, 346 (top & bottom); **New-York Historical Society**, 58, 73 (bottom), 75 (bottom), 113, 115 (top & bottom), 134 (top & bottom), 135, 137, 138, 148, 164, 165, 199, 201, 202 (top), 214, 272 (top); **Village Preservation**, 172 ; **Winterthur Library**, 91, 100 (top & bottom).